"Powerful. Encouraging. Real. These stories touched my life at a very deep level, and I found the applications to be something I could use and apply to my life."

—Sharla Jackson

"*Refresh* is a perfect balance of real-life stories, Scripture, and thoughtful, deep-reaching exercises. I was able to look at my personal issues from different perspectives and—by taking my time and truthfully answering the questions—kick through my blockades squarely at the base. The best part of all was that I felt safely accompanied every step of the way by my tender, gentle God, and at the same time, by my group of cherished friends."

—Susan Rampson

"I was surprised at how *Refresh* drew me in. Reading about courageous everyday women sharing the victories they've experienced instead of staying stuck in their pain or circumstances was more than inspirational! The questions and exercises at the end of each section provided a practical way for me to make my walk with Christ more genuine and intimate."

—Cori Hill

"I have been looking for a good Bible study that will take me deeper and address some of the issues that I have been struggling with during this season of my life. I have found that resource in *Refresh*. I love the combination of real stories, relevant Bible verses, penetrating questions, and soft suggestions for making change. If I am too tired to do anything else after a long day of work, kids, and service, I can still open *Refresh* and read something, even for five minutes, that will draw me closer to God."

—Susan Merriman

"When I opened *Refresh*, I was really tired and thinking, *I will have to read this tomorrow. . . .* Then I thought, *I'll just read a few sentences and see what the feel of this is. . . .* Ten pages later I sat there riveted. I wondered, *Where am I in this story?* I was not only compelled to keep reading but also to look deeper at my insides. And as I read, it was as if someone delicately turned the light on some dark places in my life and then gently reminded me that my God is tender and loving and desires to take the darkness out of those places and bring in the Light."

—Cathy Pluimmer

"I loved this format for Bible study! It was so refreshing and engaging, relevant to my real life instead of something abstract and distant. I felt God tug my heart, nudge me to consider some things that I knew He wanted me to look at. I felt challenged and encouraged at the same time."

—Sami Bookout

Refresh

Sharing Stories. Building Faith.

This book belongs to

New Hope® Publishers
P. O. Box 12065
Birmingham, AL 35202-2065
www.newhopepublishers.com
New Hope Publishers is a division of WMU®

Library of Congress Cataloging-in-Publication Data

Greiner, Laura Ross, 1963-
  Refresh : sharing stories, building faith / Laura Greiner and Kathy Escobar.
      p. cm.
  ISBN 978-1-59669-069-1 (sc)
  1. Christian women—Religious life. I. Escobar, Kathy. II. Title.
  BV4527.G7423 2007
  248.8'43—dc22

                 2007009869

ISBN-10: 1-59669-069-0
ISBN-13: 978-1-59669-069-1

Book design by Brooks Graphic Design

N074133 • 0807 • 10M1

Refresh

Sharing Stories. Building Faith.

Kathy Escobar and Laura Greiner

Q: What's your passion—each of you—and how do you live this out in your writing, other ministry work, and family life?

A (Laura): My passion is to live missionally. Partly, this is fleshed out in my writing work. Since I was a little girl, I have been drawn to people's stories because they are such a powerful way to experience God. Focus on the Family published my first book of stories, coauthored with Jean Blackmer, *Where Women Walked: Powerful True Stories of Women's Perseverance and God's Provision.* That book, and now *Refresh,* speak to my desire to have women see and experience God more in their own story. Kathy knows what I mean.

A (Kathy): Sure. One of my chief desires is to help women get "unstuck" in their relationship with God and others. My first book, which I coauthored with my good friend, Elaine Hamilton, *Come with Me: An Invitation to Break Through the Wall Between You and God,* speaks to this. I have always had a passion for people to see God moving in the midst of their stories, no matter how painful or hard those real stories are. Regardless of the many ministry roles I have been over the years, I always notice the same theme in most people—a deep desire to know and experience God's love and hope in the middle of real life.

A (Laura, continues): And hope so often comes from listening to other people's stories. In my 25 years of ministry, God has given me many amazing "story" opportunities as a nursing and hospice volunteer, on staff with Prison Fellowship Ministries, on the board of Impact for Life Ministry, outreach abroad with Rancho de Sus Niños, retreat and event speaking, and writing and teaching many Bible studies. No matter which opportunity I am in, I feel myself pulled like a magnet into the lives of other people. And I feel like each story I listen to and write is a modern-day parable in which God is teaching about Himself and revealing Himself to us.

Q: Kathy, remind us, how long have you been in ministry?

A (Kathy): I've had the privilege of being in ministry for more than 15 years now in a variety of different roles both as part of a megachurch and church plant staff and also as a lay leader. I love to lead and facilitate large and small groups in which there is a high degree of safety, love, creativity, and challenge. I have been an adjunct professor at Denver Seminary, helping train new spiritual directors. Denver Seminary is where I received my certificate in spiritual guidance. I also have a master's degree in management.

Q: Laura, what's your educational background?

A (Laura): I have a PhD in sociology from the University of Denver and a master's in journalism from the University of Colorado.

Q: And, both of you, tell us about family life.

A (Kathy): My husband, Jose, and I have five children, so our life is always an adventure. Readers can learn more about my personal background, vignettes, and faith experience in several of the "Refreshment" segments, on pages 74, 110, 131, 144, 150, and 177. Over the years I have learned to embrace the story God is telling in my life, and my hope is that sharing details of my journey and how God is continually redeeming and healing me will inspire and comfort others on their journey too.

A (Laura): My husband, Bruce, and I live in Boulder, Colorado, with our three children. You'll find infor-mation on parts of my journey on pages 33, 37–38, 56, 72, 91, 149, 161–162, 169, 177, and 178. I am not as good at revealing my story as Kathy. It has been a process for me to learn how to share and reveal my own God story and not just listen to and write other people's stories. And raising a family is a great place to practice telling your story. My kids love hearing about my mistakes and what God has taught me.

Where do the stories in *Refresh* come from?

A (Laura and Kathy): The women in these stories are all real women whose lives have somehow intersected ours. Some are good friends, some we barely knew. Over coffee or in a group or at a conference, we somehow heard their stories and were amazed by God's work in their lives. We knew their stories reflected many of the same themes shared by other women. Our perfect day is to sit with people and hear the story God is telling in their lives because it brings us so much hope too!

Q: Why did you choose this kind of format for this material?

A (Laura and Kathy): We are convinced there's a longing out there for more interaction in Bible study, more connection than only answering questions and checking boxes. We knew that the real story combined with real-life questions would bring real hope. We wanted to give women choices on how they could interact with this material on their terms; and because we know that real women are busy, we wanted to develop a tool that would meet the needs of those who want a little more flexibility and creativity in how they connect with God and each other.

Our perfect day is to sit with people and hear the story God is telling in their lives because it brings us so much hope too!

Contents

11 INTRODUCTION
Real Women, Real Life,
and Real Hope

Refreshments

14 Will Somebody Please Love Me?
Searching for someone faithful
SHAWNA'S STORY AND FEATURES

28 Bye-Bye Superwoman!
Unmasking my heart
DANA'S STORY AND FEATURES

48 Guiltbusters
Top tips for banishing self-blame
HOPE'S STORY AND FEATURES

66 I Want More!
Secrets to a satisfied soul
LYNETTE'S STORY AND FEATURES

82 How I Became Fearless
One woman's story
ALESHIA'S STORY AND FEATURES

100 Leaving Behind Good-Girl Baggage
And lightening your load
DEBORAH'S STORY AND FEATURES

116 Girlfriends
Good for your health and your hope
STACY'S STORY AND FEATURES

136 A Total New You!
Letting go of the past
NORMA'S STORY AND FEATURES

154 Learning to Show Up
Instead of shut up
JANETTE'S STORY AND FEATURES

172 Beauty Secrets
Upside down and inside out
JUSTINE'S STORY AND FEATURES

188 CONCLUSION

Extra tips

to help you use *Refresh* and its features

- Each of the ten different stories in *Refresh* can be read individually or collectively. If you use *Refresh* within a group, the stories are short enough to read out loud during group time. You could have one person read the whole story to the group or have group members take turns reading a few paragraphs at a time.

- Each story comes with a set of five application tools:

Point of Connection is a devotional type of tool, with Scripture and guiding questions, allowing you to use the story as a springboard into your own life.

Digging Deeper can take you to the next level, providing more biblical applications to chew on and consider for your individual needs and circumstances.

Tryin' It provides concrete exercises where you can experiment in your own life with some of the ideas explored.

Mix It Up includes group-related exercises that will help leaders who are facilitating this material in either a large or small group. Ideas are provided to help participants connect experientially. Several ideas are included with each story so you have several to choose from.

Multiply It is a set of group discussion questions. This will help groups process the material together and provide a guide for the discussion. The questions also can be considered as journaling questions for those of you who are working the material on your own.

You will also discover in the application sections some additional features.

Infusion shares perspectives from older women who have "been there" and learned some life lessons along the way. These thoughts provide wisdom to draw from regardless of how young or old we are. We have also provided book lists to consider on different topics along with additional thoughts, checklists, and quizzes to take to help you reflect and connect.

In Living Color shares additional, shorter stories.

- If you are using *Refresh* as part of a group, we recommend one Refreshment story per group meeting. We have found that an hour-and-a-half meeting time (or longer) works well with the *Refresh* material. At the same time, we encourage you to let God guide the process and not limit yourself to one story a week. Women may connect certain sections in a powerful way and you may want to spend additional time praying and sharing over that particular topic.

- Please don't feel like you have to use all five tools for every story. Experiment with what is most effective for you and/or your group.

Introduction

Each of us women has a unique life story—a story filled with moments of courage, hope, joy, pain, and more. Often our stories are left untold and our moments forgotten and lost because we do not share them with one another. There are reasons we don't share.

We're embarrassed because we don't want to be judged when our stories are messy and do not fit imaginary, perfect lives. Some of us wish our life stories were different. Or more "important." The culture of *surface-ism* in which we live also keeps us from opening up to one another. In many gatherings, including churches, women who look "good" on the surface are stuck within the confines of shallow sharing. In reality, most of us who appear to have it all together actually do or have struggled through major life issues. The adage "Never judge a book by its cover" applies.

Beneath the surface of every woman's appearance are those moments—courage, hope, pain, joy, and more—but we simply do not experience enough opportunities to share safely about our lives. Surface-ism fosters fear of judgment for any floundering faith, past mistakes, and personal battles. We wonder, *If no one else is sharing what's really going on in their lives, how can we?* So our stories are held hostage in our hearts' silent shame. But there is a truth we need to embrace: Our stories are worth telling!

When we yield our voices to God and allow Him to use our stories, we can be sure of one thing—He will create opportunities for redemption. Then, as we share from the chapters of our lives and as our stories unfold, great healing and growth occur. These are the stories in *Refresh*. Each reveals a real woman with real life struggles, who has found real hope. That hope has come because of Jesus Christ.

Jesus tells His followers to expect trials and hardships in this world. He adds, "But take heart! I have overcome the world" (John 16:33 NIV). When we turn our lives over to God and ask Jesus to be our personal Savior, our hope becomes anchored in this truth: He triumphs over the world regardless of the magnitude of our heartaches, mistakes, or circumstances. We pray you see His triumph through these stories and as you interact around them with other women.

Reading these stories and sharing with other women will generate light and life in a broken world. Jesus tells us, "You are the light of the world—like a city on a mountain, glowing in the night for all to see. Don't hide your light under a basket! Instead, put it on a stand and let it shine for all" (Matthew 5:14–15 NLT). When we share our stories there is a refreshing ripple effect that encourages, inspires, and brings light to the listeners. So lean in and share and listen because God has something for each of us in *Refresh*. He wants to teach us something about Himself; to transform us more into His likeness; to give us tools to live with greater peace and freedom; to infuse us with His hope.

We pray through *Refresh* you are spurred to continue in real community with others—sharing your difficulties, heartaches, and failures, and living honestly and authentically. This was modeled to us by the Apostle Paul who wrote: "We loved you so much that we were delighted to share with you not only the gospel of God but our lives as well" (1 Thessalonians 2:8 NIV). Sharing our lives with each other is what God wants us to do so we can "encourage one another and build each other up" (1 Thessalonians 5:11 NIV). When this sharing and encouraging happens we find ourselves refreshed continually!

> "I will **refresh** the weary and satisfy the faint" (Jeremiah 31:25 NIV).

> "Happy are those who are strong in the LORD, who set their minds on a pilgrimage to Jerusalem. When they walk through the Valley of Weeping, it will become a place of refreshing springs, where pools of blessing collect after the rains! They will continue to grow stronger, and each of them will appear before God in Jerusalem" (Psalm 84:5–7 NLT).

Before you dig in

- This material is meant for sharing, but you do not have to do so.

The Apostle Paul often spoke about his spirit being refreshed when he spent time in community with other Christians. If you have the opportunity, it may be a very refreshing journey to walk through this book with one or more women. But each chapter has sections called **Tryin' It, Multiply It,** and **Mix It Up** with discussion questions and exercises you can do alone or with others.

- These stories are snapshots.

Each story in *Refresh* is only a brief snapshot of a long struggle or

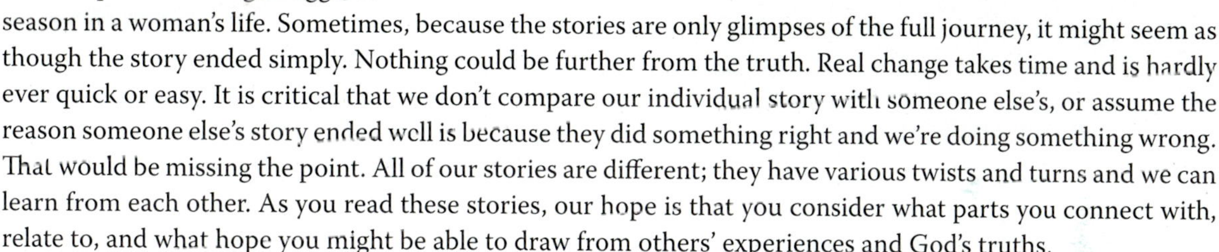

season in a woman's life. Sometimes, because the stories are only glimpses of the full journey, it might seem as though the story ended simply. Nothing could be further from the truth. Real change takes time and is hardly ever quick or easy. It is critical that we don't compare our individual story with someone else's, or assume the reason someone else's story ended well is because they did something right and we're doing something wrong. That would be missing the point. All of our stories are different; they have various twists and turns and we can learn from each other. As you read these stories, our hope is that you consider what parts you connect with, relate to, and what hope you might be able to draw from others' experiences and God's truths.

- You'll sometimes get frustrated.

Growing in our walk with God isn't always easy. Some exercises in *Refresh* may challenge you to think about things you may want to ignore, feel feelings you'd rather block, and explore your spiritual journey through a new lens through which everything appears fuzzy at first. You may wonder why one woman finds a solution to her problem and you still don't. You may question God's work in your life or get tired of reflecting on the truth of your heart, and how you feel about God and your relationships. When you hit these sorts of obstacles, we urge you to press forward. Don't stop just because you hit a bump in the road and the journey feels too hard. Keep the bigger picture in mind and strain to listen for God's voice to you.

- Take your time.

There are many activities and experiential exercises in each chapter. They are meant to be "chewed," prayed about, and enjoyed. Sometimes we have a tendency to breeze quickly through things so we can finish but, when we do this, we miss out on the luxury of soaking in the refreshment and encouragement God wants to give. Please take your time. Go slow. Soak in His truth, challenge, and hope.

We are praying for you—that you feel less alone and more encouraged in *your* life story. We hope you experience a new depth in your relationship not only with God but with others in your life. And, we pray that these stories and biblical truths water you with hope and love. Be refreshed!

Love,

Laura and Kathy

Will Somebody Please Love Me?

Searching for someone faithful

Shawna forced another bite of

meat loaf into her mouth. *Ugh.* Her stomach knotted as she watched her parents beam with approval of her sister, Jill, who rambled on about Friday night's youth group meeting. *She doesn't even have to try and be perfect. She just is.* Shawna's emotions surged as she moved some green beans around her plate. Looking over at her brother, she surveyed him as he laughed and added to Jill's story. *He doesn't even have to try either.* Shawna grimaced, her eyes clouding. *I'm an outsider. I can never be like Jill and Brian, even if I want to be. I'm just different.* Shawna thought about how her unusual dress and love of dancing and rock-and-roll music separated her from the family. They preferred everything traditional.

"Shawna?" Her mom's voice redirected Shawna's thoughts. "Are you OK? Did you have a good time at youth group too?"

"Uh-huh," Shawna mumbled and looked down at her plate. Then, before her mother could ask any more questions, she shoveled a huge bite of green beans into her mouth. Slinking down into her chair, Shawna let her mind wander to what she had been doing during Friday night's youth meeting. *Mom and Dad would freak out,* she thought as she pictured herself kissing Andrew Walker outside the church building. *Poor Dad,* her heart felt heavy as she stole a glance toward her father. *I'll never fit the image of a pastor's daughter. . . . I'll never be what he expects me to be.* Swallowing the lump in her throat, Shawna asked to be excused from the table. As she walked away, listening to the sound of their voices, tears rolled down her cheeks. *I'll never be good enough.* These words stuck with Shawna, echoing in her mind and heart as days, weeks, months, and years passed.

When Shawna married, *I'll never be good enough* controlled her life. Eight months pregnant with her second child, Shawna sat at the kitchen table to eat her seventh meal of the day. Constantly hungry, she had gained more than 50 pounds. "I hate looking like this," Shawna confided over the phone to her close friend, Liz. "I know it turns Greg off to look at me."

"You're imagining that," Liz said with conviction. "I gained tons of weight, too, and Bill still couldn't keep his hands off me."

"That doesn't make me feel any better . . . ," Shawna's voice trailed off as she thought about Greg's lack of romantic interest.

"Growing a baby is beautiful and Greg adores you," Liz assured Shawna.

"I guess." Shawna popped another pretzel into her mouth. "But at least God could have designed a woman's body so it would bounce back to normal after giving birth. After all, He's God. He can do anything. Right?"

After hanging up the phone, Shawna wobbled to the back of the house to check on her napping one-year-old. Passing by the hallway mirror, she stopped dead in her tracks. "I look like a cow!" she spat with disgust.

Never Feeling Good Enough

Down in the human heart,
   Crushed by the tempter,
Feelings lie buried that grace can restore.

—Fanny Crosby, "Rescue the Perishing"

Later that night when the phone rang, Shawna lay in bed exhausted. Answering the phone meant exerting extra energy she didn't have. But after the fourth ring she changed her mind, thinking it could be Greg, who was away on a business trip.

"Hello?"

"Is this Greg Farmer's wife?" a deep male voice boomed.

"Yes," Shawna answered as she felt a slight shiver run down her back.

"My name is Ben Hamilton. I am calling to let you know that your husband is having an affair with my wife," his voice seethed. "And they are with each other right now!"

A siren went off inside Shawna's head. "No. That's not true. My husband is away on business," her voice wavered.

"Listen, you can believe what you want, but I have followed them and I know they are in a hotel together in New Falls this very minute."

When Shawna got the name of the hotel, her hands shook as she dialed the number and asked for her husband's room. As the phone rang, Shawna's heart felt as if it might explode. A shrill voice in her head kept screaming, *No! It can't be true! No! Please, no!*

When Greg answered the phone, she could hear the guilt in his voice.

"Greg?" Shawna could barely say his name as hysteria began to take over. "Are you with another woman?"

The silence on the other end of the phone burned into Shawna's ears.

Greg drove home that night and spent hours telling her that the other woman meant nothing to him and begging for her forgiveness.

Shawna spent the next week in a daze as the reality of her husband's betrayal sent fresh waves of pain crashing against her. Late one afternoon, the phone rang and Shawna answered it in a fog.

"Shawna? Is this a good time to talk?" her mother-in-law was always direct.

"I guess so," Shawna sighed, desperately wanting to hang up but knowing she couldn't.

"You know men don't do this without a reason," her mother-in-law said matter-of-factly. Slouching down in her chair, Shawna could picture the look of disapproval on her mother-in-law's face.

After an awkward silence, Shawna muttered, "I don't know what to think." Her heart throbbed as she listened to her mother-in-law talk about how to make a successful marriage.

A few days after their phone call, Shawna received three thick books in the mail from her mother-in-law on how to become a better wife. Taking the books back to her bedroom, Shawna dropped onto the bed and began to read. After skimming several chapters including, "How to Keep a Husband Happy" and "Fulfilling Your Man," she began to cry until her ribs ached. *This is my fault. I'm not good enough as a wife. I let this happen.* When her tears finally subsided, she grabbed one of the books and wildly flipped through the pages. *I will do whatever it takes to be the wife Greg needs*, she vowed to herself.

Shawna began writing Greg little love notes, buying him special gifts, and making herself available to him romantically at any hour of the day or night. It was exhausting. She often felt empty, but was desperate to woo Greg. She tried to do anything she could think of to be the perfect wife, mother, and woman. Her marriage seemed to improve gradually and for several years she and Greg grew closer. They had another child. Yet in the depths of her heart, Shawna wrestled a fierce battle against insecurity. Even though their life together appeared healthy and happy, Shawna's feelings of inadequacy festered.

Several years after the affair, Shawna got an opportunity to work in the music industry, one of her passions. Greg was supportive and they arranged their schedules so that one of them was always at home with the children. One of the men Shawna worked with, Kurt, thought Shawna was exceptionally talented. Kurt and Shawna spent long hours together as they worked on different projects. An intimate connection grew as they talked and shared their lives with each other. Kurt was always building Shawna up, making her feel good about herself. She didn't feel the need to prove anything to Kurt. It was such a huge relief. He seemed to love everything about her, including her body, which Shawna had always felt very self-conscious about with Greg, especially after two pregnancies.

One night as they were working late on a project, Shawna made a joke about herself. "See, that looks like me," she laughed and pointed to a picture of an overweight woman.

Kurt took her by the shoulders and spun her around almost forcefully. Surprised, Shawna looked into his eyes, "What?"

"Don't ever say that about yourself! You are beautiful! Your body is perfect! Everything about you is perfect." Kurt's eyes pierced hers.

And Shawna drank in his words like a parched

Faithful to You

Songwriters have penned countless lyrics and varied voices have sung endless melodies in an effort to communicate the faithful love of God. From Thomas O. Chisolm and William M. Runyan's traditional hymn "Great Is Thy Faithfulness," to Ethel Waters's halting rendition of the spiritual "His Eye Is on the Sparrow," to Jennifer Knapp's contemporary testament "Faithful to Me," or the gospel sound of Karen Clark Sheard singing "A Secret Place," all tell of God's faithful love for us.

Kurt and Shawna spent long hours together.

desert nomad. As he spoke to her about her beauty, talent, and worth, for the first time in her life she felt "good enough." Looking into Kurt's eyes, she whispered, "You really believe that, don't you?"

The longing in his eyes made Shawna's whole body shiver, and she began to give her heart to him.

Shawna crossed a dangerous emotional line with Kurt as she let his adoration and love fill the emptiness and insecurity inside of her. Although they never committed physical adultery, Shawna allowed herself to fall in love with him. Eventually, she made the decision to end her relationship with him in order to preserve her marriage and family. The ending of the relationship almost came at the cost of her life. He had been filling something so deep within her that when it was gone, she felt empty, lonely, not wanting to live without his approval and love.

Weeks after ending the relationship, Shawna curled up on her bed as fresh tears poured into a tiny pool on her pillow. *He filled me with hope . . . that I'm not a letdown, that I'm beautiful, and actually lovable.* The loss of this hope crushed her profoundly and it was years before Shawna recovered. She began a slow journey by being honest with a few close friends who encouraged her to let God—and not men—fill her. She began to confess her feelings of low self-esteem and unworthiness. It was so hard for her to admit that what she knew in her *head* about God and His love for her had not ever translated into her *heart*. Slowly but surely, Shawna recognized God's hand gently guiding her and teaching her that the hope and fulfillment she sought can't come from another human being or anything in the world. God showed Shawna that the sense of worth and value she desperately craved had to be rooted in Him.

Change didn't come all at once and she is still on a healing journey. Some days she senses the old insecurities rising up and trying to take over her thoughts. But she has learned how to run to God and let Him fill her instead of desperately searching for people to make her feel better about herself.

As Shawna talks about her journey today, she beams with a different kind of hope. "There is only one who can truly make any woman feel good enough: God. I *am* good, simply because He *made* me good. Period! He is the ultimate lover of my soul and I am learning daily how important I am to Him. I spent many years searching for a remedy from people and from my achievements to heal the emptiness within my aching heart and to make me feel as though I am good enough. But I searched in the wrong places and it cost me a lot of pain and devastation. Today both my husband and I are striving to learn how to allow God *alone* to fill us." ❈

Looking for love in all the
wrong places?

"God's still small voice . . . speaks with the accent of love."
—Claire Cloninger, *Dear Abba*

POINT OF CONNECTION **Inside each woman is a seemingly insatiable need to feel loved, nurtured, and valued.**

We often look in every direction, desperately searching for someone to fill that longing in our heart. We want someone or something to make us feel whole and complete. The problem is that other people can never satisfy us completely. We will always come up short. Because people are imperfect humans, they will fail us, hurt us, neglect us, and love us incompletely. And if that is where our value comes from, we will be left bruised, hurting, and empty over and over again. We will keep searching in vain to have someone make us feel "good enough," even if only for a moment or a season, and even if it only brings shame and pain into our lives.

God can satisfy our longings if we let Him. We can come to Him regardless of what we have done or how we look or feel. Believing that in our *head* is one thing, knowing that in our *heart* is quite another.

This is not a new struggle for women. In the Bible, in the fourth chapter of the Book of John, we learn about an encounter Jesus had with a woman whose struggle looks like Shawna's.

Read from the Gospel of John, reprinted here, about Jesus's interaction with a woman at a well.

This woman had been looking for love repeatedly. She had been married five times and the man with whom she was currently living wasn't

John 4:4–10, 14, 28–30 (NIV)

Now he had to go through Samaria. So he came to a town in Samaria called Sychar, near the plot of ground Jacob had given to his son Joseph. Jacob's well was there, and Jesus, tired as he was from the journey, sat down by the well. It was about the sixth hour. When a Samaritan woman came to draw water, Jesus said to her, "Will you give me a drink?" (His disciples had gone into the town to buy food.) The Samaritan woman said to him, "You are a Jew and I am a Samaritan woman. How can you ask me for a drink?" (For Jews do not associate with Samaritans.) Jesus answered her, "If you knew the gift of God and who it is that asks you for a drink, you would have asked him and he would have given you living water." . . . "Whoever drinks the water I give him will never thirst. Indeed, the water I give him will become in him a spring of water welling up to eternal life." . . . Then, leaving her water jar, the woman went back to the town and said to the people, "Come, see a man who told me everything I ever did. Could this be the Christ?" They came out of the town and made their way toward him.

her husband. She was probably filled with shame, doubt, and self-contempt. She kept looking for love and never felt satisfied. Then, she met Jesus. A skeptic, she wasn't quite sure what it was that He was telling her. Yet, His words penetrated her heart, and He knew exactly what was going on in her life—she was looking to satisfy her "thirst" in places that would never quench her dryness.

Shawna also looked to satisfy her thirst in places that would never quench her need to feel good enough: the approval of her parents, her husband, and another man. The woman at the well went through five husbands and was working on a sixth. She longed to feel quenched. So do we.

Our "husbands" might not be literal ones as in the Bible story, but we all have "wells" that we may run to in an effort to fill the longings of our heart. Our "husbands" might look like relationships in which we always try to get noticed, approved, and validated; or careers that we invest in so that we feel important; or exercise we engage in excessively and eating that we overly control so that we are "valued" for our bodies. Or children and family, whom we pour our everything into, working hard to feel as though we're *worthy* wives and mothers.

What are some of the "husbands" in your life?

Do they satisfy you? Why or why not?

Jesus, in His encounter with the woman at the well, says that the typical water we drink will cause us to become thirsty again, but that *"the water I give them takes away thirst altogether. It becomes a perpetual spring within them, giving them eternal life"* (John 4:14 NLT). He is telling the woman that He is the only true thirst quencher, and He is the only One who can fill us up so that we are satisfied. But how do you get this *Living* Water? What does letting God fill us look like?

For Shawna, it looked like getting honest about her need for approval and unconditional love and admitting that she never felt "good enough," even as a young child. Sometimes the hardest step of all is to say out loud, "I need to feel valued and loved and I know I am looking in the wrong place." Yet, without it, we will never taste freedom. Once we surrender and say, "I know I am looking in the wrong place to get my needs met," we can begin to allow God to fill us with the one source that fully satisfies—His love.

His desire is that we know how much we are loved, treasured, and valued. If we know that more deeply in our hearts, it is less likely we will look elsewhere to be filled.

What does God say about His love for us?

Read Ephesians 3:16–19.

I pray that from his glorious, unlimited resources he will give you mighty inner strength through his Holy Spirit. And I pray that Christ will be more and more at home in your hearts as you trust in him. May your roots go down deep into the soil of God's marvelous love. And may you have the power to understand, as all God's people should, how wide, how long, how high, and how deep his love really is. May you experience the love of Christ, though it is so great you will never fully understand it. Then you will be filled with the fullness of life and power that comes from God. **(NLT)**

Describe God's love for you based on this passage.

Now read Romans 8:38–39.

And I am convinced that nothing can ever separate us from his love. Death can't, and life can't. The angels can't, and the demons can't. Our fears for today, our worries about tomorrow, and even the powers of hell can't keep God's love away. Whether we are high above the sky or in the deepest ocean, nothing in all creation will ever be able to separate us from the love of God that is revealed in Christ Jesus our Lord. **(NLT)**

What words in these verses make a special impression on you?

If you believed

in God's love for you more fully, what might look different in your life? What would you do more of? Less of?

If I believed in God's love more fully, I think there would be…

> **More** __________ in my life.

Think of thoughts, feelings, or actions.

Now fill in the columns provided.

Glimpsing His love for us begins to transform us. This does not always happen in a rush; but if we continue to rely on the truth God says about us instead of leaning into the lies that distract us, life begins to shift. Like Shawna and the woman at the well, we can become less inclined to seek "husband after husband" and more inclined to rest in the truth that we are loved, valued, and "good enough."

Less __________ in my life. <

Think of thoughts, feelings, or actions.

We waste so much of our lives trying to measure up to the inconsiderate evaluations that significant people in our lives make of us—callous statements that do not consider the frailty of our souls. What a glorious acceptance and encouragement we have from God, who offers us through His painful degradation and death, the gift of full acceptance, total love, and a purpose that is tailor-made, fulfilling, and true.

Mary, 57

1. Are you leaning into lies or truth?

THE LIES WE SOMETIMES BELIEVE THAT LEAVE US FEELING EMPTY:	THE TRUTH THAT HE CAN FILL AND SATISFY US:
"I'm unlovable."	His love for us is sealed and permanent, regardless of how we think or feel. (Romans 8:38–39)
"I'll never measure up."	In people's eyes we may not be, but in God's eyes we *are* complete in Christ. (Galatians 1:10; Romans 5:1)
"I must prove myself to others so that they will love and like me."	As God's daughter, there is nothing to prove. (Romans 8:15–17)
"If I just try harder, things will get better."	God's grace—a free gift—is what sustains us, not what we do. (Ephesians 2:8)
"I'll be left alone."	Jesus's promise to us: "I'll never leave you, I'll never forsake you." (Deuteronomy 31:6)
"I'm not worth fighting for."	God delights in us, will fight for us, and will work to save us. (Zephaniah 3:17)

Mark with an *X* each lie you sometimes believe.

Now using the statements you marked, look up the scriptural truths on the right-hand side of the chart and, from what you discover in the Bible, insert your own words into this sentence:

Even though I sometimes believe that ____

___________________ *(statement from "The Lies We Sometimes Believe")*, God's truth says that

____ *(statement based on Scripture).*

Repeat this thought process for each of the statements that you marked, mentally challenging the lies with God's truth.

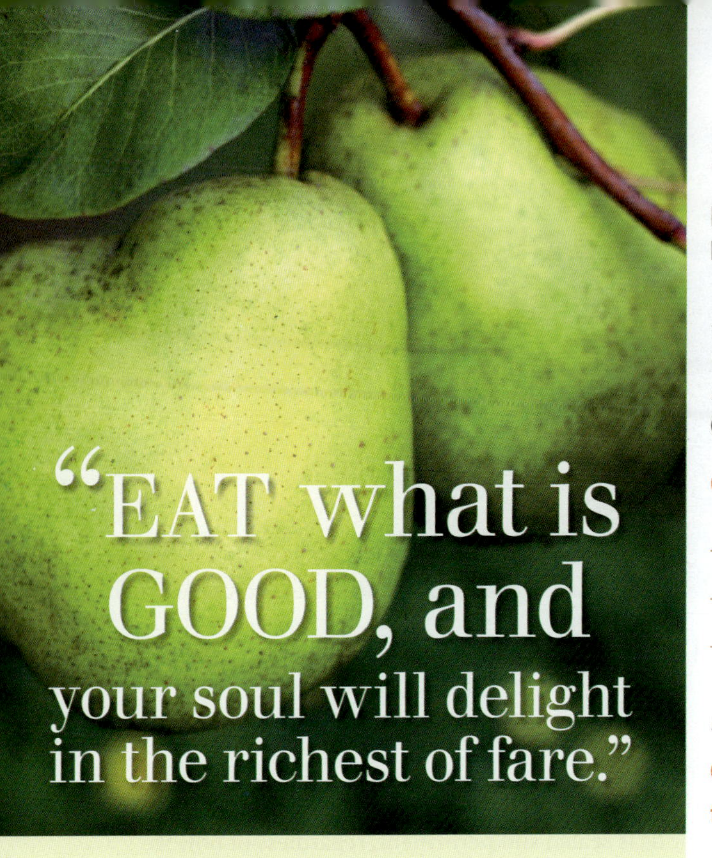

2. Satisfied

In the Old Testament Book of Isaiah, we are challenged with the question, *"Why spend money on what is not bread, and your labor on what does not satisfy? Listen, listen to me, and eat what is good, and your soul will delight in the richest of fare"* **(Isaiah 55:2 NIV)**.

How are these words similar to what Jesus shares with the woman at the well in John 4?

What do these statements mean to you?

3. Cry out!

Pray through Psalm 107:4–9 (NIV) in your journal by using the prayer launchers here:

Some wandered in desert wastelands, finding no way to a city where they could settle. They were hungry and thirsty, and their lives ebbed away **(vv. 4–5)**.

God, I am hungry for:

Then they cried out to the Lord in their trouble and he delivered them from their distress **(v. 6)**.

God, I cry out to You now. You know how I am troubled about:

He led them by a straight way to a city where they could settle **(v. 7)**.

God, I think that the straight way You may be asking me to think and act is:

Let them give thanks to the Lord for his unfailing love and his wonderful deeds for men, for he satisfies the thirsty and fills the hungry with good things **(vv. 8–9)**.

Lord, I thank You for:

1. A new direction

When you start to fill yourself with something that isn't good for you this week, imagine a huge red stop sign right in front of you, blocking your path. Next to it is an arrow pointing *Go this way . . . toward God.* Then spend some time praying in the quiet of your heart, read your Bible, and drawing from the verses provided, write in your journal and tell Him what you are thinking and feeling instead of filling yourself with things that don't satisfy.

2. Soak in His love

Each day this week, start your morning by reading Ephesians 3:16–19, reminding yourself of God's love for you. At the end of the week, journal about what happens to you, in the space provided.

I pray that from his glorious, unlimited resources he will give you mighty inner strength through his Holy Spirit. And I pray that Christ will be more and more at home in your hearts as you trust in him. May your roots go down deep into the soil of God's marvelous love. And may you have the power to understand, as all God's people should, how wide, how long, how high, and how deep his love really is. May you experience the love of Christ, though it is so great you will never fully understand it. Then you will be filled with the fullness of life and power that comes from God. **(NLT)**

Did meditating on this truth more intentionally change your week? How?

3. Share the emptiness

Sometimes feelings of emptiness come from sensing we are alone in our struggle. Letting it out with someone safe—telling the truth—can be freeing. Tell someone close to you about what's going on in your heart. Tell some of the things you are feeling inside (empty, satisfied, scared) and your longing for something different.

The emptiness I want to share about with someone is:

Who did you tell? What was it like for you?

1. What are some of your "husbands," the things that you run to, in order to feel loved?

2. Do these things ever satisfy you? Why or why not?

3. Look at the chart you completed in "Digging Deeper." What would there be more of, less of in your life if you believed more fully in God's love for you? Share what you wrote with the group.

4. Look at the "Are You Leaning into Lies or Truth?" chart in "Digging Deeper." Which of the statements on the left-hand side of the chart do you relate to? Read one Scripture application you wrote, replacing a lie with truth.

5. Closing round: Finish this sentence in one or two words: *I really want to feel like I'm "enough" in my*___________________ (to be answered after thoughtful reflection about relationship with God, others, and self).

Check These Out...

Abba's Child
by Brennan Manning

The Search for Significance
by Robert S. McGee

Be Restored! God's Power for African American Women
by Debra Berry

1. In advance of your group time ask someone from the group who has experienced freedom in the area of approval and seeking love from others instead of God to share a part of her story for five minutes. A good time to insert this in the group activity would be following activity number 4 below.

2. Start your group time by playing a song about God's faithfulness, such as "Faithful to Me" by Jennifer Knapp from the CD *Kansas* or another song. Or invite your women to sing an appropriate song from a hymnal.

3. Have all the women take everything out of their purses. When purses are empty, every woman should choose one item to put back into her purse—something that she "can't live without." (Note: cannot be wallet or keys!)

Everyone takes a turn and shares in response to these questions:

Why did you pick your one item?

How does it feel to let go of the other things in your purse?

If your purse only held items that were *absolutely necessary,* what would be in your purse?

What is *necessary* in your life to feel whole?

4. Hand out an index card to everyone in the group. Ask everyone to write down some "things" in their lives they use to fill themselves up (i.e., activities, money, approval). Share some of the responses in the large group or in smaller groups or in pairs.

5. Ask the woman who is prepared to share her story.

Bye-Bye Superwoman!

Unmasking my heart

Dana gave a polite smile to the women sitting around the circle. "OK, time for prayer requests." She pulled out her fabric-bound notebook and pen. "Marge, why don't you start." She nodded at the redheaded woman sitting next to her.

Marge glanced at Dana and then gazed down at her own shoes. "Well, I guess. . ." she hesitated. "My mother-in-law is visiting and it's just I find myself doing everything to win her approval," Marge's eyes welled up with tears. "But I never feel like I'm meeting all of her expectations."

Dana rested her hand on the well-worn Bible in her lap. "You know the Book of James might be a good place for you to spend some time. It has some really good things to say about needing other people's approval."

Marge sniffed and looked at Dana. Her eyes blank. "OK."

Dana patted Marge's leg and shifted her attention to the next woman. "How 'bout you, Sylvia?"

After all the women shared their requests, Dana closed the Bible study with a prayer and then stood up. "I'm sorry, ladies," she said as she smoothened her navy wool slacks. "I need to go. I have a meeting with a few elders in a couple of minutes. Thanks, everyone. See you next week."

Her heels clicked along the cement floor as she took brisk steps down the hallway to the church conference room. At the meeting, Dana was asked to consider being a key leader for the church. "We really respect your Bible knowledge and your disciplined lifestyle," one older gentleman told her. Dana assured the men she would pray about the decision and get back to them as soon as possible. As she left the meeting, a smile nudged its way up the corners of her mouth. Unlocking her car, she pulled her cell phone out of her purse and called her husband. "Jeff! Guess what?"

she asked with a surge of pride. "The church asked me to be part of the volunteer leadership team!"

"That's great, hon. I've got someone on the other line. Can we talk later?"

"Sure," she chirped. Pushing the red End button, she began making more calls as she drove to pick up her daughters from school. Before she pulled into the school parking lot, Dana had scheduled teeth cleanings for everyone in her family, left a message for the piano teacher to reschedule a lesson, and called the holistic nutritionist's office to ask for advice on a new rash that had broken out on her four-year-old daughter, Grace.

That night, after cooking a stir-fry dinner with brown rice, she gave the girls their baths, read to them, recited their Bible memory verse for the week, and tucked them each in bed with a prayer and a kiss. After picking up some scattered toys in the hallway and putting them away, she found Jeff sprawled out in front of the television watching a football game. "Hey, hon. Can we go over our calendars? I want to schedule some date nights and find a good time for us to meet with the principal."

Jeff nodded, his eyes glued to the screen.

Dana walked over to the kitchen desk and picked up her calendar. "Where's your Blackberry? I'll get it for you," she called to Jeff.

When Jeff didn't answer, Dana walked back into the family room. "Honey, where is your planner?"

He glanced at her briefly. "Uh, I think in the office."

After digging under papers on his desk, Dana found it. She grabbed a pen and plopped herself down on the couch next to her husband. Opening her calendar, she patiently waited for a commercial break. "OK, sweetie. I was going to try to get a babysitter for next Saturday night so we can go on a date. Does that work for you?"

Pushing some buttons on his Blackberry, he shrugged. "Sure."

"Great!" she wrote *7:00 P.M.— Date night* on both their calendars. "How 'bout a time to meet with Mr. Mackey?"

"I'm pretty packed next week. Do I have to be there?"

Swallowing her disappointment, Dana forced a smile. "I think it would be good if we were both there."

"Just set a time. I'll try to make it."

"OK." She bit her lip forcing herself not to lecture

What do you thrive on?

Part of breaking out of the superwoman syndrome is to understand what we "get" out of living this way. We don't act or behave a certain way because we think it's a good idea. There is a payoff that is sometimes addictive. Dana thrived on being respected by other people, being seen as the capable, competent Christian woman who had the right answers and did the right things. Being respected made her feel better about herself.

What do you thrive on? What are you hoping your efforts will get you? Check which one(s) might fuel you:

- ☐ Respect—being regarded highly by other people
- ☐ Control— maintaining power and control over a situation or people
- ☐ Approval—getting praise and affirmation from others
- ☐ Position, promotions, awards, leadership positions

What are some other ones for you?

him. The football game came on again and they watched it together until another commercial break. "Hon, I also wanted to get your opinion on something." She rested her hand on his leg. "Do you think Molly should stay with her current piano teacher, who is cheaper but doesn't really push her to stay on top of her practices; or should I move her to Mrs. McKenzie, who I hear challenges her students?"

"Whatever you think." Jeff stood up and walked into the kitchen to get a beer.

"I think she needs to be pushed a little more."

He nodded. "OK. Then change teachers."

After he sat back down, Dana snuggled into him and they watched the game. When a yawn escaped her mouth, she closed the calendars. "I'm gonna go to bed." She pecked Jeff's cheek. "Night."

"Night." He didn't look at her as she walked out of the room.

Brushing her teeth, Dana analyzed how she could improve the communication in their marriage. *I need to figure out better times to try to connect with Jeff.* She pulled out the floss and silently reprimanded herself. *He was too preoccupied tonight. I need to wait until we have some solid time together and not force it when he is tired and distracted.*

The next morning when Dana's alarm went off at 5:00, she slipped out of bed careful not to disturb Jeff. Padding softly downstairs, she made herself a cup of herbal tea. She sat down on her favorite overstuffed chair and pulled an angora throw blanket over herself. Picking up her journal from the side table, she opened to her list of people she prayed for. It was Tuesday, which meant it was her day to pray for unbelieving friends and family members. She prayed for each name on the list and then worked on her Bible lesson for the following week. After she was done with that, she picked up her prayer journal and began to write.

Dear Lord,

I try so hard to make our marriage better, but Jeff is inattentive and uninvolved. I find myself so let down by him all the time. Lord, help me to try harder to engage him as a dad, to communicate with him more effectively; to serve him better. . . . Help me have the energy to try harder.

After an hour of studying and prayer, Dana noticed

How'd it get there
in the first place?

None of us woke up one morning and suddenly became a certain way. Patterns develop over a long period of time. Most of the patterns we are living out as adults came from significant relationships we had in our families. As Dana learned to move from her head to her heart, she looked back on her childhood and remembered how anything she expressed emotionally was labeled "dramatic" or "silly" by her parents. She learned at an early age that emotions weren't valued, so she adjusted and shut down parts of her heart to live more peacefully in her family's culture.

GROWING UP, how were your emotions valued in your family? Was it OK to express your emotions freely? Why or why not?

THINK ABOUT THE PRESENT, Is it easy or hard for you to express your emotions in your current family? Why or why not?

IF YOU HAVE CHILDREN, what messages are you passing on to them about feelings? Do you encourage them to feel or is it hard for you to let them be angry or sad? Why?

Abby shuffling into the room dragging her tattered pink blankie. "Good morning, sweetie." Dana set down her journal and scooped Abby into her lap. She buried her nose into her daughter's hair, inhaling the sweet scent of baby shampoo. With her arms tightly wrapped around Abby, she rocked back and forth as her thoughts swirled around everything she needed to get done that day.

She fed the children pancakes made with whole-wheat flour, flax-seed oil, and honey; then packed lunches, did the girls' hair, helped them each brush and floss their teeth and make their beds. Before driving them to school, she kissed Jeff. "Don't forget our meeting with Grace's teacher today at 3:30."

Jeff looked up from reading the newspaper. "OK. Did you get my dry cleaning?"

"Yes. It's hanging in your closet. Need anything else?" Pleased by her own efficiency, a smile tugged at her cheeks.

He shifted his eyes back down to the paper. "No thanks."

She kissed him again. "Have a good day."

That afternoon Jeff did not show up for the teacher's meeting. Dana's disappointment turned to anger as she drove home from the meeting. "Why didn't you show up?" she snapped when he got home that night.

"I'm sorry. I totally forgot."

"That's not good enough." Her voice got louder.

"I don't know what to tell you, Dana. I forgot."

"I'll tell you what you can tell me. Why aren't you more involved? Why do I do everything around here?" She walked after him as he left the kitchen. "I do all the discipline." Her voice rose to a higher pitch. "I'm the only one implementing what we've learned from our parenting class."

"Dana, I've had a long day." His words were clipped.

"And I didn't?"

He shrugged, went into the bathroom, and closed the door.

She stomped out of the room muttering under her breath. Anger boiled inside her as she banged around the kitchen making dinner. Later that night after putting the girls to bed, her emotions simmered down and she began chiding herself. *Instead of blowing up I need to take my marriage to God.* Taking a deep breath she prayed. *Lord, I'm sorry for my impatience. I know I need to love him better. Help me do a better job.*

Dana's "try harder" spirit spiraled downward after she had her fourth child. Besides the sheer energy drain on her from taking care of four small people, life began piling up: Abby was drawing daily on furniture and no punishment seemed to be effective; Grace's chronic food allergies continued to get worse despite Dana's superwoman efforts to treat the condition with naturopathic remedies; and Molly's teacher thought Molly had attention deficit disorder (ADD). On top of all that, Jeff's business had taken a serious financial hit and they had lost a lot of money. Nothing Dana said or did lifted Jeff's spirits and every day he seemed to become more withdrawn and depressed. Tired, overwhelmed, and disappointed, Dana was void of any energy to pursue her husband, and they drifted further apart.

One morning during her routine quiet time, Dana pounded her fist on the chair. *Why, God?* She looked up at the ceiling as tears drizzled down her cheeks. *Why won't everything I am studying . . . all the verses I have memorized . . . translate into my own life?*

A turning point in Dana's crumbling world came when her newly divorced, alcoholic brother visited from Chicago. For years Dana had prayed for Jack

and she was glad he was visiting but, the truth was, she was so emotionally and spiritually depleted she didn't have her usual vigor to pour into him. She did manage to find out about a local church that held a great recovery group for hurting people and made a phone call to find out when they met. To her surprise, when she told Jack about the group, he agreed to go. The night the group met, Jeff and Dana had their couples Bible study. "We should be home by 9:30," Dana said to Jack while furiously writing down notes for the babysitter.

"OK," he said bleakly.

Glancing over at the kitchen table where her brother sat watching her, Dana noticed the bags under his eyes were bigger and darker than usual. Her heart pinched. She wanted to help him. Save

Becoming Better Lovers

Jesus summed up the entire law in two commandments: "'*And you must love the* Lord *your God with all your heart, all your soul, all your mind, and all your strength.' The second is equally important: 'Love your neighbor as yourself.' No other commandment is greater than these*" **(Mark 12:30–31 NLT)**.

When we are living in the head instead of the heart, striving instead of being, there is a great likelihood we are missing out on the most important thing in the Christian life: *love*. Without love, the Apostle Paul tells us that we are like a clanging symbol that makes meaningless noise **(1 Corinthians 13:1)**. All of the Bible knowledge in the world can't replace *living* the Bible. Jesus calls us to love above all things; to love God and to love other people as we love ourselves. The old adage "Actions speak louder than words" comes from God. Spiritual transformation, then, should be measured not by how much we know but how well we have loved.

I (Laura) was on the phone the other day with a friend who was recently diagnosed with stage 4 ovarian cancer. She had just been through a day of chemo and was very weary. Before we hung up she said in a weak, tired voice, "Love each other well." As I hung up the phone my heart stung. Just before talking to her I had been too busy with my to-do list to help one of my kids. Earlier that day I had ignored something my husband had asked me to do because I was so focused on all the work I had to get done. My very sick friend's words reverberated inside my head, reminding me about what was really important: loving each other well.

How are you missing out on loving others because you're caught up in doing? Who do you want to love more freely?

Joy Zapper

him. Mustering up enthusiasm for his willingness to go to the group, Dana offered, "I think you'll get a lot out of tonight."

"Sure."

After the sitter arrived, Jeff and Dana drove to the Bible study in silence. Dana hated the chasm between them. *Why am I the only one who tries to fix us?* she thought as resentment brewed inside her. Looking over at Jeff her throat tightened. His face and shoulders sagged and it felt like he was slipping away from her. *We need help.* Desperation took hold of her. "Jeff," she blurted. "I'm going to tell them about us tonight."

For a minute he didn't answer. "Whatever you want, Dana," he finally responded with a flat voice.

Once they got to the sprawling ranch home where their Bible study was held, Dana and Jeff nibbled on warm brownies and sipped decaffeinated coffee with the other couples before they gathered in the family room and began their ritual of starting out with prayer requests.

"I'd like to ask for prayer for my daughter's transition into middle school," one woman shared.

Everyone nodded.

"Please pray for the stress at my office," a man next to her said. "We are moving this week and we have some big deals we are trying to close by Friday." He raised his eyebrows. "Everyone is a little tense."

Holding his hand, his wife gave a nervous laugh. "And you can pray for me because he's gone every night this week."

Dana was the last one in the group to share her need for prayer. "I'm sorry," she said drawing a deep breath, "I can't do polite anymore."

The room grew still.

"Life's just too hard right now." She raked her hand through her hair. "Jeff is really struggling with depression because our finances are so bad." She avoided looking over at Jeff. "Grace's eczema is so awful she cries and bleeds every day. My kids are fighting all the time and I feel like I don't know how to effectively discipline anymore." Gulping for air she continued. "And Jeff and I aren't talking. We're like strangers in the same house. I guess I'm just out of ideas

> Dana was the last one in the group to share her need for prayer. "I'm sorry," she said drawing a deep breath, "I can't do polite anymore."

on how to make things better." She looked around at the faces staring at her.

No one said anything.

Biting her lip, Dana looked down. "And out of energy," she mumbled. Discomfort rose inside the room like a hot-air balloon.

Finally one of the women cleared her throat. "What comes to mind is Philippians 4:6–7." She opened her Bible and read the verses. Dana knew the words by heart, but as the woman read them they rang hollow in her heart.

She looked up and forced a smile. "Thanks."

Another woman said, "We'll be praying for you. I know God will use these hard times to refine you."

Dana nodded weakly but something inside her withered.

"Well, let's start this week's study," the host said opening his Bible.

As the men and women talked, Dana didn't hear a word they said. She wanted to disappear into thin air and never see those people again. During the car ride home, Jeff's silent anger burned into her skin but she was too humiliated and defeated to say anything.

When they got home, Jack was in the kitchen munching on leftover pizza.

"Hi," Dana forced a false cheerful note into her voice. "How was it, Jack?"

Jack's face lit up. "Great! Those people were amazing."

"Really?" Dana leaned against the refrigerator.

"Everyone there has hard stuff in their lives, but the cool thing was they were all really into God."

Dana noticed a small spark in her brother's eyes. "Wow, Jack. That's great."

"Yeah. And the speaker talked about codependence." He paused long enough to take another bite of pizza. "How some people get into relationships with other people who are unreliable or emotionally unavailable." Jack chased his pizza down with a gulp of root beer. "He said the codependent person tries to provide and control everything within the relationship without addressing his or her own needs."

Dana's heart quickened. "That's codependence?"

"MmHm," Jack nodded and pulled another piece of cold pizza from the cardboard box. "These people were so honest and no one was scared of anyone else's story."

"Sounds like a great group," Dana said, pouring herself a glass of water. Bone weary, she reached over and squeezed her brother's shoulder. "I'm really beat. Do you mind if I head up to bed?"

He shook his head with a smile.

"Go right ahead."

Lugging herself up the stairs, her mind spun around what Jack had said. She stopped halfway up the staircase and held onto the rail. *I need to go to this group—don't I, Lord?* The answer seared her heart. *Yes.* As Dana got ready for bed, she thought about what it would be like going to a group for "messed-up" people. Cringing, she squeezed toothpaste into a neat line on her toothbrush. *How embarrassing. How can a person like me need a recovery support group? What if I see someone I know?* When she crawled in bed, she felt the cold distance between her and her husband. "I'll go," she whispered into the dark.

The following Friday night,

Dana found herself sitting among people with a wide range of problems and issues in their lives. She watched in awe as different men and women humbly opened up and shared their struggles. One woman shared how crushed she was at work because all of her efforts to please her boss didn't fix the situation. *Me too,* Dana thought as tears pooled in her eyes. *All of my efforts haven't worked.*

Dana began to attend the recovery group on a weekly basis and she also became plugged into a 12-step Bible study which was geared toward helping people honestly look at their issues and grow in a safe environment through studying the Bible. It was powerful to be around a group of Christians who were longing to live a different way and committed to truth and honesty. Dana marveled at how they were unafraid to say the hard, unedited reality of their struggles.

As she reflected on herself, Dana began to see how all of her life she had operated from her head—logically, systematically, and efficiently. But in doing so she had shut down living from her heart. "I realized that as a kid what was valued was head stuff and not heart stuff. If I was ever emotional, it was written off by my parents as silly or dramatic. What was respected in my home was 'getting the job done.' So that's how I operated. I became a proficient, knowledgeable doer and learned to thrive on how well I could do a task. I actually thought that was what God wanted from me—striving for excellence in all things. Aren't we supposed to be 'women of excellence'?"

But, as Dana began to explore a relationship with God from her heart, she started to realize she had been trying to play God in her home, always rushing in and saving people, including her husband. To change her ways, she had to accept that God cared about her heart and not how many Bible verses she knew or how expertly she ran her household. Her whole sense of self was based on her hard-earned respect, and now she had to learn to believe she was valued beyond how competent and capable she was. It was a huge shift for Dana. ❁

striving all of the time that anything else felt unnatural. But through the support and love of honest friends, I finally got to a place of surrender that is really the opposite of striving," she explains. "I came to a place where I was OK being a messy person that didn't have it all together and who couldn't fix everything by trying harder. And the shift from my head to my heart changed how I see life and what I value. I feel so much more relaxed and free. It's sometimes still hard for me not to try to control and overcompensate, but I'm slowly learning to let go and laugh more at myself. And, I've discovered a much more satisfying relationship with God that I always longed for but never could find."

The Long **Journey** from Your **Head** to Your **Heart**

POINT OF CONNECTION

**Striving for excellence. Trying harder.
Being better.
Working smarter. Accomplishing. Succeeding.
Doing more.**

Isn't that what good Christian women are all about? Ingrained into many of us is the belief that our spiritual walk is based upon how hard we work . . . how much we *do*. We feel valued for our competency and efficiency. But we need to stop and ask ourselves: *Is this how we are supposed to live? Is this the free and abundant life Jesus talks about?* (See John 10:10.)

God makes it very clear in Scripture He wants us to be with Him and not just do for Him. After all, He made us human *beings*, not human *doings*. What does this mean? It means He cares more about a relationship with us than anything else. He wants to connect with our heart in the deepest places and be our friend.

Jesus said, "But I have called you my friends."

John 15:15 (AMP)

And a true friendship requires a heart connection. A friendship is not about skills, competencies, and abilities. It is not about Superwoman efficiency and Wonder Woman strength. It is about relating to one another with vulnerability and openness. Just as you enjoy being with your friends, God enjoys being with you. Think about it for a minute. If you hadn't seen a close friend for a long amount of time, would you rather her come over and organize your spice rack or sit in front of the fireplace and talk with you? Talk

with you, right? Same with God. He'd rather be with you than have you running about in a full-blown frenzy doing things for Him.

Another problem with living like superwoman Dana is a tiresome lack of freedom. When we live a life centered on striving, we miss the whole point God intended for us. God wants to be in a wild, deep, beautiful intimate relationship with all of us that is full of freedom. Freedom to be ourselves. Freedom to make mistakes. Freedom to love God. Freedom to receive His love. Freedom!

Working for God is slavery and bondage. Loving God is freedom. Here is a picture of how different the two look. Years ago I (Laura) was asked to be the nursery director at our church. At the time, I had two nursery-age children and the last place I wanted to be was in a nursery crammed with more small children. But, I did it. I did not do it out of love for God. I did it out of a dutiful obligation to do my share of work for the church and God. I hated every minute of my nursery work. Years later, after we had moved and began attending a new church, I was asked again to get involved in the children's ministry. This time I said, "No." And I didn't feel guilty one bit. I was in a different place with God. A place of freedom. A place where I knew He didn't frown on me for not "working" for Him in a volunteer job I had no passion for and didn't enjoy.

Many of us live our walk with God as slaves to Him and slaves to other people.

When you think of the words *freedom with God,* what do you think about?

Read Hosea 2:14–16.

"Therefore I am now going to allure her; I will lead her into the desert and speak tenderly to her. There I will give her back her vineyards, and will make the Valley of Achor a door of hope. There she will sing as in the days of her youth, as in the day she came up out of Egypt. "In that day," declares the Lord, "you will call me 'my husband'; you will no longer call me 'my master.'" **(NIV)**

In this verse, God is talking about His relationship with the Israelites, but it is also meant to be a beautiful metaphor for His heart toward *us.* He doesn't want to be the master with us as His dutiful slaves. He wants us to be free in our relationship with Him, to break out of the bondage of doing and trying and learn how to live in a free, heart-connected love relationship with Him.

Go back to Hosea 2:14–16. Reread it, knowing that this is God's heart for a relationship with you. What words impress you from this passage of Scripture?

Dana could only view God as a master, someone to work for, someone to please. And in her striving she was a slave. Look what God says about living like a slave.

Read the following passages.

• Romans 8:15–16

So you should not be like cowering, fearful slaves. You should behave like God's very own children, adopted into his family calling him "Father, dear Father." For his Holy Spirit speaks to us deep in our hearts and tells us we are his children." **(NLT)**

• Galatians 5:1

So Christ has really set us free. Now make sure that you stay free, and don't get tied up again in slavery to the law. **(NLT)**

Dana lived in slavery to the law. She was controlled by a need to do the right things for God and didn't know how *to be with* God. Second Peter 2:19 says, "For you are a slave to whatever controls you" (NLT).

Reflect on your relationship with God and other people. What are you a slave to right now?

Dana felt tired most of the time. She also felt empty, unfulfilled, and angry; but she was afraid to admit these feelings because it was not how she was supposed to feel.

What are some of your feelings right now? Circle the ones that describe you. Below are some to choose from. Be honest.

Sad	Angry	Shame-filled
Disconnected	Discouraged	Tired
Ambivalent	Encouraged	Filled
Scared	Lonely	Thankful
Broken	Hurt	Happy
Anxious	Suicidal	Excited
Hopeful	Dissatisfied	

Getting in touch with some of the real feelings is a big step for many women. Many of us have been taught, intentionally or unintentionally, that feeling anything negative isn't good. The sad truth is many of us are like Dana, controlled by what we think we're supposed to feel instead of living in freedom.

To change her life, Dana had to admit that she was tired of how she was living. Being valued for her competency, independence, and efficiency felt empty and frustrating. To change she had to begin to risk her heart with God and some new, safe friends who were trying to live from the heart too. She had to be courageous and make herself vulnerable. She had to rock the boat in her Bible study, in her marriage, and risk being seen as scandalous. Let's face it. Talking about the real stuff going on in our hearts is messy business. It means some people will look at us and think we're clearly not as *spiritual* as we're supposed to be. When Dana initially shared the truth of her life and negative feelings with some Christians, she was met with stony silence. It would have been easy for her to retreat back to the bondage of living dishonestly and trying harder, but instead she pursued something different.

And in her pursuit of living differently she found a very rewarding payoff. Dana actually began to experience genuine peace, joy, and love for the first time.

Freedom in her relationship with God. Freedom in her relationship with other people. She let go of controlling others and overcontrolling herself. Remember the words in 2 Peter 2:19—we are slaves to whatever controls us. When we are controlled by striving, doing, and trying, our hearts are absent of peace, joy, and love.

Read Galatians 5:22–23.

But when the Holy Spirit controls our lives, he will produce this kind of fruit in us: love, joy, peace, patience, kindness, goodness, faithfulness, gentleness, and self-control. **(NLT)**

Many of us who have been Christians for a while might be able to recite these fruits of the spirit without even blinking. But how do we experience them more in our daily lives? Striving harder? Dana tried that but it didn't work. We can't make any of these things magically appear. Maybe you're trying hard to get more of them in your life, too, but keep coming up short. Instead of striving for more joy and peace and patience, we need to know God wants to freely give them as we connect with Him through our hearts, not our heads. If you're a doer like Dana, making this shift won't be easy; but we have to start somewhere. **Let's start with this prayer:**

God, I am tired of striving and living like a slave. I yearn to live from my heart and be in a deep fulfilling friendship with You. Teach me how to do this, Lord, and give me friends who can encourage me in my journey. I confess that I often thrive on my own self-sufficiency and don't come to You enough. Help me let go of this, Lord. I long for Your fruits of love, joy, peace, patience, kindness, goodness, faithfulness, gentleness, and self-control. And I know these come from You alone. So help me to draw close to You and receive these fruits instead of striving for them. Teach me how to risk more, feel more, and take hold of the freedom found in You.

Digging Deeper

1. Rest for the weary

Rest. Ah, isn't that what so many of us long for, to just rest? To get filled up, replenished, and rejuvenated. Strivers never rest. We know how to *do* but we don't know how to simply *be*; how to stop and deeply connect with God and let Him nourish us with truth, love, and grace. Part of learning to connect with God with our hearts and not our heads is to talk with Him in a conversational, real way that's raw. And then to stop and ponder and listen to what He might be trying to say back to us. Some of you are already good at this. Keep going! For others of you, this is new and it will be harder. Here is an exercise that can help you practice.

Read Matthew 11:28–31.

Then Jesus said, "Come to me, all of you who are weary and carry heavy burdens, and I will give you rest. Take my yoke upon you. Let me teach you, because I am humble and gentle, and you will find rest for your souls. For my yoke fits perfectly, and the burden I give you is light." **(NLT)**

Now, breaking down this passage, answer the following questions. Try to respond from your heart, not your head. Don't think about the "right" answers. Give answers based on how you feel in this moment.

Jesus starts out this passage saying, *"Come to me . . ."*

Do you want to come to God right now? Why or why not?

"All you who are weary and carry heavy burdens..."

Tell God what you are weary of right now.

God, I am really weary of . . .

What are the burdens you are carrying right now?

I am carrying these burdens, Lord . . .

"I will give you rest."

What would rest look like for you?

What do you need rest from?

"Take my yoke upon you."

A yoke on an ox is something that guides the ox so that it can do its job more efficiently. It's not a burden; actually it makes the ox's load lighter.

Why is it hard for you to take God's yoke upon you? What scares you about His yoke?

....

....

....

....

"Let me teach you . . ."

What is something you know God is trying to teach you right now?

God, I think You are trying to teach me . . .

....

....

....

....

....

....

"Because I am humble and gentle, and you will find rest for your souls."

Do you see God as humble and gentle? Why or why not?

....

....

....

"For my yoke fits perfectly and the burden I give you is light."

Practice giving your burden to God.

God, I give You . . .

....

Tell God why you are giving this burden to Him; what you hope will happen; what you want to be released from.

....

....

....

....

The older I get, the more I know a couple of things for sure! "Try harder" Christians often live a life of shame and defeat in a somewhat self-centered pursuit to serve God.

I know because I have been there! There is an accuser who has been on a relentless pursuit to barrage my mind and assault me with negative "facts" about myself! I have spent much of my life agreeing with him!

After all, I know the messages. I play those tapes over and over in my head—the replay of my own sins, inadequacies, failures. This nagging endless tirade has robbed me of reaching out to others and loving them.

No more! The spiritual armor includes the belt of truth and I confront the enemy and my own mind with Scripture. "I can do all things through Christ" (Philippians 4:13 NKJV). My sins are forgiven and removed from me (Psalm 103:12). He delights in me (Psalm 18:19). The Bible is full of truths. I choose to believe the truth. Life is full and God has brought freedom to my soul and spirit as I believe His Word instead of lies.

Jane, 62

2. Heart truth

But you desire honesty from the heart, so you can teach me to be wise in my inmost being.
Psalm 51:6 (NLT)

In order to move from our heads to our hearts, we need to become more honest about the truth of what's going on inside our hearts. It took time for Dana to be able to connect with what she really felt and be honest about it. The connection was not automatic. First, she saw other people being real and it felt refreshing. Then she had to practice it in her own life. To grow in this area, we'll need to practice too. We need to tune in and begin noticing what's happening inside us and then be able to say it to God, ourselves, and other safe people. Here's a chance to practice.

In the heart below write out all the emotions you are feeling. Look at the list in the "Point of Connection" section if you need a little help getting started.

Read what you wrote. Take a minute to reexamine your heart in silence, asking God for His help. This is digging deeper His way. Is there anything else there?

Would you be embarrassed to share what you've written with close friends? If so, why?

3. Playing God

In the Sermon on the Mount, Jesus gives us some fairly clear instructions on living. He starts out with what are called the Beatitudes, heart attitudes that can guide us toward Him and a new way of living. These attitudes are against our basic human nature to live life our way instead of God's way. He starts out with the most critical one for strivers.

Read Matthew 5:3.

God blesses those who realize their need for Him, for the Kingdom of Heaven is given to them. **(NLT)**

Here are how some other Bible versions translate this verse:

Blessed are the poor in spirit: for theirs is the kingdom of heaven. **(KJV)**

You're blessed when you're at the end of your rope. With less of you there is more of God and his rule. **(The Message)**

Blessed (happy, to be envied, and spiritually prosperous—with life-joy and satisfaction in God's favor and salvation, regardless of their outward conditions) are the poor in spirit (the humble, who rate themselves insignificant), for theirs is the kingdom of heaven! **(AMP)**

Those of us who work harder—try harder—are trying to control our lives and usually also the lives of those around us. Who is supposed to be in control? Us or God? Striving is like playing God because it is a dependence on ourselves and not on Him. It is self-reliance instead of God-dependence. There's no room for God when we are doing all of the work ourselves. But God says that we are blessed when we realize our need for Him.

Reflect on areas of your life where you are "playing God" by trying to control and manage through your own efforts instead of relying on God's help. Write them in the space below.

4. Who are you?

If we think about it, a lot of Christian women are valued for being self-reliant, capable, and extremely efficient.

Self-reliant. Capable. Extremely efficient. Which of these are you?

Do self-reliant, capable, extremely efficient women need God? Do they connect with God on a heart level? Do they need others? Do they connect with others on a heart level? No, no, no, and no. When we protect ourselves by doing instead of being, we miss the whole point. Wouldn't it be wonderful if Christian women were valued instead for being bold, unguarded, and risky? These are powerful and challenging words, especially for superwomen who spend a lot of time maintaining their image by working and trying harder.

Bold means a degree of courage. What if we'd be women willing to break out of fear, to have courage to say hard things, feel hard feelings, stay engaged in relationships instead of hide?

Unguarded means we don't pretend we have it all together. We can admit we don't know the answers. We can show our true hearts to people and let them speak into our lives.

Risky is the word that probably scares us the most because it means we will have to trust. Risky women are willing to upset the apple cart. Think of men and women in the Bible. Weren't all of them (including Jesus!) extreme risk takers? To really live the life God calls us to means that in some way we are going to have to take some risks, stop playing it safe, and rock some boats.

Bold. Unguarded. Risky. Which of these words do you connect with? Why?

Being Instead of Doing

Part of learning to live from our heads instead of our hearts is learning how to *be with* God instead of simply *do for* God. Being with God is not an easy task for most of us. We'd rather be doing. But sometimes real spiritual connection means going to a quiet place and resting with God.

In Mark 6:31, Jesus says, *"Come with me by yourselves to a quiet place and get some rest"* (NIV).

The following are some short exercises you can do in a quiet place to help you reflect on being with God instead of striving to do something for Him. Some of these might be helpful; others might feel uncomfortable. The bottom line is, in order to become healthy and strong spiritually and emotionally, we must learn how to rest. We must find ways to let go of the doing, the controlling, the managing, and *be.*

- **Sit quietly** in a comfortable place. Try to breathe deeply, inhaling God's peace, exhaling the anxieties that you are carrying inside of you. Do this at least ten times. Inhaling the peace of Christ; exhaling the burdens, the worries, the fears.

- **Focus** in on the Scripture Isaiah 40:11 (NIV) for a few minutes. **He gathers the lambs in his arms and carries them close to his heart.** Think through quietly in your heart what a little lamb is like. Describe that lamb. How are you like that lamb? Imagine that you are that lamb and that Jesus is gathering you up and nuzzling you close to His heart. What does that feel like for you?

- **Go for a walk** around the block by yourself. As you walk, look around to see if you notice a sliver of God's beauty. Is it in a flower sprouting up in the sidewalk's cracks? Is it in a baby being held by its mother on the front porch? Is it in a puddle rippling? Where do you see God's beauty in a place that you normally don't notice?

- **Go to an art museum** by yourself (this will be hard for some of you but worth the effort). Take at least an hour and walk slowly through the art gallery. What pictures provoke your eye? Which do you connect with? Why? How do you see God in these art pieces? What does it feel like to be still and silent and soak in something that you're not used to observing? Did you notice God's presence?

- **Try this** spiritual discipline where we take time to reflect on our day, noticing where we sensed or felt God's presence—called by some an examen. When we are busy working for God and disconnected from our hearts, we often miss God's presence. But as we discipline ourselves to slow down and stay more connected to our heart, we don't miss as much. A daily examen helps us reflect on where we felt God in our day. Here are some questions to ask:

  Where did I sense God's presence today?

  Where did I feel less alone?

  Where did I see His work?

  Where did I feel His comfort, protection, challenge, or help?

- **Do a heart check.** What is the truth of your heart right now? Be honest and in a quiet moment with God tell Him. *God, right now, my heart is really . . .* Then sit quietly and try to still your mind. Listen to what He might be trying to say to you. Does a word, a Scripture, a poem, a song, something you heard or saw in a movie, a picture, or vision come to mind?

- **Imagine** a big, rugged cross atop a hill. Picture yourself carrying your bag of burdens up this hill. What burdens are in your bag? Now, imagine laying them at the foot of this cross, giving them to God. Take a moment to thank God for taking these burdens from you. See yourself walking away, back down the hill without the bag. How does this feel?

1. Which of the "Tryin' It" exercises did you try? What was it like for you?

2. Which of the following do you relate to and feel most valued for/? Self-reliant? Capable? Efficient? How so?

3. Which of the following do you want more of in your life? Do you want to be more bold, unguarded, risky? Explain why.

4. Reflect on the activity "Playing God." What areas of your life are you "playing God" by controlling and micromanaging instead of relying on God's help?

5. Closing round: Go around the group to wrap up the sharing, and finish this sentence in a couple of words: *One thing I got out of this chapter that I hope to transfer into my heart is . . .*

Check These Out . . .

Satisfy Your Soul
by Bruce Demarest

I'm Not Wonder Woman; But God Made Me Wonderful
by Sheila Walsh

Love Beyond Reason
by John Ortberg

1. Read this slogan for the modern super-woman: She can go to her kickboxing class, manage her in-home business, and still make it to all of her kids' afterschool activities. She can whip a trans-fat-free gourmet dinner and serve it to her family with a smile on her face. She doesn't look tired and wears a size 4. And when her husband wants to be intimate after the kids are in bed, she never says no.

Bring a dartboard (or something that you can pin things to) to your group and have each woman write on a small piece of paper one thing about the modern super-woman message that she'd like to see eradicated. After each woman shares, she gets to pin her paper to the dartboard.

2. Rest and quiet sometimes need to be intentional. Do the following exercise together to help the group recognize how hard it is to stop even for just five minutes and receive God's rest.

Read the following Scripture aloud three times and then tell the group to open their hearts to try to rest with God for a few minutes: **In Mark 6:31, Jesus says, "Come with me by yourselves to a quiet place and get some rest" (NIV).**

Now be still for five minutes. *(Tell women they can get comfortable, close their eyes, and so on.)*

Invite feedback from the group afterward.

What was it like for them to be still and quiet for five minutes?

What did they experience?

3. Bring in a piece of chocolate and set it out in front of the group. Ask the women, "What does your head tell you to do when you look at this chocolate bar?" After some discussion ask, "What does your heart tell you to do when you look at this chocolate bar?" Discuss living more from our hearts and not our heads.

HOPE

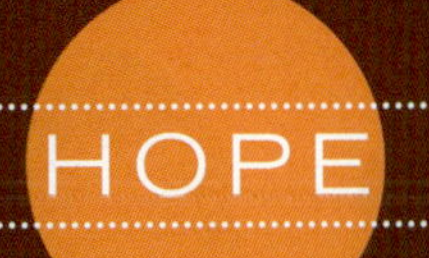

Guiltbusters

Top tips for banishing self-blame

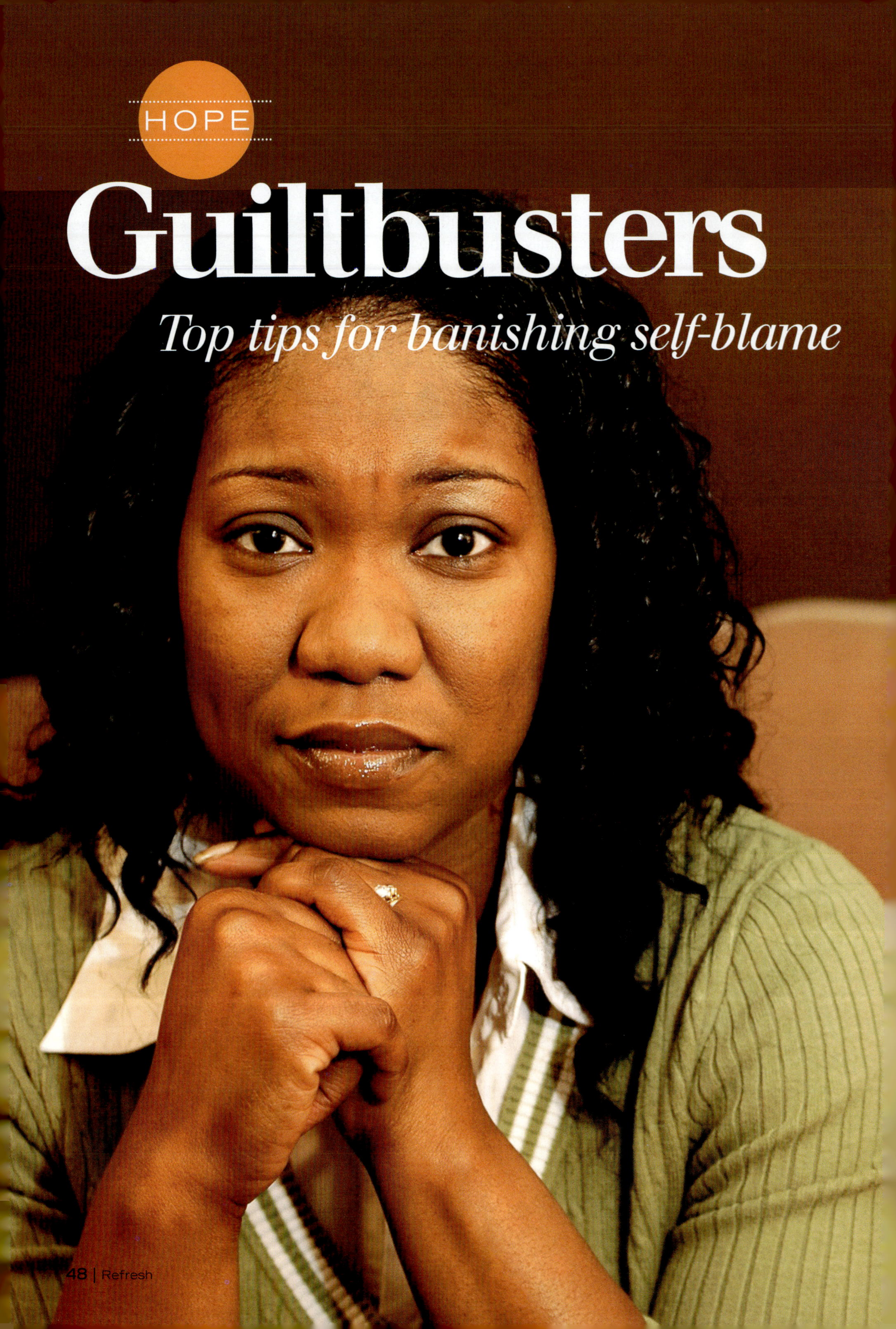

Hope drained the last of her

lukewarm coffee just as the phone rang. "Hello?"

"Mrs. Kresper?"

"Yes."

"This is Miss Patty. I'm so sorry to call you, but I was wondering if you can come get Jeremy. He's been screaming for an hour now."

"What happened?" Hope could hear Jeremy's screams in the background and her heart lurched.

"He fell off a chair. But don't worry. He's not hurt. When I helped him, he got embarrassed and upset." Miss Patty sighed into the receiver. "I'm so sorry, but we've tried everything and he's scaring the other children now."

"I'll be right there." Hope hung up the phone, whisked two-year-old Emma into the car, and drove to the church preschool. When she entered the building, she could hear Jeremy's loud crying. Rushing down the stairs to the preschool room she made a beeline into the office where a teacher's aide sat with Jeremy. His tear-streaked face was puffy and his nose was running. Kneeling down in front of him, Hope wrapped her arms around him and pulled him into her. "It's OK. Mama's here."

Jeremy's cries simmered down to a series of dramatic sniffles. "Come on, sweetie." She pulled a tissue from her purse and wiped his nose. "Mommy's going to take you home." Taking him by the hand, she led him through the classroom and she mouthed "Sorry" to Miss Patty, who glanced up while reading a story to the other children. Hope's chest tightened as her eyes swept across all the cross-legged children who sat quietly in the circle, their little faces attentive to the story. *Why isn't he able to be like the other kids?* Hope asked herself. A whirlpool of emotions swirled inside her as she and her son walked outside.

Strapping the seat belt across Jeremy, she gave herself a silent lecture. *I really need to get this temper tantrum thing under control. He can't be a disruption like this anymore.*

The strong-willed battles and temper tantrums didn't let up as Jeremy entered kindergarten. In an attempt to get their household under control, Hope read a mountain of parenting books. She and her husband, Brock, also signed up for a ten-week Christian parenting class. After taking the class for several weeks, Hope felt frustrated because she still wasn't winning any battles at home. One night during class she boldly raised her hand. Normally she would have been embarrassed by her question, but after the two-hour tantrum Jeremy had thrown that afternoon, she felt desperate for advice. "What do you do if your child runs out of school every morning and tries to get back into the car?"

The instructor cleared his throat. "You need to show the child who is in control. If the child senses he can get away with it, he will."

Hope nodded.

Another mom in the class jumped in. "I've found if I am consistent, Joey behaves better."

Hope swallowed. Joey was the most well-behaved five-year-old boy Hope had ever seen. *I need to be more like her.*

"Consistency is critical," the instructor nodded with an approving smile. "Discipline has to be consistent if you want to see change."

Brock and Hope drove home that night without talking. When they pulled into their driveway, Brock stopped the car and turned toward Hope. "I'll go with you tomorrow to take Jeremy to school."

"That would be great." She held his gaze noticing the empty space between them.

"We really do need to be consistent," he added before opening the car door and stepping out.

His words stung. She knew he was talking about her. As she got ready for bed that night, guilt pressed down on her. *If Brock was the one staying at home with the kids, we wouldn't have this problem. I'm the one to blame for his bad behavior.*

The next morning, Jeremy ran out of the classroom four times, and Brock spanked him four times before Jeremy finally stayed inside the classroom. Although Brock "won" the battle that day, Hope continued to struggle with Jeremy at home throughout the school year.

On one afternoon, Hope asked Jeremy to pick up his room before dinner.

"No!" he glared at Hope with eyes of steel.

Bracing herself, she spoke each word slowly. "Jeremy, you do not say no to your mother. If I tell you to clean your room, you say, 'Yes, ma'am.'"

Jeremy's face stiffened. He stormed into his room and Hope heard something crash against the wall.

Bolting after him, she watched in horror as he picked up a brand-new alarm clock and threw it.

"What are you doing?" Hope shrieked. "Jeremy, stop!"

When Jeremy picked up another toy, Hope grabbed both of his arms and squeezed his one hand, forcing him to drop the toy. Still holding his arms, she wrapped them around his middle and held him. He fought wildly, howling for her to let go. As Hope's mind raced and her heart ached, all she could think was, *Please, Lord, calm him down!*

After a long and fierce struggle, his limbs finally melted into hers. She held him for a long time until his breathing became heavy and she knew he had fallen asleep. Easing herself up off the ground, Hope lifted her son onto his bed. Kneeling beside him, she touched the soft curls on his head. Her heart continued to ache. He looked so innocent. *Lord, help me figure out what I am doing wrong.*

Hope ramped up her efforts to be consistent, but no matter how hard she tried, Jeremy's behavior did not improve. After Brock and Hope had their third child, the stress of mothering and dealing with Jeremy's outbursts took a toll on their marriage.

"I think we need to go for help, to talk to someone," Hope told Brock late one night after the kids were in bed.

Brock exhaled. "If you would be more firm, he would respect your authority."

In a flash of anger Hope snapped, "I'm trying the best I can. You're not at home. You don't have to deal with it all day." But inside her head, another voice confirmed his words. *He's right. I am the one to blame.*

"I'm just saying . . ."

"I know what you're saying. He acts this way because of me."

"Hope," Brock reached out to touch her but she pulled away. "I think you're right," he sighed. "Why don't we go talk to a counselor?"

The following week, Hope made arrangements for a babysitter to come watch the kids while she and Brock went to their first counseling appointment. The counselor made Hope feel worse, indicating Jeremy was having difficulties as a result of the problems in their marriage.

"Jeremy has been difficult to handle before we ever had any struggles in our marriage," she bemoaned to Brock on the car ride back to their house.

When they got home, Hope paid Jessie, the babysitter, and went into the kitchen to start dinner. Weighted down by more guilt, she was lost in her thoughts as she boiled pasta.

"Have you seen Jeremy anywhere?" Brock asked walking into the kitchen.

"Jessie said he was still upstairs. They were playing 'hide-and-seek.'"

"I was up there and he isn't there."

"Maybe he went outside. Dinner will be ready in ten minutes. Have the kids wash their hands," Hope called after Brock who was already headed out the front door.

When Brock came inside again, his brow was wrinkled. "I can't find him outside either."

"I'll go check upstairs again." Hope wiped her hands on a dish towel. "Jeremy?" she called as she climbed the stairs. After checking each room thoroughly she found Brock in the front yard. "He has to be out here."

For a half hour Hope and Brock combed the area while neighbor kids formed a search party on their bikes to find Jeremy.

When Hope walked into a neighbor's backyard that had a hot tub, she was no longer able to swallow the anxiety that was building inside her. "Jeremy!" she shrieked, picturing her child floating inside the tub. Her heart pounded against her ribs as the neighbor checked under the lid. The empty hot tub only shook her further. *Every minute counts. We have to find him.*

Soon more neighbors were pouring out of their houses and joining them in the search. After an hour of searching, Hope no longer could mask her hysteria. "Brock, we have to call the police!"

Instead of telling Hope she was overreacting, Brock nodded his head. "Yes." His voice was barely a whisper.

An icy quiver ascended to the back of Hope's neck as she watched her husband walk in the house to make the call. Brock's reaction confirmed her worst fear—Jeremy had been kidnapped, abducted, stolen. *This is how people get on the* Oprah *show,* she thought staring blankly at her house.

After an hour and a half of searching, Brock and Hope stood embracing each other on their driveway as police searched for any signs of Jeremy. When Brock buried his head into Hope's neck and began to sob, panic became a tidal wave around her. *Please, God! No!*

Suzanne, a friend of Hope's, pulled up in the driveway, jumping out of her car to embrace Hope. Hope shook with choking sobs as her friend held her tightly.

All of a sudden Suzanne pulled away. "What was that?"

"What?" Hope blew her nose into a tissue that someone had handed her.

"Hope, I just saw someone in your window."

Hope turned and looked up. No one was there.

"I promise I just saw someone up in your room." Suzanne pointed at their bedroom window. "There was someone up there."

"The police checked everywhere inside." Hope looked toward the window again and a flicker of hope stirred inside her. Without another word she hurried into the house. Dashing up to her room, there she found Jeremy standing with a sheepish grin on his face.

"Jeremy! Where have you been?" she threw her arms around him.

"I won."

"What?"

"I won. No one found me."

She pulled away from him. "Didn't you hear us calling for you? Didn't you hear the police?"

Shrugging, Jeremy looked away. "I won."

That night in bed Hope stared at the ceiling as a chilling truth seeped into her skin. *This is a bigger problem than we have been wanting to admit. There is something* wrong *with our child.* She gulped. *Something very wrong.*

Hope and Brock began taking Jeremy to a child psychologist, who eventually prescribed a medication for attention deficit disorder (ADD). But the doctor warned that, if Jeremy had a mood disorder, the medication would make Jeremy dramatically worse. The first time Jeremy took the medicine he went berserk—ranting and raving and throwing things all over the house. Brock and Hope took turns restraining him until the drug finally left his system.

His adverse reaction led to further psychological evaluations and Jeremy was finally diagnosed with bipolar mood disorder. Hope and Brock spent many months experimenting with different medications

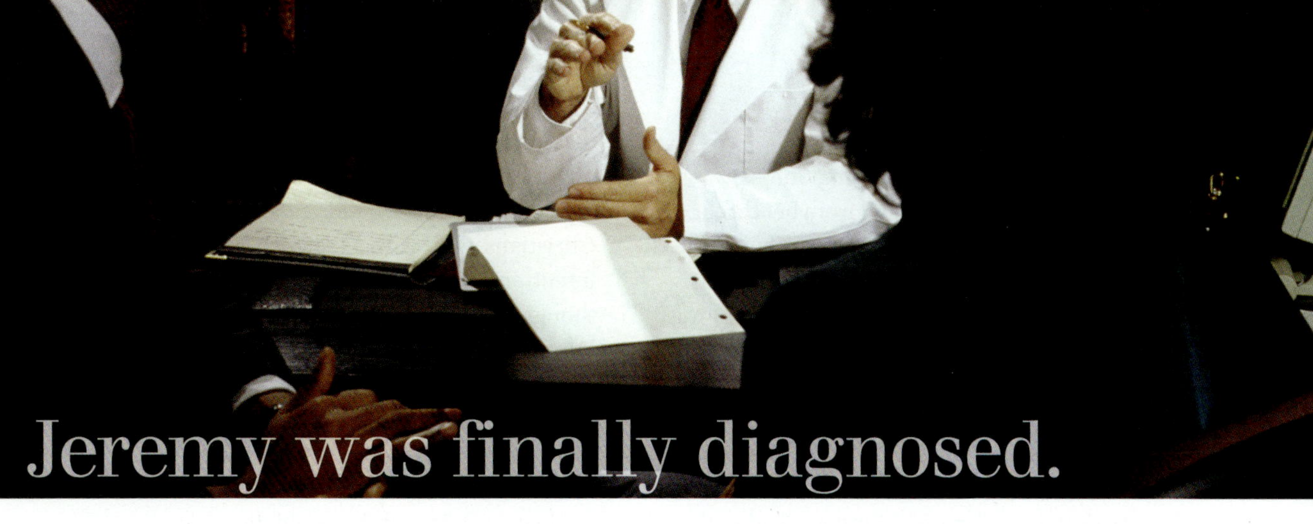

doctors provided to try to tone down Jeremy's mood fluctuations and aggressive behavior. Hope felt a mix of converging emotions in reaction to the diagnosis. Relief was one element, since there was finally some conclusive evidence about what was behind Jeremy's behavior. It was still so difficult not to feel as if somehow it was her fault. She battled the nagging voice that told her if she had only done this or that, everything would be turning out differently. Fear for Jeremy's future was another powerful emotion twisting inside her. Questions like, *Will he ever be able to function well as an adult in society?* haunted her.

On top of Hope's mixed bag of emotions, their whole house was on pins and needles as they experimented with different medications to help Jeremy.

One Saturday morning the tension in their house exploded. Hope was at home with the kids and was doing the dishes. Brock had left to go help friends move, and as Hope loaded the dishwasher she heard a loud bang upstairs. She stopped and listened again. *Bang!* Her limbs stiffened. "Emma," she called to her five-year-old daughter. "Come into the kitchen, please."

While Hope closed the dishwasher, Emma wandered into the kitchen, still wearing her pink pajamas. Putting her hand underneath Emma's chin, Hope tipped her daughter's face up so she was looking at her. "Emma, I need you to be a big girl for me."

Emma scrunched her face up. "I *am* a big girl."

"I know you are. So if Mommy tells you to take your sister and lock yourself in my room, I need you to do that. OK?"

"We're not supposed to lock the doors." Emma knit her eyebrows together.

"That's right, unless Mommy tells you to. Can you do that for me?"

"OK, Mommy."

Bang! Hope drew a shaky breath. "Your sister's watching her video. Go sit with her, Emma." Hope turned her daughter toward the family room and gave her a gentle push. "I'm going to go talk to Jeremy. Remember what I told you, honey?"

"MmHm," Emma's ponytail bobbed up and down.

Climbing the stairs, more banging rattled above her head. She found Jeremy in his room whipping a golf ball against the wall. "Jeremy! Stop!"

Jeremy didn't even look at her and threw it again. "I hate my life!" he spat as the ball ricocheted and he caught it.

"Jeremy, give me the ball." Her voice was low and steady.

He turned to her and whipped the ball at her. "I hate you!" Ducking to the side, the ball whizzed by her into the hallway.

"Jeremy, I have to lock you in here until you can control yourself." She closed the door in time to protect herself as Jeremy picked up something else and threw it at her. "I don't want to live anymore," he shouted at the top of his lungs.

Hope locked the deadbolt Brock had installed and leaned her forehead against the door. *Oh God, please don't let him hurt himself.* A shooting pain pierced her heart. *Please help him.* Suddenly a crash shook Jeremy's door and Hope jumped back.

"Emma," Hope called out. "Take Claire and lock yourself in Mommy's bedroom."

Again the door shook with another crash. Racing downstairs she grabbed the kitchen phone and dialed Brock's cell number. "Please answer!" she yelled into the receiver.

"Hello?"

"Brock," her chin quivered. "You have to come

home now! He's losing it!"

"Hope, slow down. What's going on?"

Crash! Choking sobs erupted from her throat. "He's breaking his door down. He's going to hurt himself!" Hope's breath caught in her throat, "Or hurt us."

"OK, I'm coming. But I'm almost an hour away."

"Hurry," she whimpered. *Crash!* After she hung up, she bolted up the stairs. "Emma," she knocked on the door to her bedroom. "Open up. It's Mommy."

Emma pulled the lever down and Hope stepped inside and locked her door. *Crash!*

"What's that loud noise?" Emma asked with wide, tear-filled eyes.

"It's OK, girls. Jeremy is just having a . . ." Before she could go any further, a thundering crash pounded on her bedroom door.

"Mommy, what's happening?" Emma grabbed Hope around the leg and baby Claire began to cry. The blood drained from Hope's face. *Please, God, help us.* She picked up the phone on her bedside table and called Suzanne. "Can you come over now? Jeremy is losing it." Hope was desperate.

"We'll be right there."

Suzanne and her husband arrived quickly and, as Hope had anticipated, Jeremy stopped acting so out of control because other people were present. When Brock got home, Hope's panic slowly released, like air from a punctured tire.

Over time, Hope and Brock discovered medications that have helped Jeremy and, as he has matured, a lot of the extreme behaviors have dissipated. When Hope looks back on the years before Jeremy was diagnosed, she sees so many areas in which she has grown and changed. "For so long I thought it was my fault that our son didn't behave like a typical boy. Christians who gave us advice may have had good intentions but it usually just made me feel guiltier. I thought if I could just be a better Christian parent, Jeremy would be better."

In her long, agonizing journey, Hope began to let go of the condemning voices in her head and began to listen for God's truth over the whole situation, including:

She was doing all she could do.

Jeremy had medical issues that were beyond her control.

Even though Jeremy would always struggle, Hope could still have a joy and peace in the midst of it all.

Both Hope and Brock realized Hope's apparent lack of "parenting skills" was not the cause of Jeremy's behavior. And now their united front, coupled with their individual approaches in dealing with Jeremy, has become a foundational source of strength in their home.

"I always wanted my son to simply be a normal youth group kid," Hope explains. "And for years I expended so much energy trying to make our home 'normal' instead of being accepting of what our family is like. I blamed myself for not being a good enough mother to change my child's behavior. I wanted the picture-perfect Christian family and I pretended that is what we were. Many days, though, I was weighed down by all this guilt, replaying things I should have done better. But when I finally accepted our family for what it is, I could go through the process of *grieving.* Accepting and grieving freed me up.

"Yes, I could have done things differently. But the reality is that Jeremy would still have the issues he has. No amount of beating up on myself can change that."

And, in letting go of the guilt and accepting her imperfect family, Hope has found herself in a much better position to love her son and help him be all he can be. ❀

Moving Past Self-Blame and Guilt
to the Bigger Picture

It's all my fault.

I keep messing up.

If only I . . .

These thoughts are common for a lot of us. We're experts at blaming ourselves and feeling guilty when things go wrong. Somehow, we always feel responsible. If only we had tried harder, knew more, done better, said something, been quiet. If only!

It is extremely difficult not to sink under the heaping weight of self-condemnation when things don't go the way they're supposed to or when we try hard and pray hard but things don't get any better. And, it certainly doesn't make it easier when we hear loud and clear critical voices around us. We sink deeper from the judgmental comments of teachers, family, and friends. But is this the way God wants us to live? Submerged under a thick blanket of false guilt? Of course not.

Jesus came to earth and died on the cross to free us from the bondage of self-condemnation! He came to remind us that what matters is what He says about us, not what others say.

Hope, a good Christian wife and mother, tried hard to do the best she could, and yet it wasn't enough. So, she blamed herself. Every time there was a conflict with her husband, a critical word from someone around her, a setback in Jeremy's progress, her first reflex was self-blame. *It's me. If only I could do it right, he wouldn't be having these problems.* For many of us, this is familiar territory. We blame ourselves first. We get stuck in guilt. Our perspective gets distorted, and we begin thinking, *If only I . . .*

Hope condemned herself time after time. *If only I was more consistent. If only I hadn't lost my temper. If only I knew more about strong-willed children.* In action, self-condemnation looks like beating ourselves up in our head. Sometimes we condemn ourselves for what we *are* doing and sometimes for what we are *not* doing.

Do you condemn yourself at times? Why? Think of how you view yourself in relationships, parenting, work, and church. Finish these sentences and fill in what comes to mind.

- **I sometimes condemn myself for . . .**

- **I sometimes condemn myself for not . . .**

But when we live from this place called *condemnation*, we are robbed. The word itself, according to *Webster's* dictionary, means "censure" or "blame." Yet here is a simple and powerful truth from God's Word about living under our own condemnation:

Therefore, there is now no condemnation for those who are in Christ Jesus
—Romans 8:1 (NIV)

Does God condemn us? Through Christ Jesus we are "fit for use" no matter what. That is the bottom line. Jesus came to free us from our sin, shame, and sometimes the hardest one to shake—our guilt when we do blow it.

It is hard for us to comprehend, but when Jesus died on the cross, He took on the sins of the world. He paid the price for our sin through His death so we could be free. So, even when we have instances of guilt, God doesn't want us trudging through life weighted down by our failures. I want to share a very simplistic example that also provides you with an entertaining visual.

Recently, my (Laura's) daughter went on a llama hike at a summer day camp she attended. On the hike the llama walked, with my daughter and 17 other campers, up the mountain trail, carrying all the water bottles and lunch boxes for the hikers. Although the campers had to trudge up the steep trail, they were free from the burden of carrying their stuff. God wants us to be free too. We all do sin, and sin breeds real guilt. However, Christ is the guilt remover: God, in 1 John 1:9 promises that every Christian's confession restores that healthy, freeing relationship.

Then who's condemning us? Why is the guilt factor in our lives so strong? Usually it's a triple combination.

- Satan—also referred to in the Bible as the evil one, the father of lies, the robber
- Ourselves—our own insecurities and fears
- Others—negative messages that they have passed on to us about who we are or are not.

Study the chart on the opposite page. Notice differences between the two voices. Which voice is more familiar to you?

Now think for a moment how the enemy is trying to prey on your situation. Walk through the chart and notice how these thoughts are consistent with the condemnation of the evil one. What parts do you connect with? Which of these feel familiar to you right now?

Think of a current struggle you face. Write it in the space below:

God can speak to us in our struggles. He doesn't want us to live with our ears tuned into the lies and condemning whispers of the evil one. He wants us to spend our lives listening to Him so that He can pour truth into us and demolish our guilty feelings.

Think again about your current struggle. Now look at the conviction of the Holy Spirit on that side of the chart. Walk through it carefully and think how God might have a different perspective on your situation. What parts do you connect with?

What are some negative thoughts you are thinking about yourself related to this struggle?

Out of these three voices, from which one do you receive the most condemnation? How?

....

....

....

....

Read John 10:10a.

The thief's purpose is to steal and kill and destroy. **(NLT)**

For Hope, the thief was trying to steal her peace and confidence, setting her up to step into the trap of self-blame.

What is the enemy trying to steal, kill, or destroy in your life right now? What is he robbing you of?

....

....

....

....

....

....

....

....

Discerning the Difference

CONVICTION OF THE HOLY SPIRIT	CONDEMNATION OF THE EVIL ONE
Gentle tone: Loving, imploring, beseeching, urging our return to Him.	**Accusing tone:** Nagging, mocking voice generates fear, causes confusion and a sense of rejection.
Specific: Tells you to take one specific action in response to sin. Freedom follows.	**Vague and general:** Generates a blanketing sense of guilt, as though everything is wrong and there is no action you can take to overcome. Creates a sense of hopelessness and weakness.
Encouraging: Says you can rely on His power, not your strength.	**Discouraging:** Attacks your self-image, tells you that you are weak and that you are not special to God.
Releases you from the past: Tells you your sin is forgiven, removed, never to be held against you.	**Throws your past in your face:** Replays your sin and shame. Reminds you of all your poor choices and bad decisions.
Attracts you to Him: Generates an expectancy of kindness, love, forgiveness, and a new beginning with His help. Speaks of your permanent relationship with Him.	**Rejects:** Produces the feeling that God has rejected you as unworthy and unholy. Speaks of God as your judge and you as a miserable sinner.
Draws you into fellowship: Sends others to minister to you in love. Speaks to you of His unchanging nature and His steadfast love, even when you fail Him.	**Isolates you:** Gives suggestions that cause you to withdraw from others and to assume they will also reject you
Tells the truth: States the facts about you and God.	**Focuses on negative feelings:** Tells you the way you feel is the way things are; that the guilt, despair, hopelessness, and doubt about God's love for you are truth.

Now read John 10:10b.

My purpose is to give life in all its fullness. **(NLT)**

God wants to bring us a fulfilled *life*. The only way to get this life is to listen preeminently to God's voice, and evaluate all other voices in light of His truth. We can't will ourselves to think a certain way. For instance, Hope couldn't simply tell herself early every morning not to feel guilty and—whammo!— not struggle anymore. Over time, as she called on God in the midst of her hard circumstances, she became a better listener and was able to discern the truth from the lies. As she leaned into God, she was better able to receive His truth into the deep places of her heart and tune out other voices. God is the real guiltbuster.

Read John 10:2–5, 27.

For a shepherd enters through the gate. The gatekeeper opens the gate for him, and the sheep hear his voice and come to him. He calls his own sheep by name and leads them out. After he has gathered his own flock, he walks ahead of them, and they follow him because they recognize his voice. They won't follow a stranger; they will run from him because they don't recognize his voice. . . . My sheep recognize my voice; I know them, and they follow me. **(NLT)**

In this verse, the enemy is the stranger. He has a strong voice and wants to lead us away from the fold, away from the Shepherd. Unfortunately, for many of us the stranger's voice is the more powerful voice. We may want to follow the Good Shepherd's voice, but the stranger's voice has for varied reasons become more familiar, easier to believe and to accept.

An important part of our journey out of condemnation is to listen more intently to our Good Shepherd and learn to become good at recognizing His voice. This kind of discernment takes practice. What follows is a tool to help decipher the distinct differences between the *conviction* of the Holy Spirit (our Good Shepherd's voice) and the *condemnation* of the evil one (the enemy, the stranger's voice).

For Hope, it was so important for her to see the bigger picture; that even though her circumstances didn't change—her son didn't miraculously get well—God was at work taking care of her and her family in ways sometimes she couldn't explain.

What is the bigger picture of your situation? What are you learning about God, yourself, other people?

....
....
....
....
....
....
....
....
....

As we learn to tune into God's voice of truth, to block out the condemning voices and strain to listen to the Shepherd's, life changes.

We move out of self-blame and guilt toward God's truth, His peace, and His hope.

1. A confident assurance

One of the ways we get into trouble and find ourselves stuck in self-blame and guilt is by losing confidence. Not confidence in ourselves, but confidence in the fact that in Christ we are accepted, forgiven, and loved no matter what we do or say (or don't do or say). Completely. How do we get more of this kind of Christ confidence? When we cling to God's Word, we can secure our grip.

Hebrews 10:19–23 is a picture of where we get our confidence. Read this passage:

Therefore, brothers, since we have confidence to enter the Most Holy Place by the blood of Jesus, by a new and living way opened for us through the curtain, that is, his body, and since we have a great priest over the house of God, let us draw near to God with a sincere heart in full assurance of faith, having our hearts sprinkled to cleanse us from a guilty conscience and having our bodies washed with pure water. Let us hold unswervingly to the hope we profess, for he who promised is faithful. **(NIV)**

• Where does our confidence come from?

• What is one thing you are feeling guilty about right now?

• What would it mean for you to feel "cleansed from a guilty conscience"? Describe how you long to feel in the space provided.

Sometimes it helps to look at the same Scripture in different translations. Look at Hebrews 10:19–23 in *The Message:*

So, friends, we can now—without hesitation—walk right up to God, into "the Holy Place." Jesus has cleared the way by the blood of his sacrifice, acting as our priest before God. The "curtain" into God's presence is his body. So let's do it—full of belief, confident that we're presentable inside and out. Let's keep a firm grip on the promises that keep us going. He always keeps his word. **(The Message; highlights added)**

• What part of this translation gives you hope?

2. Who makes you feel guilty?

During the time of Jesus, the Pharisees and other religious leaders were experts at heaping guilt upon people. They assumed that if someone was sick, it was because of a sin that person must have committed (John 9:2). For these leaders, God's blessing was withheld if a person did or didn't do certain things. Hope felt this same kind of Pharisee-type judgment. Some Christians around her assumed she must be doing something wrong; otherwise she and her husband and son would not have had such problems. When Jesus began His ministry, He made it clear that He loathed this type of legalistic, self-righteous attitude.

Read Luke 11:46.

"How terrible it will be for you experts in religious law! For you crush people beneath impossible religious demands, and you never lift a finger to help ease the burden." **(NLT)**

Pharisees aren't exclusive to Jesus's time—we all have friends, neighbors, parents, children, and other people in our lives who may make us feel guilty, intentionally or unintentionally, about our inabilities and deficiencies. But we need to know it is not their fault that we feel guilty. We get to decide how we are going to respond to others' demands and opinions.

Not to point the finger, but to understand better what's going on inside of us, who are some people in your life who sometimes make you feel guilty?

What do they do or say that increases your feelings of guilt?

Have other Christians made you feel guilty? What have they expected of you that you couldn't measure up to?

How did you let this affect you?

Reread Luke 11:46. What is more important to Jesus than "religion"?

How does this verse encourage you?

3. Guiltbusting

There is a spiritual battle going on for all of us—a war being waged for our freedom. Ephesians 6:10–18 is a common Bible passage that points to how we can fight this battle and stand up against prevailing feelings of guilt. Walk through this Scripture and finish these sentences.

Ephesians 6:10–18*a*

A final word: Be strong with the Lord's mighty power. Put on all of God's armor so that you will be able to stand firm against all strategies and tricks of the Devil. **(vv. 10–11)**

God, I want to stand firm against . . .

....

....

....

For we are not fighting against people made of flesh and blood, but against the evil rulers and authorities of the unseen world, against those mighty powers of darkness who rule this world, and against wicked spirits in the heavenly realms. **(v. 12)**

This battle is . . .

....

....

....

Use every piece of God's armor to resist the enemy in the time of evil, so that after the battle you will still be standing firm. Stand your ground, putting on the sturdy belt of truth and the body armor of God's righteousness. **(vv. 13–14)**

I need the belt of truth and body armor of God's righteousness to protect me from . . .

....

....

....

For shoes, put on the peace that comes from the Good News, so that you will be fully prepared. **(v. 15)**

The good news of Jesus gives me peace that . . .

....

....

....

In every battle you will need faith as your shield to stop the fiery arrows aimed at you by Satan. **(v. 16)**

Lord, increase my faith that . . .

....

....

....

Put on salvation as your helmet, and take the sword of the Spirit, which is the word of God. **(v. 17)**

I am learning that the Word of God . . .

....

....

....

Pray at all times and on every occasion in the power of the Holy Spirit. **(v. 18)**

God, right now, I pray that . . .

....

....

....

This is an exercise you can recall in different situations, when you start to feel guilt and self-blame weigh you down. God wants to help us fight this battle. You are not alone.

Should've, Could've

Looking over my backyard,
  reviewing what I've done
Looking across the view of my life,
  what I have become

Should'ves, Could'ves, taking over
Stealing time from today
Should'ves, Could'ves, fill my
  thoughts
Please take them away

Your forgiveness is my answer.
  Bringing me relief.
From my own condemnation.
  Imprisoned in my grief.

Your forgiveness has released me.
  From my inner cell.
Your forgiveness lets me release me.
  From my inner hell.

Should'ves, Could'ves cannot
  hold me
Imprisoned anymore
Should'ves, Could'ves I give to You

To hold You forevermore

Should'ves, Could'ves cannot
  haunt me
With You by my side
Should'ves, Could'ves only taunt me
When I'm trapped in my own pride

—Suzanne Hunter

Used by permission.

1. Should have, could have: letting go of regret

Regret increases guilt. We think of the things that we should have done or could have done and fail to live in the present. The energy we spend beating ourselves up could be spent living life instead! It's time to get out the regrets and begin to let them go.

In the space below, reflect on some seasons in your life. Brainstorm whatever comes to mind in these two areas of "I should have . . ." and "I could have . . .".

I SHOULD HAVE . . .

I COULD HAVE . . .

There will always be things we could have done, should have done; but if we focus on that, we will miss the bigger picture. Now finish this sentence and write whatever comes to mind in the space provided.

But even though I didn't, God still . . .

2. The bigger picture, the bigger story

Often we get so caught up in the day-to-day of our present struggles that we lose sight of the bigger story. God is telling a story in all of us and part of our journey is making sure we don't miss the bigger picture by focusing in on only what is right in front of us.

Here's a fun exercise to help us see the themes of our lives and notice that the story isn't just one chapter but the combination of many.

If your life was a book, what would the title be?

Now think of some chapter names, following the guide below:

TIME FRAME	CHAPTER TITLE
Birth to 5 years	
Elementary years	
High school years	
College age (18–25 years)	
Other:	
Other:	
Other:	
Other:	
Other:	

If you were describing this book to someone who didn't know you, what would you tell them about this story?

Question: How do you measure your goodness?

Answer: We live in a world where our value and goodness are often measured by what we accomplish. In school with grades. In the workplace with projects. In our families with our children's successes. But that's not God's standard. The Bible tells us that our goodness is not measured by what WE do, but by what JESUS has done FOR us. And I want to keep learning to let Him live through me.

Carol, 62

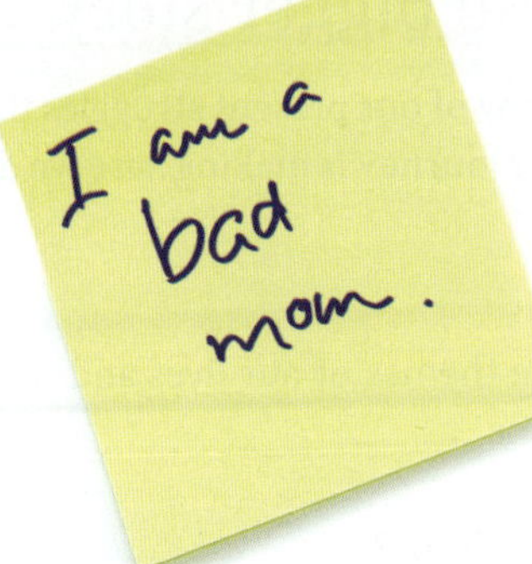

1. Read Suzanne Hunter's poem. Ask the group for their thoughts and reactions.

2. Give everyone a sticky note. Have each person write on her note a lie that she battles (i.e., "I am a bad mother!" or "I am unlovable."). Ask each person to state her lie and then post her note on a whiteboard. Then, ask the group members to take another sticky note and write God's truth related to that lie, and share the truth with the group and place that truth over the lie on the whiteboard. In the end, there will be a whiteboard full of truth.

3. Bring in a backpack filled with very heavy objects. Have a woman put on the backpack and walk around the room. Then have her take the backpack off and walk around the room. Ask her to use adjectives to describe the difference between walking with the backpack on and walking with the backpack off. Relate this to condemnation in our lives and the weight it brings, while conviction brings freedom.

4. Hand everyone a blank piece of paper and ask them, whether they are artistic or not, to draw a picture that represents someone saddled with guilt. Ask each person to describe what she drew and why. Does the drawing connect with how she is feeling? How so?

1. What part of the "Discerning the Difference" chart did you connect with?

2. Which voice is easier for you to follow? Why?

3. What are some things you feel guilty about and that are robbing you of peace?

4. Share with the group your responses to "The Bigger Picture, the Bigger Story." What is the title of your book and some of your chapters?

5. Closing round: Finish this sentence: *A way God encouraged me through working this chapter is . . .*

Check These Out...

Telling Yourself the Truth

by William Backus and Marie Chapian

Real Moms

by Elisa Morgan and Carol Kuykendall

Stepping-Stones for Stepmoms

by Karon Phillips Goodman

I Want More!

Secrets to a satisfied soul

After hanging up the phone

with her mother, Lynette plunked down on the couch with a bag of potato chips. Picking up the remote she began surfing channels with one hand and shoveling chips in her mouth with the other. She increased the volume, trying to drown out the shrill noises coming from the basement where her children played with some neighborhood kids. "They sound like monkeys on speed," she mumbled to herself through a mouth full of chips. When she found an old *I Love Lucy* rerun, she set down the remote and leaned back into the cushions.

"Mom, do you have a bucket we can use?" yelled her oldest son, Trent, barging up the stairs.

"Check in the garage."

"Can we have a snack?"

"In a minute." Lynette's eyes stayed glued to the television.

"We're hungry."

Irritation rippled through her. "I'll make lunch in a minute, Trent!" When the show was over, Lynette reluctantly pushed herself off the couch, crumpling up the empty bag of chips. A craving for something sweet swelled up inside her. Without thinking, she went to the pantry and reached to the back where she hid a stash of candy bars. She chose her favorite, and devoured it in four quick bites. She stuck the wrapper inside an empty milk carton and buried the carton at the bottom of the trash can.

Her mouth still savoring the sweetness from the candy, Lynette pulled ham and cheese out of the fridge to make sandwiches for the kids. Eyeballing the meat, she scolded herself. *I really should have some protein and not all this junk.* She wolfed down three slices of ham as she made the sandwiches.

"Lunch is ready," she hollered.

In mere seconds a stampede of legs and arms barreled into the kitchen. "Can we have Popsicles after lunch?" Her daughter, Taylor, had a sweet tooth just like Lynette.

"We'll see." Lynette handed a plate piled full of sandwiches to Trent. "Eat these downstairs." She gave a bag of seedless grapes to Taylor. "Try not to make a big mess," she called after them as they scampered back downstairs.

Standing in the kitchen, Lynette fought the urge to sit back down in front of the television. She reprimanded her urge, *Do something constructive.* With a huff, she made herself tackle the never-ending pile of laundry. She sorted through it and started a load of whites.

Then, passing by the hallway mirror to get the vacuum, she stopped dead in her tracks. *Ewwww!* She ran her fingers through her hair and cringed. Her wavy brown hair fell flat around her face and a thick fold of flesh hung below her chin. She raised her lip and scowled to herself. *Ugly pig.* She had no makeup on and her deep blue eyes looked dull and puffy. As she stared at her reflection, self-hate took off inside her like a runaway train. *Fat piece of crap. Worthless cow.* Unable to stand looking at herself another second, she turned away. A sinking

despondency pressed down on her chest and she forgot all about vacuuming. When the phone rang a few minutes later, she stuffed down the emotions churning inside her. "Hello?"

"Hi, hon."

The sound of her husband's, Randy's, voice set off a wave of vulnerability and tears pooled in her eyes. "Hi." She tried her best to sound upbeat.

"What's wrong?"

"Nothing," she lied.

"You don't sound good."

"I'm fine." She didn't want to burden him yet again with her emotional roller-coaster rides.

"OK . . . well," he hesitated. "I . . . uh . . . I hate this, but I'm going to be home late tonight. This project is . . ."

Lynette didn't let him finish. "I know. Same project you've had for the last two weeks." Her voice turned to steel.

"I'm sorry, honey. I'll be home as soon as I can. I'll bring you a surprise."

"Don't bother." She clicked the phone off. Her tears turned bitter and she stomped to the cupboard and pulled out a box of snack cakes.

"Mom, can we have Popsicles?" The children reappeared from the basement.

Lynette instinctively dropped the box of cakes behind a stack of pots and turned around. "Eat them outside."

"OK." Trent opened the freezer and pulled out a colorful box. "Come on, you guys." The kids followed him out as he opened the sliding glass door as if he were the Pied Piper. When the door closed behind them, Lynette reached for the cakes and popped one in her mouth as quickly as she could. The sweet icing tingled the roof of her mouth and a small sigh leaked from her lips.

She took the package of cakes and ambled back toward the television. Her knees ached and the short walk to the family room made her short of breath. Collapsing onto the couch, she clicked on the television and ate another cake. After watching a popular talk show, she channel-hopped until an infomercial grabbed her attention.

"You can be everything you dreamed you would be," a tanned, toned, blonde woman smiled, flashing her perfect teeth. "I was wandering through life without any direction," the woman shook her head, distraught. "I wanted more. I knew there was more. But I didn't know how to get there."

Lynette sat up.

"I didn't like myself and I gained a lot of weight. I was so miserable." The woman blinked and her eyes became somber.

How did you change? Lynette thought, her eyes glued to the woman.

"When I hit rock bottom, a friend told me about these tapes." She held up a cassette in her hand. "I listened to them and my life took a new direction." The woman's whole face expanded into an explosion of delight. "Now I've learned how to make good decisions about taking care of myself."

Feeling her heart clutch for hope, Lynette went to the kitchen and found a pencil and piece of paper. After scribbling down the 800 number she sat and listened to more of the woman's story. "I have purpose. I feel fulfilled. I am healthier than ever before."

Lynette squeezed her eyes shut. *Oh God, I want to get to that place. I'm so sick of this year-after-year battle against my weight.* She dabbed at two silent tears. *And I want my life to count . . . for something. I want fulfillment and meaning, but look at me—a worthless-stay-at-home-nobody-fat blob?* I sob rose up her throat.

"Mom, we're going over to Tommy's!" her youngest son, Brandon, bellowed from the kitchen door.

Clicking off the television, Lynette forced a chipper tone. "OK, honey."

"Bye."

The sliding glass door slammed shut again and silence filled the house. She sat staring at the black screen for several minutes. "That's it!" Lynette stood up and tugged her shirt down over her waistline. "I'm going to do it. I've had it with this pathetic life. I'm going to lose the weight I've talked about forever and start living like God intended." Bolstered by her new resolve, she went into the bathroom, brushed her hair, and put on some makeup.

Feeling brighter, she cleaned the kitchen and then shuffled downstairs to the basement with a damp rag and a bottle of spray cleaner. She wiped off the table and picked up chunks of ham and bread that dotted the carpet. Something wet hit her in the top of her head. Lynette looked up. What in the world? She squinted at dozens of greenish spots splattered on the ceiling. "Oh, great!" she grunted realizing they were grape skins. Annoyance sizzled within her.

She pulled a chair underneath the mess and with a loud grunt thrust herself up on the chair and began

"That's it!...
I'm going to do it.
I've had it with this
pathetic life."

to wipe up the mess. "This is my life. All I do is *wipe* things!" she whined to the empty room. "I wipe noses, I wipe countertops, I wipe windows, I used to wipe bottoms all day." A bead of sweat trickled down her forehead as she scrubbed the ceiling. "Now I wipe ceilings. Where's the value in this?" Anger and despair crashed together inside her. "I'm all wiped out!" she stepped down from the chair and sat down, her joints aching.

The familiar dark cloud of defeat began hovering over her again. Suddenly, a gripping need for something sweet surged inside her. Forgetting her new resolve, she wheezed up the stairs and grabbed a carton of ice cream from the freezer.

Several months later, Lynette sat at the kitchen table flipping through photos

she had had developed. Anxious to see how the shots from her birthday party turned out, she quickly went through the stack until she got to the photos.

Yikes. And I thought I looked good that night. Flurries of panic rose inside her as she looked at herself. *I can't believe I've gotten this big!* Paralyzed, her eyes became glued to a picture of her blowing out the candles on her cake. *I look like a cow wearing a moo-moo.* Her mouth went dry. *I'm going to die.* Her thoughts catapulted to her funeral and she dropped the photo like it was on fire. *Oh God, help. I don't want to die like this.*

The next day she made an appointment with her nurse practitioner, Joyce.

"I'm thinking about Weight Watchers again," she confided as Joyce wrapped the blood pressure belt around Lynette's arm. "I have to do something about this weight or it's going to kill me."

Joyce gave a quick nod and squeezed the blood pressure bulb. After writing down some numbers, she unfastened the belt and set it down. Lynette could see the concern in her eyes. "You have tried Weight Watchers two other times."

Joyce flipped through Lynette's chart and continued. "You've also tried Jenny Craig, Dexatrim, NutriSystem, the grapefruit diet, the hard-boiled egg diet, the cabbage soup diet, Slim-Fast, Atkins, Susan Powter, the Richard Simmons weight-loss program, the Weigh Down program. What am I missing?" She looked up from the chart with a raised eyebrow.

"I know." Lynette bit her lip. "I've tried everything."

Joyce set the chart down. "Lynette, I want you to consider gastric bypass surgery."

For a moment Lynette couldn't move or breathe.

"You weigh nearly 300 pounds now and, you're right, this kind of weight is very, very hard on your heart. On your whole body."

"I . . . uh . . .," Lynette stammered.

"Just think about it. You don't have to decide right now."

As Lynette drove home from the doctor's office, she called Randy on her cell phone and relayed everything Joyce had said.

"I'm going to do it," she blurted out.

"Whatever you decide, I support you."

"Thanks," she whispered.

Several months later Lynette had the surgery. She was scared to have it, but she was even more scared not to go through with it. Through the surgery, her stomach shrank from the size of a football to the size of an egg and she began to lose weight steadily. More than a year later, her stature had plunged to a healthy, strong, and satisfied 146 pounds. Lynette's physical changes are not the end of her story.

She has found her journey of weight loss to be much more than a road to looking and feeling better. Lynette discovered how her preoccupation with weight was a barrier between her and God, and robbed her of peace, purpose, and soul satisfaction. "I believe Satan uses weight as a distraction for women because it takes us away from God. For me, weight struggles were the dominating force in my life for so many lost years. It took so much time and energy from my life. My time, my heart, my mind, my stomach were all focused in a direction that never satisfied the deepest longings of my heart."

Once her weight wasn't a constant fixation, Lynette was faced with the pain in her heart. "There are lots of different pieces to this puzzle, but one piece of my pain was feeling insignificant as a stay-at-home mom. I really wanted to be at home with my kids, but at the same time I felt so worthless doing it. I wrestled daily with that painful question—*Is this as good as it gets*? I kept trying to fill myself up, to make myself feel better. But, all I really did was fill myself out."

After the surgery, she found herself opening her heart to God more and looking at her destructive patterns of avoiding feelings and hiding behind food. When she allowed herself to feel, to run to God instead of food, she learned a secret: *I am much more than "just a stay-at-home mom."*

A gifted communicator and natural people person, Lynette has been realizing her dream of making a difference in people's lives through her zany humor and heart for encouraging others. She began pursuing one of her dreams: launching her own speaking ministry. It hasn't been easy because she has still struggled with feelings of worthlessness; but as she kept listening to God, praying for help and guidance, and pushing through her pain, she soon realized that she had good things to offer others, both inside and outside of her home. She began to love her family better and had found a job she loved too.

"I knew there was value in staying home, but I didn't feel valuable. God's plan and purpose for everyone is different. For me, I felt there was a calling on my life that I wasn't stepping into because I was preoccupied and distracted with the weight game. I now find the more I live out who God made me to be instead of hiding in shame and unworthiness, the more my deep cravings are satisfied. God, not food, has become my comfort, friend, encourager, and greatest cheerleader."

Lynette still wages a battle with food. "This is not a story titled, 'And She Lived Thinly Ever After.' Food is still a temptation. But I've found healthier tools to turn to when I feel sad or stressed. I do replacement therapy; I replace food with something that is good for me. Something that will help me work through the emotions instead of anesthetizing myself. I go on a walk and pray it through. I call a friend and talk it through. I take a bath and relax myself. I drive someplace beautiful and admire God's handiwork and get refocused on Him. And, once I deal with what is going on inside me, I can see more clearly. I'm in growth mode instead of self-destructive mode, which helps me reach for the dreams He has put in my heart."

Filling the Void And Still Feeling Empty

> "What we dwell on is who we become."
> —Oprah Winfrey

Food. Exercise. Work. Cleaning. Shopping. Friends. Caring for kids.

All of these things aren't "bad." They're part of life. We need to eat to survive. Exercise is good for our health. Work, well, most of us need to pay the bills. These things done without excess are part of healthy living. The problem for many of us, though, is that we can use these benign, even "good" things to distract us from what's most important—a fulfilling, meaningful relationship with God.

Lynette distracted herself with food and losing weight. She used it as a way to fill the empty void in her life. As a stay-at-home mom raising young children, she felt insignificant and worthless so she used food as her comforter and companion. The problem was overeating only added to her pain and separated her further from the work of God in her life.

Some of us don't get distracted by eating. But all of us get distracted by something. We all have things that can derail us, taking us away from the only One who can truly satisfy.

I (Laura) have led a church Bible study for the past five years and every year there is one woman who starts off in the fall full of enthusiasm and excitement to dig in and learn more about God. But every year around November she starts missing our meetings and before too long we don't see her anymore. She has a gift basket business and it gets busy before Christmas. Once Christmas is over, new orders come in and it is hard for her to get back on track.

What derails you? What distracts you? What takes your time and attention away from God?

How do these distractions make you feel?
Circle the ones that apply.

Satisfied   Empty   Lonely

Longing for more   Ashamed   Fulfilled

Tired   Unsatisfied   Discouraged   Happy

Frustrated   Angry at yourself   Anxious

The tendency to look in directions other than God has been going on since the beginning of time. Think of Adam and Eve in the garden. The serpent (Satan) distracted them with an alluring assurance they'd be fulfilled by something outside of God's plan. Guess what? Satan lied. They ate from the tree of life, they weren't fulfilled, and their distraction ended in disaster.

Adam and Eve learned this profound, everlasting truth that we need for our lives today: **Distractions from God never satisfy us.** So why are we such slow learners? Why are we so easily distracted? Let's look into the life of Martha, a woman in the New Testament, who also gets distracted.

Read Luke 10:38–42.

As Jesus and His disciples were on their way, he came to a village where a woman named Martha opened her home to him. She had a sister called Mary, who sat at the Lord's feet listening to what he said. But Martha was distracted by all the preparations that had to be made. She came to him and asked, "Lord, don't you care that my sister has left me to do the work by myself? Tell her to help me!" "Martha, Martha," the Lord answered, "you are worried and upset about many things, but only one thing is needed. Mary has chosen what is better, and it will not be taken away from her." **(NIV)**

We can relate to Martha, can't we? Come on, now. The house is full of people, it's time to eat, and the food must be prepared. Picture yourself in her shoes. What would you do? Be the "lazy" one and sit at Jesus's feet or get up and get the job done?

One of the reasons we are so easily distracted is that we are women! There is work to be done! We're doers—multitasking machines who can ride circles around most men. We get distracted because doing (like Martha did) feels better than sitting (like Mary did). Doesn't it?

Jesus uses this Martha-Mary moment to teach women today about His secrets about how to live life and not get distracted. In the King James Version of the Bible the words used are: "Martha was cumbered by . . ." In the Greek, the root of the verb is: *perispao* or περισπαω.

10 sure ways to lessen the distractions

1. **Prayer.** Make time to seek, question, and connect with God

2. **Bible infusion.** Soak in God's Word, especially the Book of Psalms if you are really going through a hard time.

3. **Community.** Hang out with friends, stop focusing on yourself, and serve someone else!

4. **Journal.** Pour out your heart to God instead of into a bag of chips.

5. **Continual confession.** Slay current instead of letting shame build up.

6. **Silence and solitude.** This is not isolation but a time of quiet focus on God.

7. **Nurture yourself.** Make time to do something you like to do.

8. **Laugh.** Call someone who reminds you to lighten up or find a mud puddle and jump in the middle of it.

9. **Exercise.** Get your bike out and take a joyride around a park or find something else physical you can do to clear the clutter from your head.

10. **Daily check-in.** Email or phone a good friend daily and celebrate the victories. For example, "I ran to God instead of to __________." And ask for prayer for the hard days.

Here's the definition:

1. To draw around, to draw away, to distract
2. To be driven about mentally, to be distracted
3. To be overoccupied, too busy, about a thing

Now put your name where Martha's is and put in the leading distraction in your life:

"________________________________ is cumbered

by ______________________________."

Reread the secret Jesus revealed to Martha about living this way. What do you think He would say to you?

....

....

....

....

OK, now it's time to get real. Another reason we get so distracted is because distractions often translate to avoidance—us trying to avoid something going on inside of us that is much deeper. For Lynette, it was her struggle with feeling less valued and even worthless as a stay-at-home mom. For others of us it might be trying to avoid the deeper pain of a broken relationship, a marriage that is in shambles, a hidden addiction, childhood abuse, financial bondage, loss, or grief.

Is there something you are trying to avoid?

....

....

....

....

I (Kathy) know this feeling well. I always have a tendency to get distracted away from God, to fill myself with food, ministry, and friends to avoid connecting with God on a deeper level. He's what I long for, but in reality I run to these other things to avoid going to Him. Often, these distractions bring me pleasure in the moment and push down the stresses and other difficult emotions churning inside me. The bottom line is: I get distracted because I don't trust that God can fill me in the moment. I turn elsewhere. I avoid dealing with what's really going on underneath. The sad part is, that moment passes in a snap and I'm left feeling further separated from God and more dissatisfied! Distractions initially quench our thirst, but only briefly, and never deeply.

Listen to what Jesus reveals to us:

Jesus said, "Everyone who drinks this water will get thirsty again and again. Anyone who drinks the water I give will never thirst—not ever. The water I give will be an artesian spring within, gushing fountains of endless life."

—John 4:13–14 (The Message)

Jesus is telling us, as He told Martha, that there is something better than what the world offers—something better than even serving and giving—and that is Jesus Himself. He alone can fill the void inside us and quench our thirst.

Now take a moment and read Jesus's call to you:

Jesus stood and said in a loud voice, "If anyone is thirsty, let him come to me and drink."

—John 7:37 (NIV)

What are you hungry and thirsty for? What do you long to receive from God?

....

....

....

....

The secret to satisfaction is to stop running, to stop filling ourselves with other things that never satisfy, and to be still and stop long enough to ask for a drink.

Digging Deeper

1. I confess!

No matter how many times we worship false gods (such as food), take matters into our own hands, and sin against God, He will always forgive and draw us back to Him. To live a life of freedom, we must become women who continually confess, turn back to God, admit where we've been separating ourselves from Him, and move again toward His love and truth. It starts with confession: *God, here I am again. In that same spot. I am sorry. Please forgive me. I want to turn to You and not other things.* Biblical examples help us.

King David got easily distracted too. He sought satisfaction and comfort in things other than God and ended up having to cover up his sins. Then something shifted in his heart and he repented, confessed, and turned back to God.

Read Psalm 51:1–12.

Generous in love—God, give grace! Huge in mercy—wipe out my bad record. Scrub away my guilt, soak out my sins in your laundry. I know how bad I've been; my sins are staring me down. You're the One I've violated, and you've seen it all, seen the full extent of my evil. You have all the facts before you; whatever you decide about me is fair. I've been out of step with you for a long time, in the wrong since before I was born. What you're after is truth from the inside out. Enter me, then; conceive a new, true life. Soak me in your laundry and I'll come out clean, scrub me and I'll have a snow-white life. Tune me in to foot-tapping songs, set these once-broken bones to dancing. Don't look too close for blemishes, give me a clean bill of health. God, make a fresh start in me, shape a Genesis week from the chaos of my life. Don't throw me out with the trash, or fail to breathe holiness in me. Bring me back from gray exile, put a fresh wind in my sails!
(The Message)

Underline which words speak to you.

Now take time to pour out any confessions you might need to make to God about what you've been focused on, distracted by.

2. Remove the obstacles, dream again!

And it will be said: "Build up, build up, prepare the road! Remove the obstacles out of the way of my people."

—Isaiah 57:14 (NIV)

Our distractions are blocks to our ability to see, hear, and feel the living God. As Lynette began letting God fill her instead of food, she began to feel more alive, free. Although it was initially scary and unfamiliar, she began to live out some of her dreams professionally. He wants to remove obstacles in your life too.

What are your dreams? This is a time to let what's in your heart flow. Don't hold back, thinking *This will never happen so it's not worth writing down.* Write down whatever dreams for your life are in your heart.

....

....

....

Which one of these dreams jumps to the top of the list as the one you feel most excited about?

....

....

....

....

One of the reasons we get distracted from God is that the obstacles to our dreams feel too big and not worth talking to God about.

Now take a look at the road to get to that dream and the many boulders along this road. These are the obstacles, the things that make realizing this dream harder. Write them on each of these rocks.

Yes, it might look like there are many obstacles along the road toward this dream, but none of these are impossible for God to break down. God is the greatest obstacle breaker!

Read Isaiah 45:2–3.

I will go before you and will level the mountains; I will break down gates of bronze and cut through bars of iron. I will give you the treasures of darkness, riches stored in secret places, so that you may know that I am the Lord, the God of Israel, who summons you by name. **(NIV)**

Ask God, in the space below, to help remove some of these obstacles. No matter how small or big they seem, He wants to help.

....

....

....

....

Keep dreaming and cling to this truth found in Jeremiah 29:11!

"For I know the plans I have for you," declares the Lord, "plans to prosper you and not to harm you, plans to give you hope and a future." **(NIV)**

3. Valued!

One of the reasons we often get distracted and go looking elsewhere to meet our needs rather than seek God is that we feel unvaluable and unimportant. Yet, the truth is, we are daughters of a King! What does that make us? Princesses. Think about it. How many women do you know who are really living that way? It's about time for some change! It's time for God's women to rise up out of the muck and mire of feeling worthlessness, self-condemnation, and shame and stand on a firm foundation of living as the King's daughters. This is easy to say and hard to do, but this is why we consistently have to be filled with God's truth about who we are as women. Regardless of age, education, socio-economic background, cultural and individual life history—we are accepted, secure, and significant.

Take some time to look up these verses in your Bible. Highlight those that help to remind you of your value in God's eyes.

We're Accepted

We are children of God.
(John 1:12)

We're Jesus's friends.
(John 15:15)

We've been made right in God's eyes through Jesus.
(Romans 5:1)

God bought us with a high price.
(1 Corinthians 6:20)

We're a special and necessary part of the body of Christ.
(1 Corinthians 12:27)

We're chosen by God and adopted as His children.
(Ephesians 1:3–8)

We've been redeemed and all of our sins have been forgiven.
(Colossians 1:13–14)

We're complete.
(Colossians 2:9–10)

We have direct access to God's grace through Jesus Christ.
(Hebrews 4:14–16)

We're Secure

We're free from condemnation.
(Romans 8:1–2)

We're assured God works for our good in all circumstances.
(Romans 8:28)

Nothing can separate us from God's love. **(Romans 8:31–39)**

We're sealed by God and identified as His own.
(2 Corinthians 1:21–22)

We're confident that He'll finish the good work He started in us.
(Philippians 1:6)

We're citizens of heaven.
(Philippians 3:20)

We haven't been given a spirit of fear but of power, love, and self-discipline. **(2 Timothy 1:7)**

We're held securely by God. The evil one cannot touch us.
(1 John 5:18)

We're Significant

We're a branch of Jesus, the true vine, receiving His life.
(John 15:5)

We're chosen to go and bear fruit for God. **(John 15:16)**

We're the temple of God.
(1 Corinthians 3:16)

We're Christ's ambassadors to the world, ministers of reconciliation.
(2 Corinthians 5:17–21)

We're Christ's workmanship, His masterpiece. **(Ephesians 2:10)**

We can approach God with freedom and confidence.
(Ephesians 3:12)

We can do all things through Christ, who strengthens us.
(Philippians 4:13)

Help Can Be Habit-Forming

1. SOS … 911 … help!

Are you good at asking for help? A good habit to form is learning how to ask for God's help when we are being tempted to run to things for comfort other than Him (overeating, excessive shopping, over-spending, too much exercise, busyness). God always provides a way of escape.

"No temptation has seized you except what is common to man. And God is faithful; he will not let you be tempted beyond what you can bear. But when you are tempted, he will also provide a way out so that you can stand up under it."
—1 Corinthians 10:13 (NIV)

Write this verse on a notecard or sticky note and keep it on your dashboard, your mirror, or your refrigerator.

This week, notice when you are about to let distractions take over, and draw strength from this verse. Try to slow down. Think about what you are about to do and ask yourself these questions:

❋ Will it draw me closer to God or away from God?

❋ After I do this, will I regret it and feel ashamed?

❋ What is something more positive I can do in its place? (Remember Lynette's replacement therapy and write a list of alternatives you can use when you are tempted by distractions.)

Nevertheless, if you end up giving into the temptation, seek His forgiveness and grace.

God, please forgive me for . . .

....

....

....

....

....

....

....

I know this distracted me from experiencing You.

Remember this truth: *"But if we confess our sins to him, he is faithful and just to forgive us our sins and to cleanse us from all wickedness"* **(1 John 1:9 NLT)**.

If you were able to withstand the temptation, praise Him for it. Write a prayer of thanks in the space below.

God, thank You for giving me the strength to not give into the temptation/distraction to . . .

....

....

....

....

What do you love to do?

....

....

....

....

....

....

How often do you participate in these activities? Often? Never? Why or why not?

....

....

....

2. What makes you feel alive?

One of the reasons Lynette ended up stuck is that she didn't have healthy outlets—activities she enjoyed doing. Part of growing in our walk with God is learning to notice what makes us feel alive and how to pursue good behaviors in an effort to honor the way God has designed us. The more we walk toward activities that make us feel alive, the less likely we will be pulled toward the things that bring death.

Pick one of these pursuits and pray about making space in your life to experience it more. Think about building the pursuit or activity into your schedule and following through and enjoying it, even more than once. Ask a trusted friend to keep checking in to make sure you are pursuing some of the activities that are good for your soul.

INSATIABLE WOMEN ...	SATISFIED WOMEN ...
Keep eating, working, exercising, or spending to try to—but never seem to—feel better.	Turn to God instead of unhealthy actions for comfort.
Make new resolutions to change their lives almost every month.	Make small changes that are realistic, almost unnoticeable in the short-term, but have more lasting results.
Are angry and ashamed at themselves.	Offer themselves grace when they make mistakes.
Feel isolated and alone.	Have a few good friends with whom they can share from the heart.
Don't believe they are worthy of God's love because they keep "failing" Him.	Understand their worth in Christ's eyes no matter what.
Find every reason possible not to turn to God.	Seek Him first because they know He is their only hope.

1. Give each woman a rock (as large as possible) and a permanent marker. Ask them to write on their rocks some of the distractions in their lives which take them away from God—the habits, pursuits, or things that they are running to instead of letting God fill them. Ask each woman to share their distractions and then place their rocks in a pile. After they are done, stand on one side of the pile, demonstrating how we're on this side and these distractions keep us from God. Brainstorm together: "How can we get rid of some of these distractions?" Then pray for God to remove these distractions so that you can experience Him more fully.

2. Have a time of confession. Read Psalm 51 in *The Message.* Have the women write on a piece of paper, *Lord, I confess that I am looking to ______________ to fill me instead of You.* Gather these papers in a basket, read aloud (anonymously), and then pray over them.

3. Ask for five volunteers. Assign one to be the listener and four to be "voices." Have the listener stand facing those who will be the voices. Hand the four voices each a piece of paper with her or his statement on it. (See the lines below.) When you say, "Start," the voices are to say their statements repeatedly to the listener. After a minute or so, say, "Stop." After the exercise, ask the listener how it felt to try to listen to so many voices at one time. Discuss as a group these and other voices in life that compete with God's voice.

Voice 1: You've got so much work to do. Have your quiet time later. There's too much to do. Come on, you're already late.

Voice 2: God works for other people but not for you. Even if you did pick up the Bible, you wouldn't understand it. He can't do anything for you anyway.

Voice 3: You're too far gone. You'll never really change. What's the point? Give it up. Stop trying.

God's Voice: Come sit with Me. Let Me take your burdens. Talk to Me. Do you know how much I love you? I do. I love you. Come sit with Me.

INFUSION

What's your cure for distraction?

We are all called to love God with heart, soul, mind, and strength, but this always gets complicated by our human condition of being distracted. My favorite description of Jesus is that He was full of grace and truth—grace to understand our distraction and truth to keep calling us to put Him at the center of our attention. The longer I walk with Him, the more I want Him; the more I need Him, the more I want Him at the center of my life and nothing else.

The best thing about God is that He calls us to *Himself,* not to good works or even being "a good person." Those things are a result of our devotion to Him. My best prayer these days when I'm distracted is, *Above all, give me You.*

Jayne, 57

1. What is the number one distraction in your life that takes you away from God?

2   Why is it easier to run to than to God?

3. What are you hungry and thirsty for in your relationship with God?

4   What are some of your dreams? How are the distractions getting in the way of realizing those dreams?

5. Closing round: In just a couple of words, finish this sentence. *This week, I really want to be less distracted by . . .*

Check These Out...

Born to Be Wild
by Jill Baughan

I Married Adventure
by Luci Swindoll

Silent Hunger
by Judy and Arthur Halliday

The Purpose-Driven Life
by Rick Warren

For One More Day
by Mitch Albom (A story that shows us it's never too late!)

ALESHIA
How I Became
Fearl

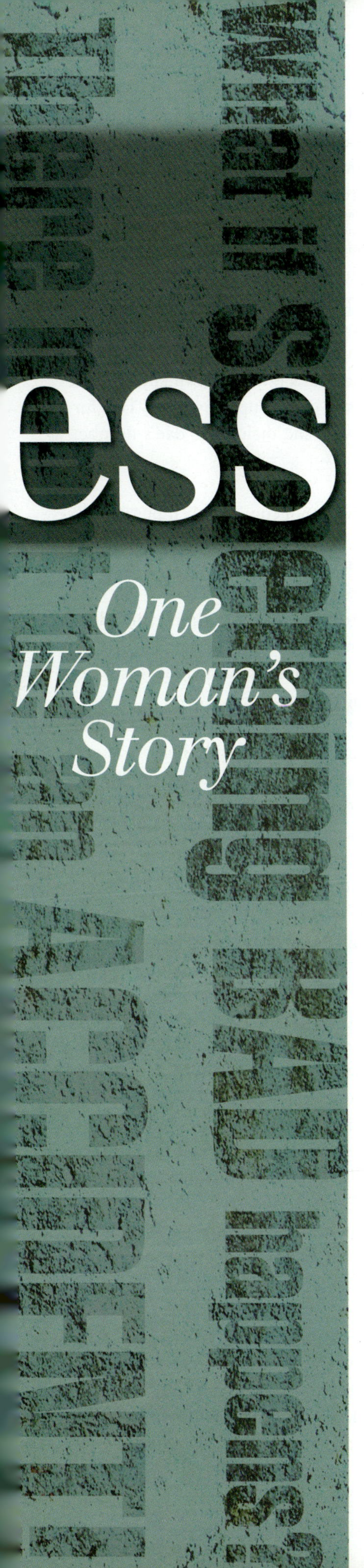

Aleshia sat at the computer, playing solitaire, and feeling the familiar burn in her stomach. Church camp was coming and she knew that her daughter, Denise, really wanted to go this year. *There's no way. Camps are way too dangerous,* Aleshia thought. The phone rang. Aleshia flinched. *I hope it's not the school. Please, God, let Denise be OK.*

"Hello.

"Hi, honey."

She sighed with relief. "Hi, Dad."

"I wanted to give you a date to put on your calendar. I'm going to have a family reunion at my house next month."

"Sure, Dad. What's the date?"

"Saturday, June 12."

"OK."

Somberness took over his tone. "It's important for you to be there, honey. Your grandparents really want to see you and Denise."

"We'll be there." Even as she said the words her heart hammered against her ribs.

I can do this, she thought, hanging up the phone.

As she lay in bed that night, thinking about the reunion, she massaged her aching jaw with her right hand. Years of grinding her teeth and clenching her jaw had taken their toll. She couldn't even chew her dinner that night because the pain was so severe. *What if they don't think I've done a good job raising Denise?* She moved her hand to the other side of her face and pressed her fingers into her jaw muscle. *I haven't seen them in years. . . . What if they don't like me? . . . What if they don't like Denise?* Rolling on her side, she looked at the clock. 3:06. *Please, God, let me fall asleep.* She clutched her pillow and squeezed her eyelids closed. *What if they make fun of me?*

As the reunion day crept closer, Aleshia felt more ill. She couldn't eat or sleep and withdrew from Denise. Aleshia's mind was preoccupied with what might happen if she went to the family gathering. The night before the reunion, she didn't sleep at all. She couldn't stop thinking about her dad and her fear of disappointing him. Her whole life, he had patiently loved her through her irrational fears. Tossing over on her side, a smile nudged the corner of her mouth as she pictured her dad sitting by her bedside.

"What's it going to be tonight, Leshia? 'Hansel and Gretel' or 'Goldilocks and the Three Bears'?"

"Dad, what if I die while I'm asleep?"

In a gentle, soothing voice, he replied, "You're not going to die, sweetheart. You're not. You're going to be all right."

"But what if the world ends tonight?"

"Honey, I'm pretty sure that the world won't end tonight. It's not going to happen."

"Will you check under my bed? What if there's someone in my closet?"

He got on his knees, looked under her bed, and then went to her closet and poked around. Sitting back down on the edge of the bed, he smiled reassuringly. "Nothing there. Now which story would you like?"

"'Hansel and Gretel.'" Aleshia wrapped her arms around her teddy bear and watched her dad until her eyelids got too heavy to hold open.

The sweet memory warmed Aleshia. When her thoughts went careening back to the reunion, she let out a loud groan. "I just can't do it!" She curled into a ball and rocked back and forth.

By the time the sun lit the sky, Aleshia's pillow was soaked with perspiration and her stomach felt as though poisonous toxins were taking over her insides. She got out of bed and tried to occupy herself on the computer for a few hours. Finally, an hour before the party, she picked up the phone. Her fingers moved slowly as she dialed her dad's number. "Hi, Dad."

"Hi, honey."

"I'm sorry, but we're not coming. My lupus is really acting up."

She knew he knew she was lying.

"Well, we'll miss you."

"I'll miss you too. Maybe next time," she added quickly. "Let's plan another time."

"Sure, honey." The disappointment in his voice stung her ear.

After she hung up, Aleshia took a shower. A fusion of sadness and relief whirled inside her. *At least I can start paying attention to Denise again.* She got dressed and found Denise in her room listening to music.

"Do you want to go to a movie?"

Denise raised her eyebrows. "Really?"

"Uh-huh," her heart swelled with love as she looked at her daughter. She hated how her fears stole her away from Denise and she wanted to make up for it. "After that we'll go have some ice cream."

"OK." Denise jumped off her bed, a smile lighting up her face.

A few weeks later, Aleshia received a call from Denise's youth group leader, Mike. "We would love to have Denise join us for the summer camp."

Aleshia wasn't surprised by the call because she knew Denise would never ask her to go. Denise knew her mom too well. In her 11 years of life Aleshia had said no to everything: No to sleepovers. No to after-school activities. No to any sort of camp or risky sport. No. No. No.

"I don't think so," Aleshia rubbed her forehead. "Isn't it in Utah?"

"Yes, but our van drivers are certified and the camp is very well supervised."

Aleshia liked Mike. He did a good job with the kids at their church and Denise loved the youth program.

"That's so far away."

"I will be on the trip," Mike continued in earnest. "And I have a great team of competent leaders."

"I don't know." A big part of her wanted to be able to let her daughter go and have fun. But another part of her froze with fear. *What if something happened to her?* "I don't . . ."

Mike jumped in before she could finish. "A lot of Denise's friends are going and I think it could be a great opportunity for her."

Oh, I want that for her. "Isn't it a whole week?" Aleshia's heart shuddered as she tried to imagine Denise gone for a week.

"Really it ends up being just five days because we have two days of travel."

"What happens if a kid gets sick?"

"There are local medical facilities nearby."

"She needs someone watching her at all times if she goes swimming."

"Of course. There will be counselors as well as a lifeguard."

"She is not good about putting on sunscreen and she absolutely has to wear it every day." Without taking a breath, Aleshia continued. "And she needs bug spray if she's outside at all. If she's on a bike, she has to wear a helmet. Same with horseback riding, or I don't want her going."

"The camp has strict guidelines about those sorts of things. All kids need to wear helmets or they can't do certain activities."

"I just don't . . ."

"Really, Aleshia, she would be very well supervised and safe."

"Well . . ."

Several weeks later Aleshia drove her daughter to the church so Denise could load into a van headed for camp with dozens of other church kids. On the drive to church, Aleshia's fears skyrocketed. *I know something bad is going to happen.* She wanted to scream but she pursed her lips together and kept her eyes on the road. A dull buzzing vibrated through her body. She pictured herself whipping the car around and telling Denise she had changed her mind. *I'm sorry, sweetie, but you can't go!* Instead, Aleshia pulled into the parking lot and robotically helped Denise get her bags out of the car.

Swallowing the giant lump in her throat, she hugged her daughter. "I've put a note in your bag for every day. You need to read those." Creases lined Aleshia's forehead.

"I know, Mom." Denise rolled her eyes. "You've told me a hundred times."

"But I don't want you to forget about the helmet thing. Promise?"

"I got it, Mom."

Aleshia stayed until the camp vans pulled out of the parking lot. When she could no longer see them, she gulped for air but her lungs seemed too crowded to breathe. Dizzy, she got in her car, put her head on the steering wheel, and forced herself to take deep breaths. *I know she is going to be taken from me. . . . I'd better just get used to it.* Still short of breath, she began driving aimlessly around the city. She turned up the music, trying to smother the horror scenes flashing through her mind.

That night she barely slept. *Dear God, please protect my daughter . . . even though You probably won't. Please, please, I beg You. . . . Don't let anything happen to her.* At one point, around 2:30 in the morning, she convinced herself she was going to take off from work the next day and drive the ten-hour road trip to the camp so she could make sure Denise was OK.

A few days later, Aleshia was called into her supervisor's office. "You have a phone call." Her supervisor held out the phone to Aleshia.

Something happened to Denise. She took the receiver with a trembling hand. "Hello."

"Hi, Aleshia. It's Mike. How are you?"

"Don't be making small talk with me, Mike. What happened to Denise?" She squeezed the receiver so hard her knuckles turned white.

"She's OK. We just wanted you to know she fell when she was mountain bike riding and cut her leg. She'll be fine."

"I'm coming to get her."

"Really, you don't need to do that. We have cleaned it out and she'll be fine."

She swallowed the hysteria rising inside her. "Call me if it gets worse."

"Yes, we will."

"Can I talk to her?"

"She's actually back in the dorm right now. But don't worry, she's fine."

Aleshia spent the next two days asking friends and family if they thought she should drive up and check on Denise. Everyone she asked reassured her that a trip to camp was unnecessary. She went through the motions of life, but the anxiety mounting inside her made her feel as if she were losing her mind. Finally the time to pick up Denise arrived and she drove to the church parking lot. *Don't ask to see her leg until we're in the car,* she lectured herself as she waited. When the vans pulled up, Aleshia threw the car door open and hurried to greet her daughter. She gave Denise a tight hug then, before she could stop herself, blurted out, "Let me see your leg."

"Mom, can't we wait until we get in the car?"

Aleshia was already pulling her daughter's pant leg up. "Denise, that does not look good." She glanced up from the cut to her daughter's face. "And you look so pale."

"Mom, I'm fine."

Hearing the embarrassed irritation in Denise's voice, Aleshia waited until they were inside the car to ask more questions. "Do you feel OK?" she reached over and felt Denise's forehead. "You're burning up!" I knew it! You're leg is infected and now you're running a fever!" She started the car. "We're going to the hospital!"

"Mom, please. Not again. I'm fine." Denise sounded desperate.

When they got home, Aleshia rushed to the phone and called Ask-A-Nurse, a number she knew by heart. Because of the fever, the nurse recommended Denise see a doctor. It turned out Denise had strep throat and that was causing the fever. But the doctor confirmed Aleshia's fears about the cut, saying it had not been cleaned well.

"I'm going to sue that camp!" Aleshia ranted. "You could have gotten a serious infection! People die from that kind of thing."

"Mom, you're being ridiculous."

"See? I was right about that place!"

"Mom!" Denise shouted. "Kids get hurt." Her face burned as she turned toward her mom. "It's normal!"

Aleshia didn't respond. She knew anything she would say would only agitate Denise further. Looking straight ahead she pursed her lips together. *I knew something would happen. Guess I'm not so crazy. My fears were totally valid.*

Aleshia's fears continued to monopolize their lives. At times, she became totally immobilized, so afraid of everything that she did nothing. She spent days not going out of the house except to work. She avoided any extra contact with people because that increased her anxiety. People who knew her thought she was simply overwhelmed with being a single mom and having financial stresses. They had no idea the life inside her head was wrought with fears. But when Denise entered middle school, and started acting out, a new journey in Aleshia's life was set in motion and she couldn't hide the anxiety anymore.

The first sign of a problem was when Denise began throwing temper tantrums. Then Denise's teacher called Aleshia and said Denise was crying uncontrollably in class. When Denise stopped eating, Aleshia knew she needed help for her daughter. Her love for her daughter superseded her paralyzing fears and she reached out to a women's leader at her church and shared with her what was going on at home. Through their conversations, the woman gently suggested that, in order for Aleshia to help her daughter, she needed to help herself first. Aleshia knew her counselor was right. She began attending a support group to deal with her fears and also started going to a professional counselor, Vicky.

Through several sessions, Aleshia described to Vicky her seemingly endless list of fears and how they governed her life. "You have a choice to make," Vicky explained. "You can walk through your fears and live or you can continue on this path and not live."

Desperate for a better way of life for her daughter, Aleshia nodded. "I don't want this kind of life for Denise."

She had never really considered what was at the bottom of her fears.

Slowly, Aleshia began looking at the roots of her fearful and anxious state of being. She had never really considered what was at the bottom of her fears. She simply thought this was how she was always going to be. With professional help and the support of others, she began to examine carefully why she lived in such bondage.

"A lot of abuse happened to me in my childhood, but instead of acknowledging it and working through what happened, I just sort of stuffed everything into a dark closet and shut the door."

By opening up, Aleshia has brought hurtful experiences she had as a child into the light instead of keeping them in the dark where they had silently festered and become infectious. As she has talked through her past, she has learned that it doesn't have to dominate her life today. "I have found that I really don't have to live this way. I get to choose not to allow it to rule my life and keep me stuck in fear."

Through counseling she has learned to categorize life events into one of two categories: (1) a big thing that she needs to process and emotionally deal with, or (2) a small thing that she needs to release.

"The horrible events in my past used to define me and steal away my life so I couldn't even cope with small challenges."

Aleshia still sees a counselor to process through various pieces of her past, but the fears that paralyzed her no longer have their vise grip. "Every day, when things happen that could cause me to fear, I am learning to put them right away into one of the two categories. If it's a huge problem, then I walk through it with the help and support of others.

"But now, most often, I see the things that used to paralyze me as small and I let them go. Like going to a family function—I ask myself, *What if something that scares me actually happens? What if someone laughs at me or doesn't like me? Is that going to kill me?* No. Processing it through in that light helps me keep a perspective instead of allowing my fears to grab the steering wheel and take over."

As Aleshia has learned to unpack her closet of painful memories, to release the past and face the reality of her irrational fears, she has found a new way of living. She recently took a job that uses her skills. She also started taking classes at a community college. "Now I can go to public places without freaking out and I say yes to most things Denise wants to do. Through this unpacking process, I've learned to trust God with my life and my daughter's. That gives me a new sense of security, something I never had before." ❁

Irrational Thinking, Fear, and Anxiety: POINT OF CONNECTION
Vise Grips on Our Lives

> "I've lost so much time feeling afraid. I don't want to lose any more of it."
>
> —Ann Reierson

Fear can be paralyzing.

Anxiety and worry snatch away peace.

And often no one can see the battle from the outside because it is an internal war of the mind and heart. The enemy's forceful mind games keep taking more territory with lies that sound like:

> **That's too hard.**
>
> **Something bad is going to happen.**
>
> **It's just too scary and risky.**
>
> **It will never get better.**
>
> **Don't trust because look at what's happened before.**
>
> **If you do that, you'll fail.**
>
> **You're a loser and everyone thinks so.**
>
> **How can you really believe God when He's allowed bad things to happen?**
>
> **You have to be in control or things are sure to go wrong.**

Deep inside every woman—and man too—is a certain amount of fear and anxiety; it is part of the human condition. Is there a difference between fear and anxiety? Not really. They go hand in hand and are nearly impossible to separate.

Here are some "symptoms" of fear and anxiety. Check which ones you sometimes feel or experience:

- ❏ Churning in your stomach when thinking about difficult things
- ❏ An overly stimulated mind; you can't stop racing thoughts
- ❏ Shortness of breath
- ❏ Unable to make decisions so you stay stuck
- ❏ Controlling situations so you don't have to risk failure
- ❏ Lack of eating because of stress
- ❏ Overeating to relieve stress
- ❏ Your inside doesn't match your outside; inside feels tumultuous; outside looks put together
- ❏ Adrenaline rushes when meeting new people or trying new things
- ❏ Imagining all the bad things that can happen in a given situation
- ❏ Consuming thoughts about a situation or circumstance

If you checked any of these, then you can relate to living with some level of fear and anxiety. And, if you don't engage in the battle of fear, you can probably relate to a healthy dose of irrational thinking and sometimes blowing things out of proportion—which is really just a different manifestation of fear.

Fear Factor:
What Women Are Afraid Of (When They're Being Honest)

Here's what some real women had to say when they were asked the question, "If I am being honest, sometimes I am really afraid that . . ."

- I might end up alone.
- Something bad will happen to my kids.
- I am not as smart as everyone else.
- My mother disapproves of me.
- I might die.
- I will give my heart and then get rejected.
- I may never feel completely healed.
- I might be unfaithful.
- He might be unfaithful (again).
- My plane is going to crash.
- I'll get cancer.
- I won't really forgive my parents before they die.
- My kids won't end up OK.
- I'll never make enough money to support myself and my kids.
- I'll get fired.
- I'll end up in a nursing home.
- My husband will never really help me with the kids.
- I'm not a good mom and I'm messing up my kids.
- I'll do something to make my older kids mad and they won't want to be around me.

Which of these are things are you afraid of too?

For some of us our fears are bigger than they need be. They can become irrational, overwhelming. They are like a bulldozer in our lives, overtaking how we make decisions. They can keep us from moving forward and enjoying the confidence and freedom that comes with living in Christ. For others, fear isn't irrational at all. We are facing big battles in our lives—an impending divorce, children who keep rebelling and making scary choices, financial woes that keep building with no end in sight, job losses, health issues, and the list can go on. Regardless of the type of fear, God has something to say about it.

Read Joshua 1:9.

Be strong and courageous. Do not be terrified; do not be discouraged, for the LORD your God will be with you wherever you go." **(NIV)**

In this passage, why do we not need to be afraid?

If you really believe that God is always with you, what would feel different right now?

Sometimes, when we truly believe God is with us, the fear subsides like a thunderstorm passing overhead. Other times it doesn't. The lightning keeps striking and we don't feel any different. This is why we can't put our trust in how we feel. Instead, we put our trust in what God says to us.

In college, I (Laura) volunteered with the ministry of Young Life. When I was a sophomore, the Young Life area director asked me if I would speak about the work I was doing at an area fund-raising event. Even though it sounded a little scary, I said I would. When I found out there would be more than 300 grown-ups at the fund-raiser, it became even scarier. Then I found out it was parents' weekend at the university and my parents were going to be in town. I started to sweat when my mom said they would like to attend the fund-raiser. They already had questions about my "born-again"-ness. Now what were they going to think?

The day of the fund-raiser came and I was more scared than ever. I had prayed a lot and a friend had come over and we prayed together the words in Joshua 1:9. But I still felt very scared. I remember right before it was my turn to speak I repeated the words from Joshua 1:9 over and over again. I closed my eyes and made a determined choice to believe His Word despite how I felt—God was going to be with me. And He was.

Fear, regardless of whether it is rational or not, can be an overpowering force in our lives. God doesn't want that. He wants His truth to rule in us above fear. That doesn't mean we won't feel fear. It just means God's truth trumps our emotions.

Read Proverbs 3:5–6.

Trust God from the bottom of your heart; don't try to figure out everything on your own. Listen for God's voice in everything you do, everywhere you go; he's the one who will keep you on track. **(The Message)**

If we look at this verse carefully, there are three verbs that are assigned to us and one verb that is assigned to God.

Our job includes: (1) trusting, (2) not trying to figure it all out, and (3) listening to Him.

God's job includes: Keeping us on track.

Out of those three jobs, which do you need to work on most? Why is this one the hardest for you?

....

....

....

....

....

We do not believe in formulas for our spiritual journey. Life is far too complex for simple formulas! However, there are a few formulas that are very accurate, including: **More trust always equals less fear.** Take a moment and see how life would be different if you trusted more.

IF I TRUSTED GOD MORE WITH . . .	I THINK I'D FEEL LESS . . .

Take some time now in prayer and do this. Cast all of your anxieties on Him. Pour out your heart to God in the space below. Tell Him what you're afraid of, your irrational thoughts, and with what you long to trust Him.

Try not to feel "bad" for not trusting more. This is where the enemy, the evil one, wants to get to us and tell us we are losers for not trusting God properly. Remember, trusting God with our lives is a lifetime journey, not a quick destination. It is something we can never fully master. But, as we continue to be honest with ourselves, other people, and Him about our fears, He can teach us new ways of living with peace and freedom instead of anxiety, fear, and irrational thinking.

What we need to do is bring our fears and anxieties before Him, repeatedly, minute by minute, day by day, hour by hour.

Read 1 Peter 5:17.

Cast all your anxiety on him because he cares for you. **(NIV)**

Let's end with this: Write Psalm 27:1 on a piece of paper and keep it close to you this week. Every time you start to feel afraid, meditate on this truth.

The LORD is my light and my salvation—whom shall I fear? The LORD is the stronghold of my life—of whom shall I be afraid? **(NIV)**

1. **Laugh.** Rent or go see a funny movie.
2. **Hang out** with safe friends and share what's going on inside you.
3. **Go** get a coffee, tea, or a special treat and try to read a good book for a little while.
4. **Cry** with a good friend.
5. **Look** at what's behind the fear. "What's really going on back there?"
6. **Exercise**. Take a walk, go on a hike, head to the gym.
7. **Scream** into a pillow; do something to express the fear that won't hurt anyone.
8. **Write** out the whole "truth" of the situation—the facts and the emotions—so you can see more clearly.
9. **Remember** and write down the times God has taken care of you.
10. **Look** at a strong woman of faith whose loss in life is bigger than your own and find strength from her.

1. Changing the equation

You + Fear = Staying Stuck
OR You + Trust God = Change

Fear keeps us stuck. To change, move, grow, and become the women God wants us to be, we must learn how to believe even when we feel afraid.

Read the following passages about trust in the Book of Psalms.

Psalm 46:1–2

God is our refuge and strength, an ever-present help in trouble. Therefore we will not fear, though the earth give way and the mountains fall into the heart of the sea. **(NIV)**

Psalm 40:4

Blessed is the man who makes the Lord his trust. **(NLT)**

Psalm 20:7

Some trust in chariots and some in horses, but we trust in the name of the Lord our God. **(NIV)**

Psalm 28:7

The Lord is my strength and my shield; my heart trusts in him, and I am helped. My heart leaps for joy and I will give thanks to him in song. **(NIV)**

Psalm 56:3

When I am afraid, I will trust in you. **(NIV)**

Let Psalm 56:3 linger. Imagine if every time we were afraid, these words were embedded into our heart and head.

When I am afraid, I will trust in you.
When I am afraid, I will trust in you.
When I am afraid, I will trust in you.
When I am afraid, I will trust in you.

This would change the equation.

2. "Do not be afraid."

"Then Jesus said to them, 'Do not be afraid.'"
Matthew 28:10 (NIV)

In the Gospels, Jesus spoke repeatedly to the disciples, telling them not to be afraid. The disciples were with Jesus in the flesh and they were still afraid! Hopefully this provides comfort to those of us who struggle with fear because even those walking closest to Jesus struggled with it. But Jesus also promised even when He was not with them physically that He would provide a Comforter to help, guide, and direct them. He makes this promise to us today. This Comforter is the Holy Spirit.

Read what Jesus says in John 14:25–27.

All this I have spoken while still with you. But the Counselor, the Holy Spirit, whom the Father will send in my name, will teach you all things and will remind you of everything I have said to you. Peace I leave with you; my peace I give you. I do not give to you as the world gives. Do not let your hearts be troubled and do not be afraid. **(NIV)**

Make your laundry list of what you are afraid of.

I am afraid of . . .

-
-
-
-
-
-
-

Now, rewrite each of these statements and plug in Jesus's words in front of each of them. To make it more real, put your name in front too.

"____________, do not let your heart be troubled and do not be afraid of _________"

Take a minute and let the words penetrate your heart. How did this bring you comfort?

3. Ruth: A woman of trust

The Book of Ruth is just four chapters in the Old Testament packed with a powerful trust story. Ruth lost her husband. Her mother-in-law was bitter and broken. Ruth had no money. Yet she had one thing that sustained her—trust in God. She trusted Him so much that she made choices that other people thought were crazy. That is the thing with trusting God; sometimes it can look very crazy to other people. The world teaches us to live and make decisions that make "good sense." But Ruth shows us how trusting God is a better way to live even when we have no idea how the story might end. She took things one day at a time and trusted her Maker.

Read the story of Ruth. It is only four short chapters. With what part of Ruth's story do you connect? Check all that apply.

- The loss—of a loved one, a job, safety and security
- Walking into the unknown—a new job, house, life circumstance
- Having to risk your pride
- Not knowing the outcome but having to make decisions today

Describe these a little bit.

How does Ruth's story give you encouragement?

Letting go of fear

1. It's gotta come out somewhere

Sometimes we think we are so good at covering up our fear and anxiety. We mask it and pretend like everything is OK when it really isn't. We can try to push it down and make it go away, but eventually it leaks out somewhere. Maybe yours comes out through yelling at your kids, or pulling yourself out of social situations, or eating, or drinking. But one way or another it leaks. Why not find a healthy place to let out some of your fear and anxiety, to get some perspective on your irrational thinking?

Try this: Find a group of three or four women to meet with on a weekly or biweekly basis. Each time you meet, give one or two women (depending on your time) 15 minutes each to talk, share, and vent. During that 15 minutes no one else talks; everyone simply listens! After the 15 minutes, pray together. When the prayertime is over, talk about what God placed on your hearts for the woman who shared. It could be one word He impresses upon you or it could be a visual image. The idea is to really listen to God for one another and then share if and how He prompts you.

2. Cleaning your closet

Aleshia learned how to sift through the fears buried inside her and put them into two categories: (1) the fears she needed to really look at and deal with, and (2) the fears she needed to let go.

Try that right now. Make a list of your fears—big and small.

1. ....

2. ....

3. ....

4. ....

5. ....

6. ....

7. ....

8. ....

9. ....

10. ....

Circle which ones you feel are "small." Ask yourself what would happen if this or that fear actually became a reality.

Pick at least one fear you circled and ask God to help you to let it go.

3. Thinking clearly

"Do not conform any longer to the pattern of this world, but be transformed by the renewing of your mind. Then you will be able to test and approve what God's will is—his good, pleasing and perfect will" **(Romans 12:2 NIV)**.

Our minds get so cramped with irrational thoughts and fears, beliefs about ourselves and God that are influenced by the world. Think for a moment about how much the world tells us to be afraid. Car alarms, house alarms, kid alarms; the need for fire insurance, flood insurance, and every "emergency plan" in the world gets drilled into our heads. We're afraid of getting kidnapped, robbed, raped, scammed, and cheated.

What are some of the things the "world" tells you to be afraid of, worried about, which on your own you probably would never have even thought about?

How is this robbing you of peace?

Here's where God wants our minds to go.

Read Philippians 4:6–9.

Don't worry about anything; instead, pray about everything. Tell God what you need, and thank him for all he has done. If you do this, you will experience God's peace, which is far more wonderful than the human mind can understand. His peace will guard your hearts and minds as you live in Christ Jesus. And now, dear brothers and sisters, let me say one more thing as I close this letter. Fix your thoughts on what is true and honorable and right. Think about things that are pure and lovely and admirable. Think about things that are excellent and worthy of praise. Keep putting into practice all you learned from me and heard from me and saw me doing, and the God of peace will be with you. **(NLT)**

Try this short journaling exercise right now, reflecting on this passage.

"Don't worry about anything; instead pray about everything." **(v. 6*a*)**
God, here's what I'm worried about right now . . .

"Tell God what you need" **(v. 6*b*)**
Here's what I really need from You right now . . .

"and thank Him for all that he has done" **(v. 6*b*)**
God, I thank You that in the past You have . . .

"Fix your thoughts on what is true and honorable and right. Think about things that are pure and lovely and admirable. Think about things that are excellent and worthy of praise." **(v. 8*b*)**

So right now, I want to remember good things. Here's what's good right now. . . . Here's what's true right now. . . . Here's what is excellent and worthy of praise right now. . . .

1. Host your own "fear factor" show. Bring in two pogo sticks, two bowls of gelatin dessert filled with gummy worms, two blindfolds, and makeup (two lipsticks, two eyebrow pencils, two compacts of blush). Ask for two volunteers. They will compete against each other in the following events: (1) who can pogo stick the longest; (2) who can eat the most gummy worms in 30 seconds; and (3) who can put on the three items of makeup the fastest while wearing a blindfold.

2. After the contest, ask the women which event was the scariest. Why? Then ask everyone to share quick "popcorn" responses aloud to this question:

   The scariest thing I have ever done but survived was . . .

3. Give everyone a small piece of play dough. Ask them to form the play dough into something that represents what they are really afraid of in their life right now. Have them share in smaller groups or in the large group, depending on the group's size. Afterward, pray that these would shrink over the course of this week. Next week, you could start off asking the women whose fears shrank this week.

in living color

Praying the Fear Out of Me

When I get surrounded by fear, the only thing that helps me without fail is prayer. I have tried everything else: panicking, crying, calling a friend, freezing, you name it; but the relief is short-lived and the fear is still present for me. Now I go through a process where I first pray to God for His comfort and peace and then I say out loud to Him, if possible (so Satan knows exactly what I'm doing while I'm in a state of fear), all the things I believe Him to be. I will say, "You are my comforter, You are in control, You will never leave me," and so on; and I continue saying these things for as long as it takes for the fear to pass. There have been situations where the fear has lasted several hours and I will continue talking to Him like this throughout the entire time until His peace pours over me. When I am in a fear state, I want so much to believe that God is who He says He is and the out loud praying helps me get there.

—Bonnie

1. Rate yourself between 1 and 10 for how much you struggle with fear, anxiety, and/or irrational thinking (10 being the most). What does it look like for you?

2 What are some of the things you wrote in the box "If I Trusted God More with . . ., I'd Have Less . . ."?

3. Do your emotions trump God's truth in your life? How?

4 What is the number one area in your life where you want to learn to trust God more?

5. Closing round: Go around the circle or group and finish this sentence in two or three words: *This week, please pray that I feel less anxious and afraid about . . .*

Check These Out...

I Grew Up Little: Finding Hope in a Big God
by Patsy Clairmont

Ruthless Trust
by Brennan Manning

Calm My Anxious Heart
by Linda Dillow

The Awakening
by Angela Hunt

If God Is in Control, Why Do I Have a Headache?
by Debbie Taylor Williams

Leaving Behind Good-Girl Baggage

And lightening your load

Deborah swirled around in a perfect pivot as she modeled her new emerald green dress. "What do you think?"

"Oh, sis, that's sharp!" her dad nodded with approval before turning his attention back to the football game on television. Deborah smiled at her mom and then bounded up the stairs to try on her next outfit.

"Deb, try on the pantsuit now." Her mom's voice bubbled with enthusiasm. Reveling in her parent's approval, Deborah slipped on cream-colored pants and a fitted jacket that matched.

Before showing off this next outfit, she decided to check herself out in the full-length mirror in her mom's bathroom. As Deborah analyzed her figure, she heard the front door open and slam shut. She cracked the door to the bathroom and could hear Steve, her older brother, and her father arguing. As their voices got louder, tension swept through the house like a tornado.

Steve had been out all night and Deborah knew from experience that the rest of the afternoon was ruined. *Why does he always have to do this?* Deborah kicked off her shoes and sat down at the edge of the bathtub. *I wish he would just clean up his act.* A surge of anger swept over Deborah and she braced herself for the ensuing battle she knew would come. *He ruins everything.*

Deborah stayed in the bathroom until the screaming died down. Then she tiptoed to her room. Knowing the fashion show was over, she pulled off her new pantsuit and yanked on her jeans and striped sweater. Touching up her hair, Deborah's eyes locked on a family picture she had taped to her mirror.

Mike, her younger brother, looked fine but he had been born with cerebral palsy. Her mother would never refer to her brother as having a disability and spent a lot of energy to prove that everything was OK. Deborah's eyes shifted to Steve. Though he was a year older than her, Deborah had always felt she was the first-born—responsible and a pleaser. As she stared next at her brother Jonathan, she could see why he had so many girlfriends. His deep green eyes rested in a chiseled face and he looked more like a model or movie star than a small-town Kansas boy.

Shoot, Steve! Deborah said through clenched teeth, turning her back to the photo. *Why can't you just stop doing drugs and make it easier on Mom and Dad?* Flopping down on her bed, Deborah next heard her father's voice booming through the house.

"You are forcing us to take drastic action!" Deborah pictured her dad's face turning crimson red and his mouth as a pencil line, and she knew his final form of punishment would be silence.

"So what? I'll move out. You wouldn't miss me anyway." Steve's words slurred together with sarcasm but Deborah noticed his voice sounded more defeated than angry. "You've got perfect Little Debbie, nothing-is-wrong-with Mike, and GQ Jonathan. That's all you want anyway."

The sound of her name made Deborah flinch. *Perfect Little Debbie? I hate this.* She closed her eyes, wishing she could move far away. She didn't want to hear them anymore. She didn't want to think about it all anymore. Rolling over on her stomach, she tugged

the comforter around her and grabbed a pillow to pull it over her ears.

The next morning Deborah rose early to get ready for school. She made her bed carefully and folded all the new clothes crumpled on the floor. Glancing over her room to make sure it would measure up to her mom's standards, she noticed her comforter was longer on one side of the bed than the other. *Oh well,* Deborah shrugged. *She always remakes my bed anyway.* Picking up a pair of sandals from the floor, she walked over to her closet, set the sandals down on her shoe shelf, and shifted her attention to her closet.

As her hands roamed over her clothes, she mulled over what to wear. Finally, she decided on navy pants and a navy and white striped, V-neck, cotton shirt. She took the clothes off the hangers and tossed them onto her bed. After her shower, she spent a half hour blow-drying her blonde, feathered hair so that it cascaded perfectly down her shoulders, as if she were a model. She dressed, went back to the mirror, and applied her makeup.

By the time she finished, she was running late. Deborah grabbed her books, stuffed them into her backpack, and dashed downstairs to the kitchen. Guzzling a glass of orange juice, she swiped the edges of her mouth with a paper towel and called out, "Bye, Mom and Dad," before she darted out the door to catch the school bus.

When she got home that afternoon her stomach rumbled. She had been so busy working on a Science Fair project that she had skipped lunch. Deborah made a quick sandwich, grabbed a bag of chips, and plopped down in front of the television to catch the last half of her favorite soap opera. When a commercial came on, she took her empty plate to the kitchen, put it in the sink, and began rummaging around the cupboard for something sweet. She found an unopened box of cookies and sat down on the couch to finish watching her show.

When the show was over, she looked down at the box of cookies and realized she had eaten an entire row—20 cookies. *Oh no! I feel so gross.* Her stomach pushed against her pants and she felt sick from all the sugar inside her body. The thought of gaining weight made her feel even more ill. Anxiety filled her like helium in a hot-air balloon. Suddenly she was gripped with an overwhelming need to get rid of the food. She went to the bathroom and locked the door behind her.

Standing over the toilet, she opened her mouth

and tried to force the food to come up. When that didn't work, she cinched her belt as tightly as she could and bent over the toilet. She began to heave and after a minute the food she had just consumed came lurching up her throat.

Breathing hard, Deborah flushed the toilet. Then she took a step backwards. Beads of perspiration gathered at the top of her forehead and the acidy taste of bile filled her mouth. She took a hand towel and ran it under cold water. Pressing the towel to her face, she then rinsed her mouth.

As she left the bathroom, a whirlpool of feelings jostled inside her—relief, guilt, confusion, and even exhilaration. *At least I don't have to worry about gaining weight from all those cookies,* she thought. She picked up her backpack and walked to her room. Troubling thoughts about what she had done lingered the rest of the day, but she had to admit there had been something freeing and satisfying to her about that moment.

The next week, she did it again. Pretty soon, binge eating and throwing up became part of Deborah's everyday life. Yet, she hid it well. She learned to clean up the mess and hide the evidence expertly and she gracefully maintained her reputation and lifestyle as an all-American girl. She was a cheerleader, earned excellent grades, dated a star football player, and was crowned homecoming queen. She also entered and won a beauty contest in her town where nearly a hundred contestants displayed their beauty and talents to a panel of judges. Deborah's beauty queen crown fueled her need to preserve her public appearance as her town's beautiful and smart "good girl."

When Deborah graduated from high school, she attended a community college and her secret habit continued to fester below the surface where no one could see. But she discovered that *bulimia* did not necessarily keep a person from gaining weight and her clothes quickly became too tight. A round face and tight jeans only made her more anxious and vulnerable to binging and purging.

After two years at the community college, she moved away from home to attend a state nursing program where she met a new friend, Nina, a student in her program. Deborah loved spending time with her, finding it refreshing to have a friend outside her small-town circle.

This new friendship made Deborah realize that her childhood friends didn't really know her well. They thought they did, but it was only the surface person they knew—not her inside.

Nina was a devoted Christian. She worked at understanding the real Deborah, asking questions no one else asked. It was a different kind of friendship. Deborah was drawn to having a close friend, but a little afraid too. Sharing her true feelings with someone felt uncomfortable. But when fall break came, Deborah asked Nina if she wanted to go home with her and spend the weekend at her parents' house.

"Sounds great." A smile lit Nina's eyes. "I'm ready for some R and R."

"I can drive. It only takes a couple of hours and we can just hang out all weekend and watch movies." The first morning of break, the girls woke up early.

"I'm so used to waking up for my clinicals that I can't sleep in, even when I try," Nina said stretching her arms over her head. "I'm starving. You wanna go eat breakfast?"

"Sure," Deborah nodded, wanting to avoid the topic of food. "It's so nice outside." She sat up in her bed and peered out the window, admiring the cloudless autumn sky. "We should take a walk later on."

"Perfect," Nina sprang out of bed and started getting dressed.

After Nina ate a bowl of cereal and Deborah nibbled on half of a banana, the two friends grabbed sweatshirts and headed out the front door. "We'll be back in a while, Mom," Deborah called over her shoulder.

"It's chilly. Don't forget a sweater," Deborah's mom called back.

After they walked for a few minutes, Nina said in a sober voice, "I can see what you mean about your mom." Her hazel eyes were filled with compassion. "She is majorly controlling."

"I know. Every time I come home, it gets harder to be around." Raking her hair from her forehead, a wave of irritation washed over Deborah. "You just saw it. She still tries to tell me what to wear!"

Nina's brow wrinkled. "Wasn't she a nurse too?"

"MmHm." Deborah kicked a stone and watched it speed across the sidewalk into the grass. "I wanted to be an artist but she . . .," Deborah's words drifted off as she remembered how her mom had told her she could never be an artist because that would mean she might starve. "For some reason, she needed me to be like her and become a nurse. So that's what I've done." Deborah shoulders sagged as they walked along.

"Deborah, you can't live to please your mom and dad for the rest of your life." Nina stopped walking and turned toward her. "You can't base your decisions on not disappointing your parents anymore. You need to do what God wants you to do." Her voice grew soft, "Even if it means letting your parents down."

Deborah shook her head up and down, knowing what she said was true but not knowing how to live outside the only role she knew—*good and pleasing Little Debbie.*

Deborah and Nina wandered onto a playground and sat down on a bench. Lost in their own thoughts, they sat without talking. When Nina spoke again, her words seemed strained. "Deborah, I . . .," she hesitated.

"What?" Deborah looked at her friend and saw a change come over her features. "What is it?"

"I know what you do." Nina's voice was tender.

Deborah's heart skipped inside her chest. "What do you mean?"

"My roommate, Sonya, has an eating disorder. I've seen it. And I've watched you."

Tears welled up in Deborah's eyes. *No one knew her secret.*

Nina reached out and put her hand on Deborah's arm. "It's OK. I'm here for you."

Deborah swallowed. She wanted to hide because she felt so ashamed, yet at the same time, she wanted to yell with relief because now she had someone to share her heavy burden.

Nina touched Deborah's shoulder lightly. "Let me pray for you." Deborah squeezed her eyes shut and bowed her head, tears streaming down her cheeks. "Dear God, I come to You right now and lift up Deborah to You. She needs You. Holy Spirit, come and take this away from her, please. Jesus, please help her to deal with what's behind this."

As Nina prayed, a crystal-clear vision appeared in Deborah's mind. She saw herself being carried by Jesus. Her arms hung lifelessly down at her sides as He carried her along and her body was limp. She knew instinctively that God was showing her an "old self" and it was dead. He was telling her that, in Him, she had a new life.

After Nina finished praying, Deborah sat with her eyes closed for another long moment, drinking in the vision God had given her. Waves of liberation flooded her spirit. When she opened her eyes, the sun seemed brighter and a smile edged its way across her face. "Thank you." She wiped underneath her eyes

> "It feels so good that you know because I know you still accept me."

with the back of her hand. "I've never told anyone." Inhaling, she sat back on the bench. "It feels so good that you know because I know you still accept me."

Nina's eyes were wide and glowing. "Of course I do. I love you in the Lord."

Over the next several months, food still fought to have center stage in Deborah's life. But when the urges to binge and purge pressed down on her, Deborah told herself, *No! I don't want that. I don't need that.* She began to let herself feel the pain of hiding behind the good-girl image all the time. She spent hours talking to Nina, processing thoughts and behaviors. Deborah began to understand why she had used food to fill the big hole inside.

One Friday evening, when Nina and Deborah were eating dinner together, Deborah spilled out her heart. "I feel so angry at my parents for their controlling ways." She thumped her fork on the table. "I mean, why does my mom care more about what I'm wearing than what I'm thinking or feeling?"

With her eyes glued to Deborah, Nina popped a carrot into her mouth and nodded. "It's hard to let go of anger, especially when we feel the right to be angry."

Deborah exhaled. "But I know I need to keep moving forward. I need to stop blaming my parents for my eating disorder." She took a quick sip of her diet soda and kept talking. "If I don't, I'll just be stuck. I don't want that." Deborah's eyes flashed with determination.

Nina smiled. "You're doing great. I'm so proud of you."

"Thanks." Her encouragement felt like a warm cup of cocoa on a cold winter night. "You know what else I believe?"

"What?" Nina munched on her burger.

"I think food is exactly like drugs."

"How?"

"People use drugs and alcohol to fill the hole inside, to make themselves numb to their pain, right?" Deborah didn't wait for an answer. "I did the same thing but with food."

"Just like my roommate." A cloud of sadness covered Nina's face.

Deborah thought about Sally, her bone-thin body, acid-smelling breath, and brittle hair. "I know. Seeing her made me realize how much I don't want to be like that."

"It isn't an answer." Nina sighed heavily. "It hasn't made anything go away. The hole is still there inside Sally."

Deborah blew out her cheeks. "Only God can fill that hole."

"I wish I could reach Sally and she could see that."

"You reached me," Deborah smiled across the table at her friend. "God used you as a big part of my growth and healing."

Nina stopped eating. A smile pulled up her cheeks, lifting the sadness from her face. "I'm so glad."

Deborah's new freedom from bulimia felt good, but for many more years she still battled the compulsion to be perfect and be seen as the "good girl" in the eyes of other people. She hated this about herself and yearned to be free of the need to maintain her

The Impostor's Gotta Go!

Impostor: One that assumes false identity or title for the purpose of deception.

(*Merriam-Webster's Collegiate Dictionary*, 11th ed., s.v. "impostor.")

Many good girls are living like impostors, presenting a false self to those around us, hiding who we really are because we fear rejection and disapproval. One of the reasons we "assume" another identity is we think we have to live up to others' expectations of us.

How do you connect with this definition of an impostor?

In order to live honestly, authentically, the impostor's gotta go!

An expectation of myself I want God to help me let go of is . . .

"game face." But it was hard. She fought the deeply ingrained desire to have it all together. Even after she graduated from nursing school and got married, she battled her good-girl stronghold. And when she became a mom, perfectionism reared its ugly head some more, but in new, maternal ways. But on Monday, August 28, 2000, Deborah's pull toward perfectionism was permanently altered.

She was sitting in the passenger seat in a friend's convertible when a pickup truck hit Deborah's side of the car. The truck driver died and Deborah suffered traumatic brain injuries. She spent four brutal months away from her two sons and husband in the hospital to relearn the most basic tasks, such as chewing. Her road to recovery was extensive and grueling; and even though she recovered most of her cognitive and physical abilities, she was told by her neuropsychologist that she could never return to her work as an RN—a huge blow on top of everything else.

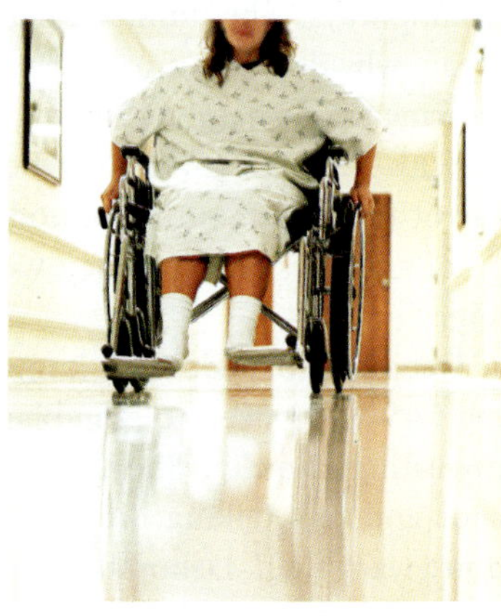

Deborah's life changed in so many ways due to the accident. She lost her career, her health, and her activities as a wife and mother changed. She no longer could be "perfect." She couldn't keep it all together anymore; and it was impossible to measure up to the image she always tried so hard to portray. One of the greatest life changes, and the one for which she is most grateful, is her need to live more authentically.

"I lost so much because of the accident. I no longer had the ability to pretend at perfection. I was such a mess," Deborah explains today as she shares her story. "I really felt healed from bulimia when I was in college, but the invisible tug-of-war that went on inside me was still there. Feeling valued for being good and beautiful had a vise grip on me. It wasn't until my accident that God forced me into a whole new zone of being real and vulnerable."

A twinkle lights up Deborah's eyes as she explains her ability to encourage other women since recovering from the accident. "God uses me in ways He couldn't before. Through all I have learned, I get to support and love other women who are fighting their own battles." Nodding her head back and forth, Deborah laughs. "Don't get me wrong. It's not that I am completely over everything. I'm still on a journey. I still worry about food a lot. I care about what other people think of me. But my heart is different, more raw and exposed. My biggest goal in life is to live authentically with God and other people." ❁

How You Can Leave Behind
Good-Girl Baggage

"I lived to please my parents, especially my father; but when I left to go away to college, I felt a new freedom. I could be more of me. The real me. Not the me they wanted me to be."

—Liz Ross

The quest to be perfect.

The desire to be the prettier, smarter, funnier, thinner, better.

To be "good" in the eyes of others.

Many of us struggle with being "the good girl"—the one who always is dependable . . . the one who achieves . . . the one who keeps everyone around them happy. But good girls usually hide something.

They're afraid to show their "true colors," their real struggles, lest they be rejected, unwanted, and unloved. They're afraid to fail. They're afraid of what people think of them. They count themselves valuable based on what they do and how others view them. But deep inside the very core of their souls is a longing to be valued unconditionally for who they are beneath the surface, raw and real.

Deborah was always the good girl. With what part of her story do you connect?

It's impossible to be "good" always. Logically, we all know that. But then why do so many women struggle with being the "good girl"? Why do we work so hard to maintain an image? Usually we are trying to live up to others' expectations of us. Often the expectations of parents, teachers, grandparents, or other significant people in our lives are cemented into us when we are young. We work hard to live up to those expectations because the message we receive is that *we are loved more when we behave a certain way.*

This is a hard message to rewire. However, it needs to be rewired, because in order to have a blossoming relationship with God, we need to believe His love is not based on how good we are. God's love is unconditional.

Reflect on 1 John 4:9–10.

This is how God showed his love among us: He sent his one and only Son into the world that we might live through him. This is love: not that we loved God, but that he loved us and sent his Son as an atoning sacrifice for our sins. **(NIV)**

God does not love you or me based upon our behavior. There is nothing we can do to cause God to love us any more than He already does—and there is nothing that will cause God to love us any less.

Do you believe that? Describe your thoughts.

Good girls get value from what they do and for what they don't do. But repeatedly in the Bible, God expresses His desire for us to understand that He loves *us*, not what we *do*. He doesn't care about what's on the outside: our looks, nor the achievements we try to earn. Those are all surface things that don't really matter in God's economy.

He cares about our heart; He values honesty and authenticity. The façade, the pretending, makes us look as though we were weeds in a garden with no real roots, no real depth. And the tricky thing is, sometimes these weeds don't actually look like weeds. They're pretenders that actually flower and grow, competing with the real plants. Usually the competition is quite fierce. But a trained gardener knows which are weeds and which are real flowers. The gardener can spot the ones that are counterfeit, getting in the way of letting the Gardener's real plants grow.

Hiding behind a good-girl image as Deborah did is living like a weed, a counterfeit life. She looked good on the outside, but like a flowering weed, it was all pretense. Most women, when they're honest, have inner battles with self-image, worth, and a lack of feeling loved.

Deborah became so entrenched in being the good girl that she didn't know how to show people the other side of her—anger and resentment toward her brother; inner battles she fought because of her controlling mother; an unhealthy need to be liked by everyone around her; and binging and purging.

What are some of your inner struggles that you are afraid others might find out about?

Sometimes people feel that unless they are "good" they can't go to God either. So they avoid Him too.

Is it hard for you to share your struggles honestly with God? Why or why not?

God wants to meet us in those honest places . . . where we struggle. He wants us to know who we truly are in His eyes—fully loved, no matter what we do or say or don't do or say. He wants to fill our heart so that our roots in Him can spread deep and it won't matter what people think about us or how they view us. We'll be rooted and grounded not by what we do or by the image we try to maintain, but rather by our confidence and trust in God's love for us.

Read Jeremiah 17:7–8.

"But blessed is the man who trusts in the LORD, whose confidence is in him. He will be like a tree planted by the water that sends out its roots by the stream. It does not fear when heat comes; its leaves are always green. It has no worries in a year of drought and never fails to bear fruit." **(NIV)**

Part of breaking free from good-girl baggage means beginning to trust God and His unconditional love for us. As Jeremiah shows us, trust is the conduit toward growth, health, peace, and fruitfulness.

But, we need to remember change will not come quickly. We will not be able to all of a sudden live authentically. We will wrestle with feeling inadequate when we are honest. We will wish people would not see our faults. We will want to hide.

Healing will take time. It will take our practice. But the reward is worth the effort: a richer, freer life.

It's time to begin to leave the good-girl baggage behind.

Digging Deeper

1. Good-girl baggage

Those of us who struggle with keeping it all together, living the role of the good girl, have voices that are strong and powerful swirling around in our heads—and not from God. They are not "truth" but they certainly can *feel* true. To which of these statements do you relate? Check those that apply.

- ◼ I am not valuable unless I'm doing something valuable.
- ◼ If I don't do it right, they won't love me.
- ◼ They are expecting me to keep it all together.
- ◼ If they really knew me, they wouldn't like me.
- ◼ Failing is not an option.
- ◼ I will let them all down if I mess things up.
- ◼ God expects perfection, so I better get it right.
- ◼ I need to live up to what they think I am.

All these statements lack a belief in the power of God's grace, His unmerited favor no matter what we do. Yet, as Jesus told the Apostle Paul, a great man of God who wrote so much of the New Testament, "My grace is sufficient for you, for my power is made perfect in weakness" (2 Corinthians 12:9 NIV). Through this passage, God is showing us that He does not expect us to have it all together. In fact, Jesus is emphasizing the power there is in weakness, brokenness, and honesty.

Is appearing weak hard for you? Why or why not?

What does 2 Corinthians 12:9 mean to you?

2. Stop faking it

Matthew 23:27

"Woe to you, teachers of the law and Pharisees, you hypocrites! You are like whitewashed tombs, which look beautiful on the outside but on the inside are full of dead men's bones and everything unclean." **(NIV)**

In this passage of Scripture, Jesus forcefully speaks to the Pharisees about their focus on the outside and people's perception of them. He is calling them *hypocrites* for pretending. This is a strong word, but when we are always faking it, trying to keep it all together, and not being honest about our real struggles and the truth of our humanness, we are being hypocrites.

In what areas of your life are you being hypocritical? How are you pretending that your life is better than it really is?

3. Addicted to approval

Addicted is a strong word. *Webster's* defines *addiction* as "compulsive need for and use of a habit-forming substance." Most good girls are addicted to approval. Approval feeds something inside of us. It becomes habitual for us to do things right because then we receive praise and approval. This helps us to feel better about ourselves and fuels us to repeat the good behavior. The problem is that when we become addicted to something other than God, we will never be satisfied.

Meditate on Galatians 1:10.

Am I now trying to win the approval of men, or of God? Or am I trying to please men? If I were still trying to please men, I would not be a servant of Christ. **(NIV)**

Are there ways in which you are a slave to people's approval?

How does this affect your life?

4. Trapped by self-expectations

Earlier we talked about expectations others have of us and how these have an impact on our lives. But as we grow up, we often begin to place expectations on ourselves too. I (Kathy) connect with playing the role of "good girl" because of expectations I adopted. My reputation with family and friends is that I'm the one who always does it right. I have always been valued for achieving, winning awards, being the best, succeeding, being positive, and not rocking the boat. No one directly told me "We expect you to . . .," but there were unspoken expectations drilled into me. And, because I was always praised for these things, I began placing the same expectations on myself.

What expectations have other people put on you that you have tried to meet? Finish this sentence:

"I think that people expect me to . . ."

What expectations do you place on yourself? Finish this sentence:

"I expect myself to . . ."

Comfort and Relief

1. What do you run to?

In Deborah's story, she shares how binging and purging became a "drug" for her. It relieved her pain, comforted her, gave her a distorted form of pleasure and control. We all have different things that we run to for comfort and relief.

Circle things that you sometimes resort to for comfort:

Overeating

Binging and purging

Exercising

Watching TV

Working

Shopping

Undereating

Spending

Cleaning

Reading romance novels

Drinking

Other________________

2. If . . ., then

Good girls live from a place of "If I . . ., then . . . ." *If I do well, then God will approve of me. If I look good, then others will notice me. If I succeed at something, then I will feel better about myself.* We do this with God, ourselves, and with others. Identifying "If . . ., thens" in our life can help us to break free of them and live more authentically.

Think of what motivates you; thoughts that go through your head about yourself and how others see you. Finish these sentences. Write what first comes to mind right now.

IF I . . .,   THEN OTHERS WILL . . .

What does this reveal to you?

areas of your life: God, friends, family, spouse, co-workers, church family. Living more honestly in these relationships requires us to trust God more fully. It's hard to do, but the fruit is a much more real and satisfying relationship with God and others.

Fill in the roots with ways you'd like to be more authentic in these relationships.

Here are a few of Kathy's to get you started . . .

4. Doing it differently

Letting go of being the good girl is not easy. We will need to practice thinking differently. God can help us if we'll let Him, but it takes some intention. Here are some actions you can try that will challenge you to break out of the box and live more authentically.

- Ask a friend to be an accountability partner for a short season and see if she'd be willing to listen when you need to confess a struggle or hurt. Set up a way of communicating (either by phone, email, in person) and commit to contacting her when you make a mistake and are tempted to cover it up and pretend.

- This one will be hard for some of you. Force yourself not to do something you think you are supposed to do, such as: attend a function, sign up for a committee, clean your house before someone comes over. What did that feel like? Was it hard or easy? Why or why not? What was the response from others?

- Before the next important decision you have to make, pull out your Bible and read Galatians 1:10.

Am I now trying to win the approval of men, or of God? Or am I trying to please men? If I were still trying to please men, I would not be a servant of Christ. **(NIV)**

As you make your decision, think through who you are trying to please—God or other people?

3. Putting down new roots

Reflect again on Jeremiah 17:7–8.

"But blessed is the man [or woman] who trusts in the Lord, whose confidence is in him. He will be like a tree planted by the water that sends out its roots by the stream. It does not fear when heat comes; its leaves are always green. It has no worries in a year of drought and never fails to bear fruit." **(NIV)**

God compares us to a tree. He says that when we trust in Him—put our confidence in Him—we will be like trees with roots that spread far and deep. Part of growing new roots is learning to be more authentic in our different relationships.

Look at the tree above. Each root represents various

1. Take a hardboiled egg with no cracks in it. Share with the group some of the elements of the egg—smooth, perfect, no cracks. Can you get to the good stuff if it always stays like that? No, part of enjoying the egg is cracking it open and letting what's inside out. This is like us. When we try to be perfect, with no cracks, we don't let our real selves out. Plus, what eventually happens to a boiled egg if it is not cracked open, shelled, and enjoyed? It begins to rot and smell. How is that like us too?

2. Bring in two dolls: the "good girl" and the "bad girl." Pass the dolls around and have each woman take a turn saying one thing for which a "good girl" is known and one thing for which a "bad girl" is known.

3. *Lectio divina* is an ancient tradition of Scripture reading and concentration. Have members of the group close their eyes while someone reads the following Scripture three times, slowly and with passion. Ask the group members to still their hearts and listen for what words or phrases stir something in them.

2 Corinthians 12:9–10

But he said to me, "My grace is sufficient for you, for my power is made perfect in weakness." Therefore I will boast all the more gladly about my weaknesses, so that Christ's power may rest on me. That is why, for Christ's sake, I delight in weaknesses, in insults, in hardships, in persecutions, in difficulties. For when I am weak, then I am strong. **(NIV)**

What words resonate most with you? Why?

in living color

"**I always got straight A's,** did everything I could to be the most popular, the smartest, the most likely to succeed. Underneath the outside persona I put on for everyone I was actually extremely insecure, lonely, and always hiding the real me from others. I remember the first B that I got in college. I bawled my eyes out, confronted my professor, and tried to do anything I could to get him to change his mind and give me an A. He didn't change his mind. And guess what? I survived. Looking back, I realize how ridiculous it was to demand perfection of myself always. Real people get B's!   —Carla

"I used to always pretend that I was doing well, even when I wasn't. It's hard to do, but now I'm more honest with the people around me and I feel so much more connected with God too."   —Lauren

"I'm starting to let God in more, instead of always trying to hide and cover up."   —Teri

"When I was really working on breaking out of always living up to others' expectations of me, my Christian counselor would give me assignments to do, and I would purposefully not do them. Not doing things just because I was supposed to was really freeing for me."   —Janelle

1. How are you hostage to maintaining the good-girl image? What are some unrealistic expectations you have of yourself?

2. Look again at the list of statements under "Good-Girl Baggage." Which of these do you hear in your head? Which statements did you check? Where do you think some of these messages came from (parents, friends, significant others)?

3. Share what you circled on "What Do You Run To?" Why is it so much easier to run there than to God or others? How do you usually feel afterward?

4. Share with the group what roots you filled in on "Putting Down New Roots." What are the ways you'd like to live more authentically in some of these key relationships?

5. Closing round: Finish this sentence in a couple of words: *I will live authentically by . . .*

Check These Out . . .

Thin Enough: My Spiritual Journey Through the Living Death of an Eating Disorder
by Sheryle Cruse

Freedom from the Performance Trap
by David A. Seamands

Posers, Fakers, and Wannabes: Unmasking the Real You
by Brennan Manning, with Jim Hancock

The Real Me
by Natalie Grant

Jesus, Life Coach
by Laurie Beth Jones

STACY

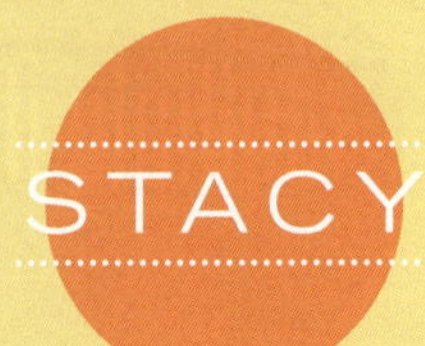

Girlfriends

Good for Your Health *and Your* Hope

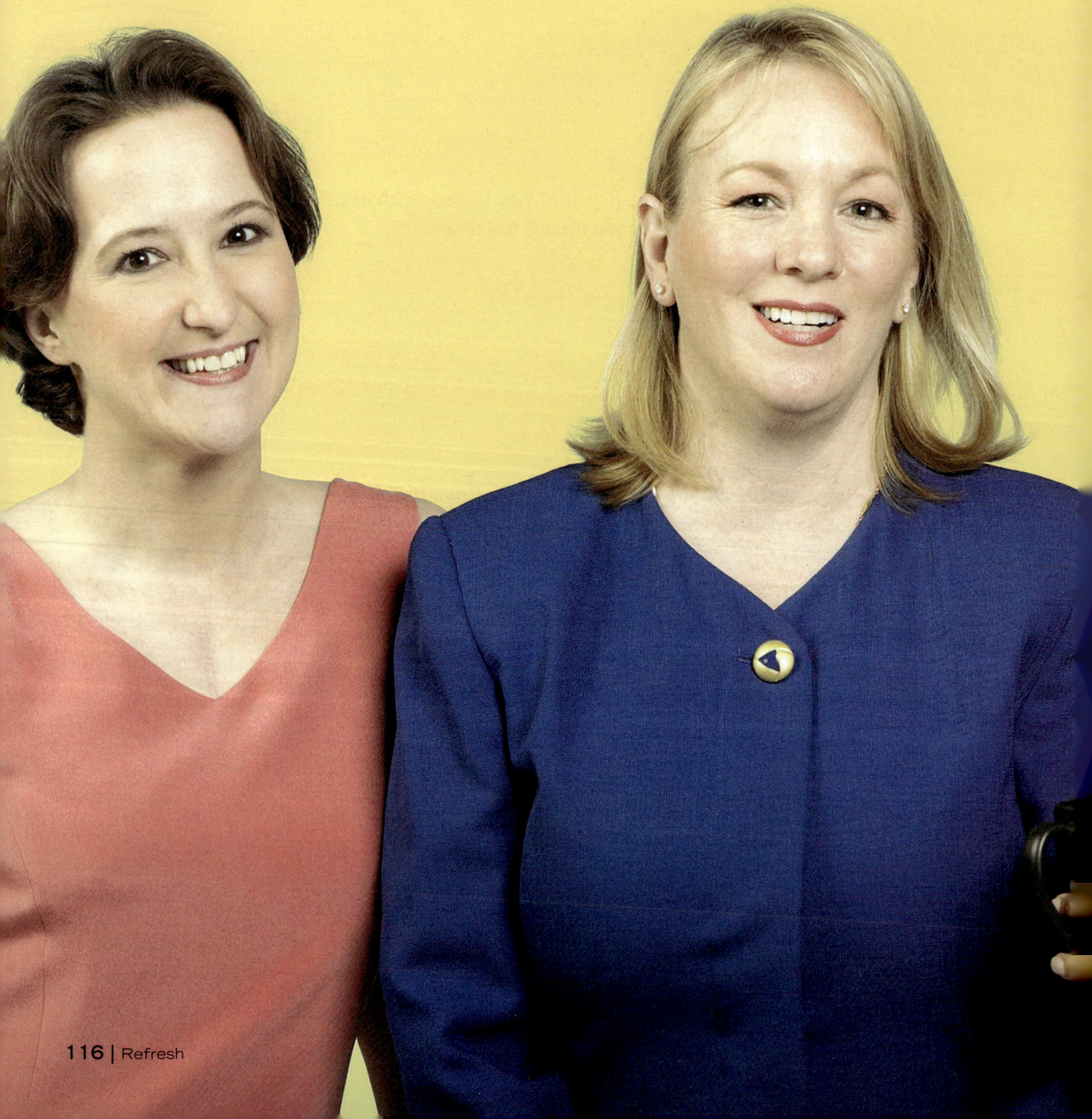

As they pulled into the gas station,

Stacy washed down the last of her burger with a diet soda. Her father parked the car and got out. Still sipping on her soda, Stacy overheard her dad speaking to someone. "That's my daughter in the front seat."

Who's he talking to? Stacy raised her eyebrows. Glancing over her shoulder she peered out the window. She gasped when she saw it was a gangly teenage gas attendant. *Oh no.* An alarm went off inside her head.

"Why don't you take her out tonight?" her dad asked.

Stop, Dad! Stop! Stacy slid down into the seat and squeezed her eyes shut.

"Come on. I'll even give you money for the date."

How could you do this to me? Groaning, Stacy covered her face with her hands. Through her half-open window she heard the boy mumble something.

"Well maybe next time then," her dad replied.

Stealing a look from the side-view mirror, Stacy watched her dad slap the boy on the back. When her father slid into the driver's seat, she clenched her jaw and looked straight ahead.

"See, honey? I'm just trying to get some dates for you, like your sisters have."

Drenched in humiliation, she forced herself not to cry. Her dad reached over and gave her arm a playful squeeze. "Don't worry. We'll get you a date one of these days."

Why does he have to make me feel like such a loser? Stacy's heart squeezed in anguish.

When they got home, she went to her room and shut the door. Leaning against the door, the humiliation still wrapped around her like a suffocating cloak. She walked over to the oak mirror above her chest of drawers and stared at her reflection. Tears burned in her eyes. *Why would anyone want to go out with me?* She ran her fingers over her face and hair, grunting at the blemishes spotting her round face. *I'm fat and ugly.* Defeated, she turned from the mirror, walked across the room, and slumped onto her bed. The curtains around her window lifted as a gentle breeze filled the room. Stacy stared out the window and watched a robin fly away from a tree. *I wish I could fly away.*

A few years later, Stacy did fly away when she left for college. She went to Brigham Young University, which was as far away from her parents' home as they would allow her to go. On Stacy's first day of classes, she walked around the campus with a swirling mixture of anticipation and trepidation tumbling around inside her. Sitting down on a stone bench, she watched students stride by.

A clean-cut boy wearing faded jeans with a florescent yellow T-shirt smiled at her as he passed by. Her heart fluttered and she stared at him until he turned a corner and was gone. Inhaling the crisp fall air, she couldn't suppress a smile. For the first time in her life, she was not living under the overpowering "You will succeed no matter what!" expectations of her father.

Laughter floated up her throat as she breathed in her new freedom. *I can do anything I want!* She swung her legs underneath her. A group of students holding instruments came streaming out of a building and

she watched as the band conductor lined them up. As she gazed at them, her smile slowly faded. The students looked so self-assured and purposeful, as though they knew the marching band was exactly where they belonged. *Where do I belong?* Her heart tugged as the students performed in unison.

Her whole life, she had lived a masquerade and tried so hard to be what her father expected her to be: a successful, confident achiever, even though none of these things were really her. In fact, she always felt the opposite: inadequate and insecure. And now, having spent 18 years putting on an act, she didn't have a clue who she really was or who she was supposed to be. A lump rose in Stacy's throat. *God, who am I?*

After a year at the Mormon-influenced campus, Stacy's parents pressured her to transfer to Westmont College. The first day of classes, she wandered down the hallways of a tan building looking for the room where her speech class was being held. Finding the class, she worked her way down to an empty seat in the fifth row.

From the corner of her eye Stacy noticed a tall, lanky student tipping his chair back to watch her as she made her way to a seat. All of a sudden, the student's arms and legs flew up in the air as he fell backwards. Several other students began clapping and the boy looked at Stacy with a sheepish grin. Her cheeks flushed and she began foraging through her backpack, silently praying her face would turn back to its normal color by the time she looked up again.

The student's name was Brian and the following week he asked Stacy out. She felt as if she were living a wonderful, romantic dream. Brian was the captain of the college basketball team, funny, smart, and everyone liked him. After dating him for a year, Stacy became pregnant.

"What should we do?" her voice quavered as she sat next to Brian on his bed.

"Well, there are ways to help you lose the baby."

"There are?" her eyes grew wide.

"There are places where you can get an abortion."

"Oh." Stacy hung her head. She could hear a group of rowdy students outside Brian's dorm room. "If I do that, then what happens?" she whispered

"We'll get married." Brian took her hand. The students passed by and it became quiet again.

The thought of marrying Brian subdued her anxious heart. Stacy nuzzled her head into Brian's neck and inhaled his musky sweet scent. "OK."

When she walked into the abortion clinic the

following week, a thick blanket of shame and guilt enveloped her. Her hope for a happy, secure future with Brian pushed her through the painful ordeal. *If I do this, he'll marry me and we'll have babies together later,* she kept telling herself.

A year after the abortion, Stacy and Brian got married. She felt lucky to have "such a catch" for a husband and she couldn't wait to start a family with him. But Brian had told her from the beginning that he wasn't ready for kids. Stacy didn't press the subject. As the years rolled by, she waited patiently and her yearning for children grew. But the time never seemed right.

One Christmas, after they had been married for seven years, Stacy and Brian were at her parents' house to celebrate the holiday. As Stacy watched her nieces and nephews rip open their packages, a gnawing loneliness consumed her. *What is Christmas without children?* Pulling one of her nephews onto her lap, she helped him put batteries in his new remote-controlled car. His little body fit perfectly in the crook of her lap and she cherished his warmth against her. As they arranged the batteries inside the control box, Stacy examined his pudgy hands. When he climbed down to try out the new toy, an ache filled her chest, making it hurt her to breathe.

Excusing herself to the bathroom, Stacy held back tears until she closed and locked the door behind her. Drawing a shaky breath, tears spilled down her face. She dabbed at her eyes with tissue, trying to keep mascara from running. *I'm 29 years old. Isn't it time I have children of my own?* Tossing the used tissue in the wastepaper basket, she pulled more toilet paper off the roll and pressed it to her watering eyes. *I want a child so badly.* Stacy closed her eyes and pinched the bridge of her nose. *Stop crying.* She bit her lip, dabbed at her eyes a few more times, and swallowed hard before opening the door and joining her family again.

Driving home, her sadness crept through the car as though it were fog, but Brian didn't seem to notice.

"I made a tee time for later on this afternoon," he tapped the steering wheel with his thumb.

"OK," Stacy forced her voice to hide the emotions raging inside her.

When they got home, Brian flopped down on the couch and clicked the remote. Stacy went into the kitchen and rehearsed what she was going to say to him. When she mustered up enough courage, she went into the family room and sat down beside him.

"Brian . . . I was wondering."

"What?" his eyes were glued to the television.

"Well, I haven't asked you for a while and I guess I'm just wondering . . . ," she hesitated.

"Wondering what?"

"Do you ever want to have children?" she then blurted out.

Brian turned toward Stacy. His hazel eyes looked into hers. "I think I've realized I'm not capable of loving children of my own. It's just not in me."

Something in Stacy's gut shriveled.

"But I could never tell you what to do. If you want to have a kid, go ahead. I'm just letting you know I will probably never love the child."

A searing pain stabbed Stacy's heart. Speechless, she nodded her head up and down as a cheerful commercial jingle for laundry detergent played on the television. A dull buzzing noise rang inside her head as they both sat looking at the television for a few more minutes before Brian got up. "I better get going."

Numb, Stacy nodded again. After Brian left, she

tottered down the hallway to their bedroom like a drunken woman and tumbled into bed. Curling up into a ball she rocked back and forth for a long time. Tears poured down her cheeks as she moaned into her pillow. As she wept, the pain seemed to multiply. She grieved for the children she had always wanted and for a future she had dreamed about. She also grieved the loneliness she had in her marriage. A gnawing hole in her heart burned for emotional intimacy with her husband. Moaning again, she squeezed her pillow. *Is there anyway to end this pain—some way of dying that wouldn't be too hard on anyone else?*

Finally, with the sheet soaked below her, she fell

asleep. When she woke up, the pain pierced her again, taking her breath away. *I just want a way out,* she whimpered as suicidal thoughts returned.

In the angst of her sorrow, she heard a soft voice whisper into her heart. *Before you do that . . . why don't you give Me a chance?*

Stacy's heart skipped. She clutched her pillow and listened again. *You've only been pretending to love Me. I want more.*

"You do?" she whispered in a ragged voice. As she lay there, she realized for the first time how true it was—she was only a Christian on the outside, pretending to love God. Clutching a pillow to her chest, a single tear dripped down her face. *Lord, I give You my whole life. I'll do anything You say.* After a few minutes, she slipped out of bed and made her way into the living room.

Sitting down at the piano, her fingers glided across the keys and she began to play "Great Is Thy Faithfulness," the hymn she had learned as a child. As the notes rose into the air, Stacy began to sing. Tears drizzled down her cheeks as the familiar words climbed up her throat. Even though she had sung the lyrics all of her life, for the first time the words felt as though they belonged to her.

Before long, Stacy was plugged into a church and meeting regularly with an older woman who taught her about the Bible and how to pray. The grief in her heart was still there, but she filled her time with working hard to live as a good and obedient Christian.

When Brian began playing more golf and spending long hours away from home, she threw herself into church activities with even more intensity and their lives drifted further apart. The drifting turned into an explosion when one afternoon Stacy received an anonymous note that read, "DO YOU KNOW WHO YOUR HUSBAND HAS BEEN PLAYING GOLF WITH?"

She was still holding the note when Brian came home from playing golf that afternoon.

"What is this?" her throat was thick with emotion as she handed him the note.

He took the piece of paper and she watched his face as his eyes darted across the words. "I don't know," he scoffed.

Unsure of what she saw on her husband's face, Stacy kept staring at him, desperate for reassurance. "Who sent it then? And why?"

With an irritated frown, he shrugged his shoulders. "I told you! I don't know." He walked past her into their bedroom.

Standing alone, cold panic sprouted inside her as the reality of Brian being involved with another woman rang true in her heart. The thought of losing him terrified her. *Lord, help me! Save my marriage.* Over the next several months, she prayed incessantly, believing that her marriage would be salvaged if she just kept doing the right thing.

But, after several more anonymous notes and phone calls, their marriage unraveled. "I don't want to end up like my parents," Brian told Stacy one night as they stood awkwardly facing each another in their bedroom. "They stayed together but had nothing to say to each other."

A tremor passed over Stacy's face. She opened her mouth to speak but nothing came out. They stood in silence for a few more minutes, and then Brian turned and left the room. As she watched him walk away, a crushing, dark emptiness consumed her.

After the divorce was final, Stacy slipped into a depression. One weekend shortly after she signed the paperwork, she couldn't get out of bed. Her chest throbbed with pain as she curled up into a ball underneath her covers. *Why, God?* A croak filled her throat and gurgled up through her mouth. "I've done everything You've asked of me! I expected You to heal my marriage! I expected You to change Brian's heart about children!" She took her fist and thrust it into the bed. "How could You fail me? I prayed so hard! I worked so hard!" Closing her swollen eyes, she rocked back and forth. "What's the point of believing if you never get what you want?" she whispered into the empty room.

In her depression, she began isolating herself from other people, which pushed her deeper into a miry pit of desolation and fear. Her parents' unspoken disappointment over her failed marriage further fueled her despair. Her family had already labeled her as the "one who never did things right" and this just confirmed it. Life was empty and gray.

On weekends, when the depression wasn't too bad, she made it to church and sang in the choir, displaying a plastic "Christian" exterior. But mostly her faith had become a series of robotic motions being played out by a woman who felt dead inside.

After years of seclusion and depression, a window of hope lit up Stacy's heart one Saturday afternoon when she was taking a walk with her sister, Sheryl. As they hiked up a winding, dirt trail, Sheryl began sharing about a conversation she had had with her husband the night before. "I wanted him to know it was OK if he didn't go with me, but I'm still going," Sheryl explained.

"Really?" Stacy arched one eyebrow. "You said that? You've never done that before."

"I know. I'm just learning to express my desires and opinions in a healthy way." Her voice was light and airy.

Stacy glanced over at her sister, and then stopped walking. Large oaks shaded them and a soft breeze rustled the leaves above their heads. "Something is different about you." Stacy slipped her hands in her pockets and studied her sister's face. "You look different."

Sheryl whistled for her dog, Kate, who came bounding back over a hill toward them. "I know. I feel different." Her face glowed.

Flustered, Stacy couldn't take her eyes off her sister. "How? How are you changing like this?"

"I'm reading this book with a small group of other women. It's by a Christian author and talks about how to make healing changes in your life." Sheryl reached down and tugged a stick from Kate's mouth. "We're telling each other the truth about our lives, how we really feel about God, what we're really scared of, and what our goals and dreams are."

Tears welled up in Stacy's eyes as she watched her sister throw the stick. For years Sheryl had lived in a difficult marriage and Stacy always felt she seemed stifled and beaten down. But now peace and confidence radiated from her. "I'm so happy for you."

Seeing her sister's tears, Sheryl began to cry too. "Thanks."

As Stacy drove home from the hike she prayed. *O God, I want what Sheryl has. Could that ever happen for me? Please help me. I am so tired of living this way . . . of being stuck. I need hope, Lord. Give me hope.*

She fell asleep that night thinking about her sister and the new, shimmering life in her eyes. When she woke up in the morning, Stacy had the names of four women on her mind. She knew the names were from God. Pushing herself outside of her comfort zone, she called each of the women and told them about her desire to meet with a small group and read a book her sister had recommended. She explained her hope of being able to authentically share their lives with one another. All of the women were eager to do so.

The first night the group met, each woman told her life story. As the women cried with one another, they all expressed an earnest longing to be real and grow together. Over the next few months, as Stacy read the book and met with the women, her heart slowly began to heal. A big piece of the healing was being part of a group of women who wanted to be with her and saw in her what she couldn't see in herself—that she was worth knowing. And, as this truth began to build inside her, she stepped into a new territory of examining who she really was.

With the other women encouraging her, she embarked on a journey of discovering what she truly enjoyed doing and embracing how God had uniquely designed her. The question "Who am I?" which she had asked God as a freshman in college began to be answered and, for the first time since her divorce, she started to see life in color instead of dull shades of gray. Sometimes she still feels like she's only taking baby steps, but Stacy continues today on a road of maturity, self-acceptance, and discovery.

"I can see how God wanted more from me than being a 'good Christian.' That way of thinking only made me depressed and stuck. I have found out that He wanted me—*individual, unique me!* For so long, I had no sense of who I was and that kept me feeling childish and trapped." A smile transforms her mouth as she explains, "I couldn't have a dynamic, two-way relationship with God because there was no *me* to bring to the relationship. My personality was flat, undeveloped, and I really didn't expect anything from anyone, including God. I wouldn't let myself hope."

As Stacy's foundational beliefs about herself have shifted, she finds she is less fragile and more willing to take adventures with God. She still struggles with depression and sometimes feels stuck, but now she has tools and a support network to help carry her through and keep her moving toward God and in her other relationships. "I know how to battle the negative thinking about myself that used to run rampant in my mind. And it frees me to explore and become all that God wants me to be. At times, it still feels very scary—but it is so much better than being stuck!"

Getting Unstuck

> "I had to begin to make a choice. Was I going to stay stuck and alone or more toward what was good for me—God and people?"
> —Stephanie Moir

Dreams get dashed.

Life doesn't go the way we planned it.

We try to make certain things work and sometimes they just . . . don't. We get tired of trying to do it all alone, of doing the right things but not feeling really alive. When this happens, it's so easy to get stuck, to fall into a low-level depression that keeps us paralyzed and unable to have life to the full as Jesus intended (John 10:10). We go through the motions, show up at church, and look fairly normal to those around us, but on the inside we feel alone and disconnected from God's hope for us. There is a lack of passion as well as a quiet desperation hovering over us like a gray morning mist that clouds the sunlight.

Stacy, although connected to God, used to feel this kind of desperation most of the time. Life felt flat, empty, and sad. She didn't have a two-way, intimate relationship with Jesus; instead, she lived her relationship with God in the same way she did with her earthly family—doing the right things but stuffing down emotions and pain, ignoring significant parts of herself to try to survive. This desperation led to depression and an ever-sinking feeling of being stuck, of having no real hope for her future.

Webster's definition of *hope* is "to desire with expectation of obtainment"; "to expect with confidence"; "trust." For Stacy, there wasn't much hope or expectation that life would ever be really full, satisfying, or good. And, this lack of hope left her stuck.

Where are you stuck right now? Think of relationships, career, finances, and other areas.

Tell God about it:

God, I feel really stuck in my . . .

....

....

....

....

Some of you may only feel mildly stuck, a little flat. You may simply need a jump-start to rev up some energy and passion in your life. Others of you are in the pit. You are afraid that life will always be like this, that there's no way out. Still others of you are in a season where you are filled with hope and excited about life and the future. (Enjoy it!) Be honest for just a moment:

Where are you right now?

Put an *X* on the continuum below that describes you best:

Energized	So-so	Stuck
Passionate	Some good days, some bad	Joyless
Excited about life	Fairly satisfied	Hopeless

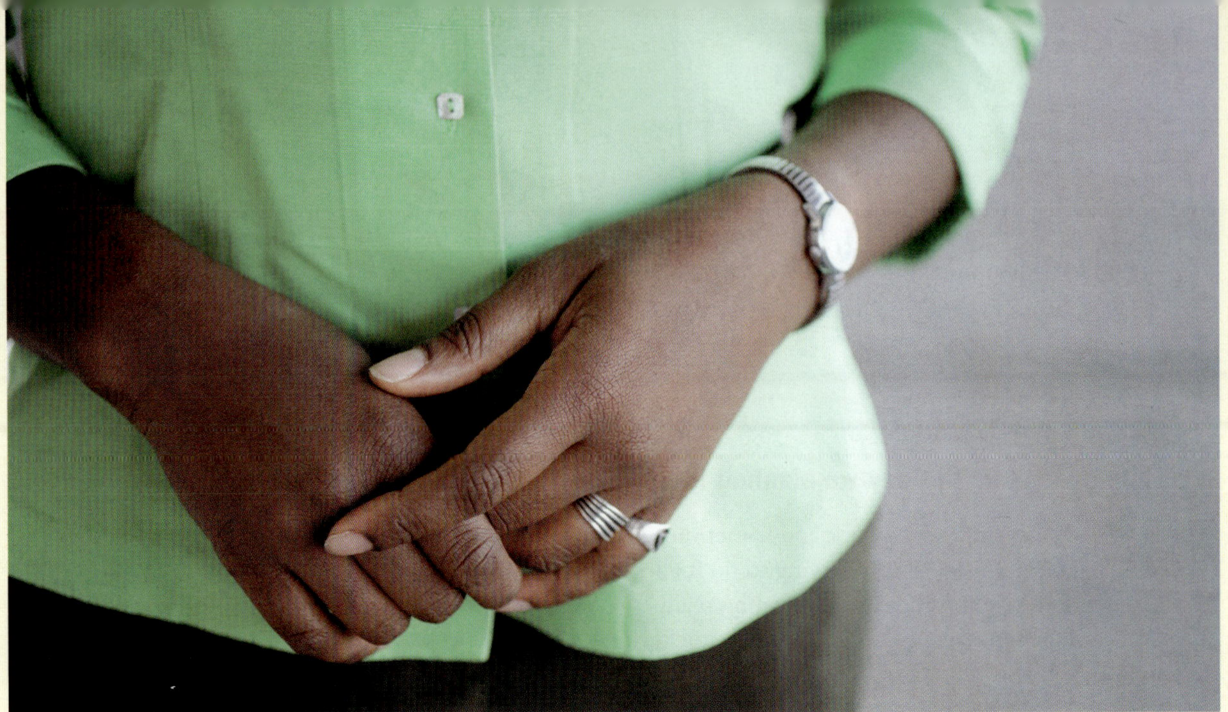

What is going on in your life that led you to place the *X* in a certain place?

....

....

....

....

....

....

We can't will ourselves to get unstuck. Have you tried? Doesn't work, does it? We wish it was that easy! Regardless of where we are on the continuum, only God's Spirit moving in our lives can shift us. We need His power, guidance, and help. And we are not alone in this struggle and need for God's hope. Throughout the Bible we see stories of God's people struggling with getting stuck, depressed, longing to move away from their pain and desperation. Moses begged God to die. So did Elijah, David, and others. David, known as a "man after [God's] own heart," struggled often with losing hope. Here are a few of the things David cried out to God in the Book of Psalms:

"How long must I struggle with anguish in my soul, with sorrow in my heart every day?" **Psalm 13:2 (NLT)**

"My God, my God! Why have you forsaken me? Why do you remain so distant?" **Psalm 22:1 (NLT)**

"Please listen and answer me, for I am overwhelmed by my troubles." **Psalm 55:2 (NLT)**

David was one of the great men of God. Imagine a great man of God saying those things. But just like us, David was human. And humans struggle, get discouraged, and lose hope. We all have a tendency to get caught up in our own struggles and lose sight of the bigger, eternal picture. But God is a God of hope, and He wants to blow a fresh wind into our hearts wherever we are, no matter what, so that we can keep pressing forward on the journey.

In the Old Testament Book of Isaiah, there is a beautiful picture of how God wants to bring hope in the midst of the struggle. Even though we get tired and overwhelmed, He doesn't. Even when we fall and don't think we can get up, He can renew our strength so we don't stay stuck.

Read Isaiah 40:28–31.

Do you not know? Have you not heard? The LORD is the everlasting God, the Creator of the ends of the earth. He will not grow tired or weary, and his understanding no one can fathom. He gives strength to the weary and increases the power of the weak. Even youths grow tired and weary, and young men stumble and fall; but those who hope in the LORD will renew their strength. They will soar on wings like eagles; they will run and not grow weary, they will walk and not be faint. **(NIV)**

Stacy needed help learning a new way to live. She was tired of living in a stagnant, disconnected relationship with God and with others. She needed the kind of hope that is described in this passage.

Stacy saw hope in her sister, Sheryl. She saw that
things were different for Sheryl and knew God was
moving in her life. She began to hope that maybe
things could be different for her too. Hope comes
from God, and includes our participation. We have to
plug into God. An electrical appliance has no power
unless the cord is plugged into an electrical outlet.
Our hope surges through a dynamic two-way relationship with God where we give and also receive.

Stacy was excellent at the one-way relationship;
she was "going through the motions with God,"
but she wasn't very good at opening up and allowing God and others to speak into deep places of her
heart and offer hope. In fact, after being hurt by her

husband and family, she was afraid to hope. What if
she wished for something again, gave her heart, and
it didn't happen? She chose instead to shut down and
operate more like a robot in her relationship with
God and others. The result? Discouragement and
depression.

One of the best places we can find hope is in God's
Word. The Bible is filled with passages about hope.
The Apostle Paul, in the Book of Romans, writes
often about hope.

**Look up the following passages and circle the
words that impress you.**

*And we rejoice in the hope of the glory of God.
Not only so, but we also rejoice in our sufferings,
because we know that suffering produces
perseverance; perseverance, character; and
character, hope. And hope does not disappoint
us, because God has poured out his love into our
hearts by the Holy Spirit, whom he has given us.*
Romans 5:2–5 (NIV)

*Be joyful in hope, patient in affliction, faithful in
prayer.* **Romans 12:12 (NIV)**

*So I pray that God, who gives you hope, will keep
you happy and full of peace as you believe in him.
May you overflow with hope through the power of
the Holy Spirit.* **Romans 15:13 (NIV)**

**Why did you circle these words? What about them
makes them meaningful to you?**

Life is hard. Without hope, it is unmanageable. In
the movie trilogy *The Lord of the Rings*, the hobbit
Frodo is chosen to go on a mission to rid the earth of
an evil ring. It is a complicated, twisted journey and on
most days he wants to give up. He gets discouraged,

depressed, and often can't find the strength to keep moving forward. It was clear in the films that if Frodo was alone, he would have died. But he had wonderful companions with him on the journey, and they gave him hope when he had none. They carried him, challenged him, and encouraged him. Like Frodo, Stacy borrowed hope from faithful companions too—godly girlfriends. She says, "It was because of the encouragement and love in my small group that I began to really live again."

God's Word says: *"Two people can accomplish more than twice as much as one; they get a better return for their labor. If one person falls, the other can reach out and help. But people who are alone when they fall are in real trouble."* **Ecclesiastes 4:9–10 (NLT)**

Do you have people in your life who give you hope, encouragement, and help you on the journey? Who?

....

....

....

....

....

How do they give you hope and help you when you feel stuck?

....

....

....

....

It is comforting to know that the great giants of God—Moses, David, Elijah, the Apostle Paul, and others—all got stuck. They were sometimes depressed and discouraged. They entered seasons of their lives where hope was hard to find, where it would have been easy to give up. But their example is one we can follow—they opened up their hearts to God and others, stayed the course, and found hope again. Like them, we will have to risk. We will have to celebrate the small steps we make. We will have to engage in a two-way, dynamic relationship with God and other people. We will have to reach out our hands and ask for help. And sometimes we will have to borrow hope.

1. Need hope?

Here's some truth from God's Word:

Look up these verses all at once or one day at a time.

God is our refuge and strength, an ever-present help in trouble. Therefore we will not fear, though the earth give way and the mountains fall into the heart of the sea. **Psalm 46:1–2 (NIV)**

Cast your cares on the Lord and he will sustain you. **Psalm 55:22 (NIV)**

Wait for the Lord; be strong and take heart and wait for the Lord. **Psalm 27:14 (NIV)**

Even though I walk through the valley of the shadow of death, I will fear no evil, for you are with me; your rod and your staff, they comfort me. **Psalm 23:4 (NIV)**

Jesus said, "I have told you these things, so that in me you may have peace. In this world you will have trouble. But take heart! I have overcome the world!" **John 16:33 (NIV)**

Yet I still dare to hope when I remember this: The unfailing love of the LORD never ends! By his mercies we have been kept from complete destruction. Great is his faithfulness; his mercies begin afresh each day. I say to myself, "The LORD is my inheritance, therefore, I will hope in him!" **Lamentations 3:21–24 (NLT)**

Which verses resonate most with you? Why?

2. Are you sinking?

Is life overwhelming? Maybe your kids are struggling in school; debts are accumulating; you can't pay the bills; you are in a dead-end job; you're single and want to be married; you have health issues; you're in

Who's on Your team?

God makes it very clear that we need people in our lives to encourage and support us. Jesus had a team. He had 12 disciples that He taught to model His ways. He also had 3 in his inner circle—John, Peter, and James—whom He journeyed with more closely. We are called to "encourage one another and build each other up" (1 Thessalonians 5:11 NIV) and to "share each other's troubles and problems, and in this way obey the law of Christ" (Galatians 6:2 NLT). In this story, Stacy began to journey with some other women who were also seeking to get unstuck and learn a new way to live. She has a team of women who are committed to each other, challenge each other, listen well, and offer grace.

Who's on your team?

If you don't have one yet, how can you begin to build one? Who are some safe women in your life with whom you might be able to pursue relationship? Is there a group at a local church or ministry you can join? Is there a support group to attend where you might meet some others who are looking for connection and encouragement too? Should you consider starting a group on your own like Stacy and gather a few people together who want to really do life together?

the midst of a painful divorce; you're grieving from the loss of someone you love; you can't seem to stop fighting with your spouse. God's presence feels far away. When life gets overwhelming, we need help. We need God's rescue.

• **What do you need to be rescued from right now?**

• **Read Psalm 18:1–6, 16–19 slowly.**

I love you, Lord, you are my strength. The Lord is my rock, my fortress, and my savior; my God is my rock, in whom I find protection. He is my shield, the strength of my salvation, and my stronghold. I will call on the Lord who is worthy of praise, for he saves me from my enemies. The ropes of death surrounded me; the floods of destruction swept over me. The grave wrapped its ropes around me; death itself stared me in the face. But in my distress I cried out to the Lord; yes, I prayed to my God for help. He heard me from his sanctuary; my cry reached his ears. . . . He reached down from heaven and rescued me; he drew me out of deep waters. He delivered me from my powerful enemies, from those who hated me and were too strong for me. They attacked me at a moment when I was weakest, but the Lord upheld me. He led me to a place of safety; He rescued me because he delights in me. **(NLT)**

Are you depressed?

Here are some symptoms of depression. Check any that you are experiencing right now. If you have more than a few of these at one time, it is important to talk to someone and seek help.

EMOTIONAL SYMPTOMS	PHYSICAL SYMPTOMS
Sadness throughout the day, nearly every day	Fatigue or lack of energy
Loss of interest in or enjoyment of your favorite activities	Sleeping too much or too little
Feelings of emptiness and hopelessness	Change in appetite or weight
Feeling stressed, nervous, or overwhelmed	Aches and pains
Trouble concentrating or making decisions	Headache
Feelings of worthlessness	Back pain
Excessive or inappropriate feelings of guilt	Digestive problems
Irritability or restlessness	Dizziness
Thoughts of death or suicide	

God, being in this place is so hard for me because . . .

• Do you believe God will rescue you? Why or why not? Tell God about this.

• Now ask Him the question:

What do you want me to be reminded of in this moment? What truth do I need to hold on to right now?

• Sit quietly and try to listen with your heart and mind.

Do any words come to mind? Any Scriptures? Any song? A vision or an image? Do you feel a physical sensation?

1. Admit you are stuck. Tell yourself, tell God, tell someone else.

2. Consider the next small step to take. When making changes, it is important to think in small steps instead of big ones. Otherwise it just feels overwhelming. Ask yourself, "What is a next *small* step I may need to take to keep moving?" (Here are a few small-step suggestions: call a friend, read your Bible or an inspirational book for a little while, go for a walk, set up an appointment with a good counselor, attend a church service, exercise for 20 minutes, clean your kitchen, do something that might be fun.)

3. Seek encouragement. From God, from others. Pray, read, listen to music.

4. Get some regular and consistent support and accountability. Attend a group or Bible study regularly; ask someone to meet with you regularly to pray and check in; consider finding a mentor or someone else who has "been there" and can stand alongside you and help you keep moving.

5. Celebrate any movement. Sometimes we think change must look drastic. Real change is a series of small movements, little victories.

• **How does this give you hope in the midst of your struggle?**

3. I've had enough! Elijah's story

In the Book of 1 Kings, Elijah was a prophet of God who was being hunted by the revengeful Queen Jezebel. He was tired and afraid and fled to the desert. He prayed that he would die. "I have had enough, LORD," he said. Take my life, for I am no better than my ancestors" (1 Kings 19:4 NLT). Does this sound familiar to you? Have you ever said to God, "I have had enough! I don't want to do this anymore!"? If we're really honest, most of us have felt this feeling more than once. Like Elijah, we sometimes just want to give up and call it a day. But in this story, God sent an angel to Elijah who fed him bread and water to give him strength and encourage him to continue (1 Kings 19:5–8). He got rest. He got filled up. And he kept going.

What is some "bread and water" God might be providing you right now? Think of some ways He is trying to encourage you and give you strength.

Changing your focus

Answer the questions below. Then, if you want, share your responses with your group:

1. Noticing

When we are stuck, we need to learn to notice ways God is working. Noticing is so hard when we are depressed; we get "ingrown eyeballs" and we can't see clearly. We miss God. We only see the negative. We focus on what's wrong instead of what's right, and we miss out on noticing any beauty in the midst of the ugliness. So much would be different for us if we noticed God more in our day-to-day lives.

I (Kathy) was in Hawaii speaking at a retreat a few years ago, and one of the women asked me if I had seen the beautiful rainbows Hawaii is famous for daily. I had been there for three days and had definitely not seen one rainbow! I was so caught up in myself, the work I needed to do, and the stress and tension of the retreat that I missed noticing anything except for myself.

Over the next few days, as I tuned in and began to notice, I found that everywhere I turned, I saw rainbows. They were there all along. It's like that with God too. We just don't notice. Part of getting unstuck is stepping outside of our small, mostly self-centered thinking and noticing the hand of God all around us.

Take a little bit of time right now to notice what is good in your life right now. Where is there beauty?

2. How did we get stuck in the first place? Looking back so we can move forward!

One of the reasons a lot of us get stuck on our journey is that we learned unhealthy patterns of relationship from our family that we are carrying into adulthood. In certain families, it may not have been OK to express feelings or have a differing opinion. Maybe you had parents who always had unrealistic expectations of you. Maybe you were neglected or abused and it's difficult to trust God or others. A lot of time we are afraid to look back because it feels like we're dwelling on the past instead of living in the present. Yes, looking back does create a dangerous tension that we need to be cautious about, but

FEELING HOPE? Offer It!

If you are in a place of hope and passion, ask God for His eyes to see those around you who are stuck, hopeless, and tired. Remember, just like Stacy, many of us put on a good act, so we need His eyes to see through the veneer. When God shows you someone who is in need of hope, ask God to help you be His tool of encouragement for that person. Maybe be His pen and write her a hope-filled note; perhaps be His ears and take her out for coffee and just listen; or be His arms and give a warm hug when it is needed.

"

the bottom line is that Jesus came to set us free (Galatians 5:1), to adopt us into his family as His own children (Romans 8:15–17), and to teach us how to live as children of God.

To grow up into mature, free, strong women, we must be set free from past unhealthy patterns and learn God's ways. That is a big part of Stacy's story—learning to develop a new kind of relationship with God that wasn't built on her past experiences with her family of origin. Every family has unwritten commandments or rules that guide how they relate to each other. These are things that were either spoken or unspoken rules of your family.

Here are a few of Stacy's:
1. Thou shalt agree with parents and never question them.
2. Thou shalt be successful. Our family is perfect.
3. Thou shalt not disgrace our family's name in any way, shape, or form.
4. Thou shalt go to church and serve faithfully no matter how you feel.
5. Thou shalt be slender, athletic, and witty.
6. Thou shalt be happy because we are always happy.

What are some relational commandments that guided your family?

1.

2.

3.

4.

5.

6.

7.

8.

9.

10.

Which of these do you still tend to live by even though you are grown up and out of the house?

1. Listen to a song about seeking God when we are stuck, such as the Ginny Owens song, "Springs of Life," from the CD *Without Condition.* (If you can, write down the lyrics before your group time and read them to the group after you have listened to the song together.) Talk about the lyrics and which ones you each relate to.

2. Pass out a blank piece of paper and draw a picture on it that describes how you are feeling right now. Ask women to share with the person next to them or in smaller groups.

3. Get a big, deflated balloon and put inside it a small toy person (i.e., a Lego guy, Polly Pocket girl, etc.) After you have put the figure into the opening of the balloon, blow it up and tie it. Hold up the balloon to the group and discuss differences in "life" for the toy figure inside the balloon (i.e., confined, limited, suffocating, etc.). Then pop the balloon and talk about "life" outside the balloon (i.e., unhindered, liberated, and so on). Where do you live? Inside or outside of the balloon? How? Why?

After the Thaw

Frozen heart
Wrapped in layers of ice
The change so gradual it wasn't even
noticed
All seemed as it should be
Cloudy, dull, cold, monotony . . .
Until Spring came
Bursting sunshine, slushy snow, trickling
creek, risen Savior—awake from the
dead
The snowman in the front yard begins to
sweat
Icy droplets drip off his brow
Sunlit jewels slide down
Carrying small chunks of ice away
The sun is warmth and freedom
A nod and a fist pumped in the air
celebrate the moment
Faces are brown and red—masks off
Breathing in the fresh, cool, sunlit air
The cold heart begins to thaw
Slowly at first—like the snowman
Small chunks of ice slide down
The ice wasn't even noticed
Until it began to melt
Then came the memory of what life
used to be like
When God lived large within me
A clinched chest with eyes closed
Trying to keep the memory from
flying away too fast
Stay
Remind me of summer
The salty, warm air blowing
across the surface of the
heart set free
But then it's gone
I reach for it too late
It flies from my grasp
Drip Drip Drip
Stay sun
Don't take your warmth away until my
heart is once again a heart of flesh
Beating full of life
Seeking God-sized answers
The icy winter is over
But can the heart find its way back
home?

—Jenny Maynard

Used by permission.

in living color

A simple lesson learned young

Eight-year-old Jenna was playing with her best friend, Maddie, one afternoon after school. Maddie told Jenna she couldn't have a sleepover that weekend because she had been grounded. Jenna asked why but Maddie wouldn't tell her. She was too embarrassed.

Jenna became frustrated. "I tell you everything! You know all the bad stuff I've ever done!" As she said it her face turned red. Maddie burst into tears and ran to the kitchen where her mom was.

"I just can't tell her, Mom," Maddie croaked through her tears. "It's too embarrassing."

Maddie's mom stroked her head. "I know. Sometimes it is hard to tell other people things we have done that we are not proud of."

Jenna appeared in the kitchen doorway, her big blue eyes narrowed. "I have waited two years for this," Jenna spoke in a firm eight-year-old tone. "I have waited to be your trusted best friend. And now you won't even tell me."

Maddie's mom nodded. "Do you understand what Jenna is saying? She just wants you to trust her like she has trusted you."

"I just can't," squeaked Maddie.

In a calm voice, Maddie's mom continued talking to the girls. "You know, everyone has done things they are not proud of."

"Really?" both girls said in unison, looking up at Maddie's mom.

"Sure." Maddie's mom smiled and told the girls stories about embarrassing things she had done when she was a little girl. Her words seemed to give Maddie confidence.

"OK," Maddie swallowed. "I'll tell her." She took a big breath and then blurted out, "I lied."

Jenna stood there for a moment without a word. Finally she opened her mouth and said, "That's it? You lied?"

"MmHm," Maddie nodded and looked down.

A huge smile lit up Jenna's face. "Good job, Maddie! You told me! You did it! Now let's celebrate."

Within a couple of minutes, Jenna had pulled out snacks, poured juice, and written a sign that said, *Good Job, Maddie, Day!* The girls were still laughing and celebrating when Jenna's mom came to pick her up a short while later. After Jenna left, Maddie looked at her mom with a new sparkle in her eyes. "I love her, Mom."

"She is a good friend."

"And you know, Mom," Maddie continued, "Once I told her, it wasn't that hard."

"That's how it is when you share hard stuff with a trusted friend."

1. Where are you stuck right now? Think of relationships, career, finances, etc.

2. Read the poem "After the Thaw" together. Has your heart ever been stuck like this, where you want more of God but you feel emotionally "cloudy and dull"? How so?

3. Share with the group your responses to "Noticing." What did you notice when you were looking for God?

4. Share with the group some of the relational commandments that guided your family.

5. Closing round: Finish this sentence in one or two words: *Something that helped me feel a little less stuck from this chapter is . . .*

Check These Out . . .

Why I Jumped
by Tina Zahn, with
Wanda Dyson

Shattered Dreams
by Larry Crabb

*The Freedom
from Depression
Workbook*
by Les Carter and
Frank Minirth

Friend to Friend
series by Edna Ellison

A Total New You!

Letting go of the past

Tears ran down Norma's cheeks in

the darkness of their bedroom as David made love to her. When it was over, she got up and went to the bathroom, careful to hide her emotions from her husband. Ever since her first son had been born, Norma had begun to dread intimacy with her husband, but she never said a word. She didn't want to hurt him.

When she climbed back in bed, David kissed her cheek. It was damp. "Honey, are you crying?"

Swallowing, Norma shrugged in the dark.

David leaned over and turned on a bedside table lamp. Propping himself up on an elbow, he stroked her hair. "What is it?"

Tears flooded down her cheeks. "It's just . . .," she stopped as a sob rose up her throat.

"Just what?"

"Every time you touch me, it feels like my dad's hands." She uttered another broken sob and closed her eyes.

David recoiled his hands from her and searched his wife's face. "I didn't know it was still affecting you like this."

"I'm sorry." Norma's heart sank. "I hate it."

"How long have you felt like this?"

Swiping away the tears on her cheeks, she looked away from her husband. "Since Joey was born."

"He's two! Why didn't you say something before this?"

"I'm sorry," her voice was barely a whisper.

Norma and David floundered for months, not knowing how to fix their broken sexual relationship. David backed away from Norma physically and they both grieved Norma's inability to enjoy intimacy. The bottled-up stress and emotional confusion began taking a physical toll on Norma and her stomach hurt all the time.

A door of hope opened for Norma when she attended

a Christian seminar with her sister-in-law, Clara. The speaker talked about finding freedom in Christ. "You can be set free from getting through the hard things in your life," the woman said with conviction to the audience. "Christ can move you to a place of freedom no matter what your past is. I know there are women here who have been sexually abused . . ."

Norma didn't hear anything else the woman said. Trembling, she got up and bolted out of the room. She fought her tears until she made it to the bathroom. Grabbing onto the sides of a sink, she began to sob. Norma didn't even notice when her sister-in-law and two other women came in and stood behind her.

"Norma, we're here for you." Clara put her hand on Norma's shoulder and squeezed.

Norma tried to stop crying but the sobs kept rising up from deep within her. One of the women reached over and held Norma's hand. "Can we pray for you?"

Norma dipped her chin down and closed her eyes. Each of the women put a hand on Norma's shoulders as one of the women began to pray. "Lord, here is Your broken daughter You love so much and yearn to heal. Help her know You and Your healing power. Help her know she can be freed from this heavy weight upon her."

As the women prayed, Norma's sobs dissipated and left only a quiet trickle of tears. Soaking in their prayers, she allowed stillness to settle over herself and, for the first time in her life, she began to see that Jesus wasn't just a historical figure who had been crucified. As they prayed, He felt close by. Listening to the women, she knew she wanted what they had and in the quiet of her own heart she prayed. *Jesus, I want You to be to me what You are to these women.*

Norma began to see a Christian counselor who helped her sift through her heavy baggage of being molested by her father, and all the reasons that experience had begun to wreak havoc in her marriage.

One night, as she was processing some of her memories, she took her mom out to dinner. Her parents had divorced when she was 18 and Norma had told her mom about the molestation during the divorce process. At dinner that night, Norma sat across from her mom. Deep lines creased Norma's forehead.

"What are you thinking about?" her mom asked, stirring sugar into her iced tea.

"I feel as though I'm going to have a nervous breakdown." Norma put her hands over her face. "Even with all this counseling, I can't get this feeling

of anger to come out of me. When I see Dad, I just freeze inside . . .," Norma's voice drifted, "and I pretend everything is normal. He still thinks we are as close as ever. . . . It's all an act on my part."

Pained filled her mom's eyes but she didn't say anything.

"Mom, do you know how old I was when it started?"

Her mother looked past her. "It had to be when you were 5 because I was pregnant with your youngest brother." She paused, looking into Norma's eyes. "When he confessed to me what he had done, I thought that was the last of it. He said he was going to get help . . . that it wouldn't happen again." She let out a shuddering breath. "Oh, Norma, I wish I had known."

"I was too scared to tell you." Norma closed her eyes and leaned back against the chair. "I didn't want to get anyone in trouble. I didn't want to break up our family."

"I know." Her mom reached out and covered Norma's hand with her own.

Later that night, Norma was giving her two sons a bath when it happened. A wave of nausea swept over her as she watched her 5-year-old splashing with innocent glee. *I was that little when Dad first touched me.* Bile rose up her throat. *How could he have done that?*

Driving in her car the next day, a sudden bubble of anger surfaced inside her then popped. Before she could stop herself, she began to scream at the top of her lungs and bang on the steering wheel. "I hate you!" she bellowed over and over again.

After her anger erupted, she no longer could pretend everything was all right. She declined all family gatherings and didn't even return her dad's phone calls. Because their family had seemed so close, her sudden withdrawal was obvious. After her dad left several distressed messages on her answering machine, she knew she had to deal with it and tell him why she wasn't able to talk to him anymore.

Dialing his number, her hand quivered. He answered on the first ring. "Hi, Dad."

"Norma-girl! Why haven't you been calling me back? I've been worried about you." His booming voice rang through the phone line.

"I've been going through some issues; a hard time."

"Issues?" She could hear the worry in his voice. "Are you all right? What kind of issues?"

"Issues that involve you."

Silence.

"When you molested me."

"Norma, does this have something to do with that new church you're going to?"

Stunned, Norma shook her head. "No. It has nothing to do with that."

"I didn't molest you."

"Yes you did, Dad!"

"That's not what that was," he countered.

"Well, I don't know what you call it, but that's what I call it. I can't talk to you anymore and I don't know when I'll be able to talk to you again." She hung up the phone and collapsed into a heap on her bed. Her whole body was shaking uncontrollably.

Over the next several weeks, her dad tried repeatedly to get in touch with Norma, but she avoided all of his calls. Christmas was only a couple of months away and Norma began worrying about what to do. Her stomach pain got worse and the muscles in her neck and shoulders throbbed. One afternoon, as she met with her counselor, James, she confided her anguished thoughts about Christmas. "I want to be with my family," tears welled up in her eyes. "But I can't be around him."

"One option is you could ask him to come to counseling with you."

She dabbed a tissue underneath her eyes. "What would happen?"

"You would tell him how what he did makes you feel and how it affects your life." He paused. "Often it is a big step in the healing process."

Norma let the idea soak in her mind for several days. She desperately wanted to move forward and work through the pain and agony of her past. One afternoon, when a burst of courage seized her, she picked up the phone and dialed her dad's number. When she heard his voice on the other end of the line, her heart pounded and she wanted to hang up. "Dad," she forced herself to speak.

"Norma." His voice was soft and humble.

"I need to ask you something. You know I'm going to counseling and trying to deal with all these sexual issues. I am wondering if you will meet with me and my counselor . . .," she took a deep breath, "to help me work through all this?"

"When do you want me there? Do you need me right now?"

"I have an appointment on Thursday at 1:00."

"I'll be there."

Norma closed her eyes as she hung up the phone. *Please help me to do this, God.* Two days later, she sat in a room with her father and James. After James asked her dad some get-to-know-you questions, he set down his pen and pad of paper. "Tell me your thoughts about what Norma is going through," he said gently.

"Well," Norma's dad crossed his arms in front of his chest. "I don't see it as molesting. . . . It was . . . ," his voice got lower, "an act of love." He glanced at Norma but kept talking to James. "My wife and I had sexual problems for a long time and Norma was the only person who showed me love."

Norma's mind flashed back to when she was a little girl. Every night when her father came home from work, she ran into his arms. He was so big and important to her and he commanded his children's attention with his dominating presence. She had loved him with every ounce of her heart.

"You know it wasn't like my childhood was perfect either," her dad was telling James. "My father would beat me regularly. I was kicked out of the house by the time I was 13."

"So you feel like you were the victim here?"

Her father nodded. "She wanted it sometimes. She would come to me." He nodded again with more certainty. "Yes. I do feel like the victim."

A siren went off inside Norma's head and her mouth hung open as she stared at her father. He looked over at her, then quickly averted his eyes. Norma's whole body began trembling as she pictured her father entering her room late at night. She could feel the overwhelming dread that seized her as if it were yesterday. She saw herself pressing her small body up against the wall, hoping to disappear before her father reached her bed.

"Let me stop you for a minute." James's voice was still gentle but firm. "This is a 5-year-old little girl and you are touching her in inappropriate places." His eyebrows lowered. "And you feel like the victim?"

Not responding, Norma's father slumped back in his chair.

James shifted his eyes to Norma. "Why don't you tell your dad what you would say to him if you were that little girl right now."

Her eyes pooling with tears, Norma opened her mouth to talk but nothing came out. James handed her some tissues and gave her a reassuring nod. She blew her nose. Looking at her dad, a surge of anger flared inside her and she found her voice. "Dad, didn't you ever stop to think how tight my body was against the wall? Didn't it ever occur to you I was squeezing my legs so tight together that I didn't want you there?" She couldn't stop trembling and her weak voice quavered. "Even though we didn't have intercourse, Dad, you raped me. You raped me of my childhood and you raped me of a healthy sexual relationship with my husband."

A tremor passed over her father's face. His shoulders hunched over and he began to weep.

When her dad's crying ebbed, James spoke. "So you do realize you did this to Norma and what you did was wrong?"

"Yes," he whispered in a strangled voice. "I'm sorry . . . I'm so sorry I put you through this." He lifted his head and looked at Norma. "I didn't realize all I had put you through." A sob croaked up his throat. "Can you ever forgive me?"

A cold knot formed in Norma's stomach. She

hated seeing her dad so desperate. "It takes time to heal, Dad . . . but, yes, I forgive you." The words felt hollow but she knew extending her father forgiveness was the choice she had to make.

After her father left the counseling appointment, James leaned forward in his chair. "So . . . how do you feel?"

Norma blew out her cheeks. "Relieved."

"It took a lot of courage to do what you did today."

"It feels so good," Norma exhaled a long breath. "I think this is the first time in my whole life I stood up to my dad. I've always been so scared to say anything. I never wanted to rock the boat."

"You were a peacemaker in your family. Speaking up or confronting your dad went against everything you knew and the role you played."

Norma met with James and her father one more time and then continued counseling on her own for many more months. She and her husband received counseling, too, and worked on their sexual intimacy. Slowly, as healing took place in her heart, their relationship was restored.

Today, many years after the confrontation with her father, Norma lives in the place of freedom she heard the Christian speaker talk about at the conference she attended so long ago. "When she spoke about freedom from the past, I had no idea how to get there. But as I asked Jesus into every part of my life, I saw I needed to expose the secret my dad wanted me to keep and confront my dad with what he had done."

After Norma made the choice to uncover and deal with the secret, she had another choice to make—what to do with her dad. "I knew I needed to forgive him, to let go of the bitterness and resentment that I carried against him. It was so hard to do, almost unthinkable because of the horrible thing that he had done to me. But as I continued to pray through the pain and hurt, God brought to mind all of the ways that I had been forgiven.

"I think the clincher was getting in touch with the forgiveness I had received when I had an abortion. I had it before I was married and I agonized over what I had done. It ripped me apart for a very long time. But a few godly people walked beside me as I grieved over the baby and my actions. They taught me how to repent and they showed me how God forgives us when we come to Him broken and sorry.

"When you experience God's forgiveness like that, something inside you changes. I was never the same and because of that I knew I needed to forgive my dad. I made a conscious choice to offer it to him. I told him directly, 'I forgive you.' This was one of the most significant moments in my healing."

It took a long time for Norma to feel forgiveness and love for her father, but as the years rolled by and she grew closer to God her heart softened along the way.

"Even though I made a choice to forgive my dad that day in the counseling appointment, I didn't really feel any daughterly love for many years. I could be around him but nothing in my heart resonated with him as my father. But today, I can honestly say I love my dad. I feel free from my past with him. And I know it is only God who could work out that sort of freedom in my life. On my own, I would have been immobilized and damaged forever." ❀

Changing Your Future: The Power of Forgiveness

"Forgiveness does not change the past, but it does enlarge the future."

Paul Boese

Forgiveness is a mystery. It's not entirely clear how it happens—that moment in time when our heart softens; indescribably the effect of a hurt ebbs away and we are changed. Something shifts. The dam breaks. The chains unshackle. Sometimes it comes in a rush, a specific moment in time when suddenly the pain disappears. And other times it happens slowly, a little letting go here, a little healing there, until after a while it just doesn't hurt as much anymore.

Part of the mystery is that forgiveness looks different for everyone; the way one person experiences it is entirely different from the next. We know it's frustrating, but the fact is that *forgiveness* cannot be wrapped up in a neat, tidy package. You can't give it to someone in a formula and it's often messy, hard, and very painful.

Yet, while it's a mystery, forgiveness is also a choice. It is intentional. For most of us, it is easy to hold a grudge, harbor hurt, and hide our difficult feelings. Meanwhile, forgiving others is often a fierce, internal battle. It comes with a cost. But it is worth fighting for because unforgiveness, regardless of how small, breeds anger and bitterness. Like a cancer, it can pervade areas of our lives for a long time without us knowing it.

God's Word says, "A little yeast works through the whole batch of dough" (1 Corinthians 5:9 NIV). Like the yeast, a little unforgiveness in our lives can go a long way. It can seep out subtly, sometimes obviously. And without a doubt, it blocks us from being able to love others freely the way Jesus intended. Norma's father sinned against her. But she and her husband were paying the price. God does not want us to live trapped in the muck and mire of unforgiveness. He wants us to live as women who are forgiven and forgiving.

Do you think that forgiveness is a choice? Why or why not?

There are many Scriptures that lead to the hard commission to forgive. Jesus doesn't say, "You *maybe* should *consider* forgiving other people." No, He makes it perfectly clear. Forgiveness is necessary and is for our sake. For example, the parables that Jesus tells in the first four books of the New Testament are powerful stories that cause us to think about important

spiritual truths. In the parable of the unforgiving servant, Jesus makes a strong point about forgiveness; it comes from our recognition of how we ourselves have been forgiven.

Read Matthew 18:21–35.

Then Peter came to him and asked, "Lord, how often should I forgive someone who sins against me? Seven times?"

"No!" Jesus replied, "seventy times seven!" **(vv. 21–22 NLT)**

This is a powerful story about what happens when we accept Christ's forgiveness for ourselves but refuse to pass it on. Like the unforgiving debtor, we can be forgiven of our debts but make others pay us back.

In Norma's story, a significant piece of her forgiveness journey was getting in touch with how Jesus had forgiven her for a past abortion. If she had been forgiven for her sins, how could she not pass it on? Not all of us have as painful a past as Norma, yet all of us have sinned, messed up, and made big mistakes. All of us need forgiveness.

So, how do we forgive? The first step is to remember. Unlike the man in the parable, we need to remember we have been forgiven. Our debt has been paid. This is God's amazing grace at work. Regardless of how many mistakes we have made, Jesus paid our debt when He died on the cross, shedding His blood

for us. Through Christ we stand forgiven. Period. No matter what.

Now if we are forgiven so freely, how can we not pass it on? Often, one of the reasons we can't pass on forgiveness is that we ourselves do not *feel* forgiven. We cannot give to others what we haven't received. We could spend volumes alone on this aspect of forgiveness and the barriers to it, but for this moment, sit and ponder this question:

Do you believe you are forgiven for your past and present wrongs? Why or why not?

Everyone reading *Refresh* is in a different place on their spiritual journey, but here's a point we hope you won't miss: Through Christ you are forgiven. For your past wrongs and your present ones. Not because *we* say so, but because *God's Word* promises it.

"Therefore, my brothers, I want you to know that through Jesus the forgiveness of sins is proclaimed to you." **Acts 13:38 (NIV)**

So also Christ died only once as a sacrifice to take away the sins of many people. **Hebrews 9:28 (NLT)**

For all have sinned; all fall short of God's glorious standard. Yet now God in his gracious kindness declares us not guilty. He has done this through Christ Jesus, who has freed us by taking away our sins. **Romans 3:23–24 (NLT)**

Circle which words you connect with in the previous passages.

Most women are fairly good at making lists—to-do lists, shopping lists, chores-for-the-kids lists. How about a forgiveness list?

Take a moment and thank God for what you have been forgiven. Start with this and list as many things as you can.

Lord, thank You for forgiving me for . . .

At the beginning of the parable in Matthew 18, Jesus tells Peter to forgive 70 times 7. Does this mean we get to stop offering forgiveness on the 490th time? Does it mean God would do the same for us? Fortunately, the answers are no and no. Rather, this is a poignant metaphor for His forgiveness toward us. If we ask for it, He offers it. He's telling us that *we need to offer it too.*

Who are some of the people who have hurt you in the past or who are hurting you in the present?

What did they do to you?

For some of you, it might be hard to write down on paper the ways you have been hurt. They may be difficult memories you'd rather ignore. For others, it might not be as hard for different reasons. You may think, *Why bother?* or *That's in the past.* The bottom line is this: Only you and God understand the pain that others have caused you, the wounds and scars that litter your heart. Like Norma, maybe you have stuffed down the pain of the past or present. The hurt feels too big. This is common for many of us. But like Norma, we may find out the hard way that unforgiveness is a silent but destructive force, slowly leaking its poison into our lives.

I (Kathy) have a similar history to Norma in that I was sexually molested when I was 14, and had an abortion in high school. I didn't tell anyone about my abortion until I was married and had two of my five children. It was just too hard and scary to say out loud. Because I couldn't acknowledge it, I couldn't forgive myself or others. The silence and shame kept me stuck.

As I came into community with some other Christian women, who were starting to be honest about their struggles, I began to say the truth out loud. At first, I became pretty good at sharing the facts without many feelings attached; it did help me feel less lonely and more authentic. But inside my heart resided a well of unforgiveness and hurt that I was terrified to look at.

As I kept forging ahead in my spiritual journey, God led me to acknowledge how abandoned, unloved, and unprotected I felt as a young person growing up. He showed me how these unresolved and damaging feelings were affecting my marriage and other relationships in my life as an adult. In order to move forward, I had to look back and peel away "onion" layers to get to some of the core issues. At the center was unforgiveness. As I pursued Jesus's truth and healing, I began to recognize the power of forgiveness. I saw that without it I would always be stuck. Forgiveness came. Not in a rush but over a season of choosing to forgive for my sake.

Like Norma, most people we have encountered started their forgiveness process in the same place—by talking about it to God as well as to close friends. Facing it and refusing to run from the painful feelings are often necessary starting points to get the ball rolling inside our hearts.

Think back to the people and circumstances you wrote down previously. Which ones have you already forgiven? Does the hurt they have caused you hold any power in your life anymore?

What did forgiveness look like for you? Was it all at once or a slow process?

Now here's the harder part. Where is there unforgiveness in your life right now? Who are you harboring bitterness and resentment against? Why? (Remember, it doesn't have to be something from ten years ago, it could be someone you just had an argument with five minutes before you picked up this book!)

What is stopping you from forgiving them?

One of the facts that makes it difficult to forgive is when the person who did the hurting is not asking for forgiveness; in fact, he or she may not even think he or she has done anything wrong. In Norma's situation, she received the greatest gift possible—repentance on the part of the person who harmed her. There is no doubt that this facilitated her healing. Sadly, this may be rare.

Often we will need God's help to find forgiveness without ever hearing "I'm sorry" from the person who caused the pain. Many times, we'll never see that person again; other times we see that person every time we wake up in the morning. We can't change his or her heart and make that person sorry for the pain he or she has inflicted. We have to let go and leave that person to God.

Read Romans 12:19.

Do not take revenge, my friends, but leave room for God's wrath, for it is written: "It is mine to avenge; I will repay," says the Lord. **(NIV)**

What comfort do you find in this verse?

....

....

Remember, forgiveness is a choice. Sometimes the first choice is, "I want to *try* to forgive . . ." That is a wonderful place to start because it means our hearts are soft and we've opened a crack to yield ourselves to God's work in us. Are you ready to take that step? If so, write it in the space below.

Lord, I want to try to forgive _________________ for

....

After you take this step, a great prayer is to tell God next that you "choose" to forgive. There is often a subtle or direct pull to take back forgiveness and we will sometimes have to choose to forgive again and again. If you feel you are ready to choose to forgive, then tell God and give it to Him.

Think of this unforgiveness as if it were a huge suitcase full of hurt, resentment, and pain. It feels heavy and you're sick of lugging it around. Heave it to God. Toss it over to the foot of the cross, where Jesus Christ died for you and for the person who hurt you.

Lord, I choose to forgive _________________ for

....

1-2-3 . . . Heave!

Take your time. Heave as many suitcases as you need, as you can, and when you can. Sometimes the suitcase is even too heavy and you might have to take out a few "garments" of unforgiveness and throw them away one at a time. There's no rush in this moment. It's between God and you.

WDJS? (What Did Jesus Say?)

We've all heard WWJD (What Would Jesus Do?). Here's a twist, WDJS? (What Did Jesus Say?).

Here are a few things that Jesus says about forgiveness:
"Do not judge, and you will not be judged. Do not condemn, and you will not be condemned. Forgive, and you will be forgiven." . . . "And when you stand praying, if you hold anything against anyone, forgive him, so that your Father in heaven may forgive you your sins." . . . "If you forgive anyone's sins, they are forgiven; if you do not forgive them, they are not forgiven" **(Luke 6:37; Mark 11:25; John 20:23 NIV).**

Now, here's a twist: WWOS (What Would Others Say?). Here are what some other prominent voices have to say about forgiveness:

Martin Luther King Jr. says:
"Hatred paralyzes life; love releases it. Hatred confuses life; love harmonizes it. Hatred darkens life; love illuminates it."

Mother Teresa says:
"People are often unreasonable, illogical, and self-centered."

Gandhi says:
"The weak can never forgive. Forgiveness is an attribute of the strong."

Abraham Lincoln says:
"Am I not destroying my enemies when I make friends of them?"

Mark Twain says:
"Forgiveness is the fragrance that the violet sheds on the heel that has crushed it."

1. It's all Greek to me!

Luke 6:37 says, *"Do not judge, and you will not be judged. Do not condemn, and you will not be condemned. Forgive, and you will be forgiven."* (NIV)

The Greek word for the word *forgive* in this passage is *apoluo* [ah-paw-LOO-oh]. It is formed from the combination of *apo*, which carries overtones of "separating," since it means "away from," and *luo*, which is used to describe "a loosening."

Here's a quick breakdown of some definitions. As you read through these, underline or circle which words you connect with when you think of forgiveness.

Apoluo:

- To set free
- To let go, dismiss, to detain no longer
- To bid depart, send away
- To let go free, release, to acquit one accused of a crime and set him at liberty
- To release a debtor, that is, not to press one's claim against him, to remit his debt
- To dismiss from the house
- To send one's self away, to depart

What about these particular words impresses you?

2. Forgiven much: a picture of humility

Read Luke 7:36–50.

Key verses (vv. 47–50): *"Therefore, I tell you, her many sins have been forgiven—for she loved much. But he who has been forgiven little loves little." Then Jesus said to her, "Your sins are forgiven." The other guests began to say among themselves, "Who is this who even forgives sins?" Jesus said to the woman, "Your faith has saved you; go in peace."* (NIV)

The Bible tells us about the woman who pressed her way into Simon the Pharisee's house, probably an outer courtyard. This is a powerful image of someone in touch with Christ's forgiveness. Not only does she cross all cultural norms by entering into a Pharisee's property uninvited, she disrupts the gathering and heads straight to Jesus and begins wiping His feet with her tears. Isn't this true humility?

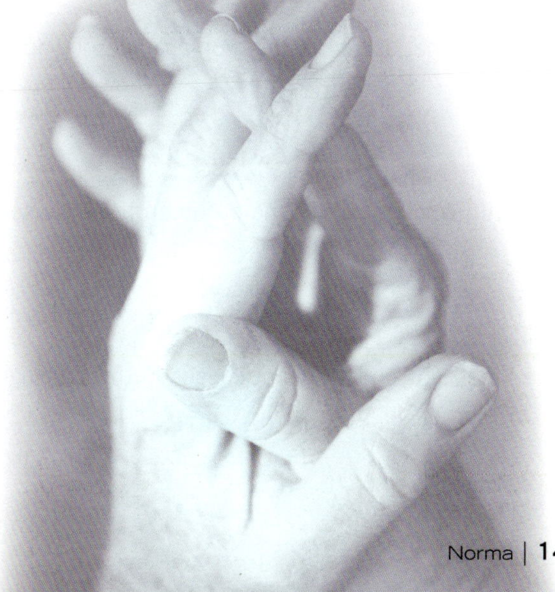

A Spoonful of
Forgiveness

Did you know that unforgiveness causes stress to our bodies as well as our minds? Research has shown a link between forgiveness and physical and mental health. Unforgiveness and the hostility and bitterness that come along with it increase the risk for mental illness such as depression, anxiety, stress disorders, and physical ailments.

Although research in this area is fairly recent, studies have shown that those who harbor unforgiveness are more likely to experience stresses to:

• **The central nervous system**—irritability, anxiety, hostility, resentment, and anger tax the nervous system

• **The cardiovascular system**—increased blood pressure and heart rate
• **The muscular-skeletal system**—increased forehead muscle tension, resulting in headaches and also stomachaches, joint aches, tiredness

The bottom line: Unforgiveness is bad for our health. To take good care of our minds and bodies, we must learn to forgive.

Meanwhile, Simon, the "religious leader," has a hard heart filled with pride and judgment. Jesus utilizes this opportunity to make a powerful point. He says these profound words, "Therefore, I tell you, her many sins have been forgiven—for she loved much. But he who has been forgiven little loves little" (Luke 7:47 NIV). This is great hope for those of us who feel like we are constantly asking for forgiveness! Jesus is saying this is actually the better thing because it means we understand our need for Him.

Read again in your Bible about this biblical woman and think through some of these questions:

• How does forgiveness affect our ability to love?

• Why is it so hard to humble ourselves as this woman did?

• With what aspect of this woman's life do you identify?

• With what characteristic of Simon the Pharisee do you identify?

• What did you learn about Jesus in this passage?

3. Does forgiving mean forgetting?

Does forgiving mean forgetting as the old adage goes? Is forgiving some kind of memory eraser? One of *Webster's* definitions for *forgive* is "to cease to feel resentment against." That's the big idea; that the pain, hurt, shame, and bitterness are lessened and cannot continue to rob us of joy and peace. What remains when the resentment has ceased? A reminder of what God has done. Forgiving doesn't mean forgetting; rather forgiving often means remembering— remembering what God has done to free us, heal us, and forgive us too; remembering where we used to be compared to where we are now.

I (Laura) had a hurtful relationship that took a lot of hard forgiveness work on my part. I wanted to forgive. Really, I did. But every morning when I sat with my Bible and journal trying my hardest to forgive, praying my best prayers, I still walked away bitter, angry, and resentful.

I shared my unforgiveness hurdle with an older, wiser woman. She asked me one simple question. "Have you ever just sat with Jesus and told Him how hurt you are? Just poured out your heart to Him? Have you ever just sat and told Him why it hurts so much?"

No. I hadn't. I had just tried my hardest. Try. Try. Try. I tried to force myself into forgiveness. But it didn't work.

The next morning as I sat with my Bible and journal I began pouring out my heart to God, bombarding Him with how I had been so unjustly wronged. It's hard to put into words; but as I sat there that first morning and grieved with Christ, I felt a spiritual balm poured over my heart. I continued morning after morning to sit and grieve with Him, explaining how mad and hurt I was. As the days and weeks rolled by, I slowly began to change. The need to grieve and lay my hurt before God no longer felt pressing. In fact, the torrent feelings of resentment and anger dissolved into a fading mist. Had I forgotten how I had been wronged? No. Certainly not. But, like Norma, my heart had changed.

And now, years later, I continue to *remember* and *never want to forget* how the hand of God reached inside me and did a transforming work in my heart that on my own I could not get done.

Forgiving and forgetting do not go hand in hand. In fact, often God wants us to remember so we can point to His handprint on our lives.

Think about your own life. Is there a time when forgiving has not meant forgetting? How can you use not forgetting to remember what God has done in your life?

Getting good at forgiveness

1. Forgiveness . . . where do you need to ask for it?

We've talked a great deal about how important it is to forgive others. Of course it is, but it is equally—if not more—important for us to be willing to ask for forgiveness when we sin against each other. Think about what a better place the world would be if we were to become good at asking for forgiveness!

I (Kathy) am learning a lot from my son, Jonas. Even though he's only a child, he is the best forgiveness-asker in our family. Almost immediately, when he makes a mistake or does something wrong, he says, "I'm so sorry, will you please forgive me?" I am challenged by my child in this area!

Asking for forgiveness requires humility, and there are many moments when I am prideful and don't like to admit it if I'm wrong. What I am learning, though, is that the sooner I take responsibility for my actions and admit my wrongs, the sooner I am able to be free of the feelings of guilt and separation from God and others. This draws me closer to my husband and my kids when they know I am willing to take responsibility for my wrongs instead of avoiding them.

In general, is it hard for you to say you're sorry?

Who have you hurt recently, either intentionally or unintentionally?

What did you do or say?

Have you asked for forgiveness? Why or why not?

If you haven't yet, *pray*, search your heart, and ask God to show you who you need to ask for forgiveness. It can be a simple request such as, *"I am really sorry for _____________. Will you please forgive me?"* You may want to do this in a letter, an email, a phone call, or in a face-to-face conversation. Although we can never fully predict the outcome, usually when we go to each other in humility, with open and repentant hearts, others are more likely to accept our request and offer their forgiveness.

2. Rockin' the boat

One of the reasons Norma had such a difficult time moving toward forgiveness and freedom was she didn't speak out for many years. She was known as a people pleaser in her family—always keeping the peace, making sure she didn't rock the boat too much. This is common for many women. Many of us tend to develop a pattern of silence in order to make sure no one gets mad or rejects us. The problem with this way of thinking is it blocks movement toward forgiveness. It can be a form of managing our world instead of trusting God, regardless of how messy a situation gets. When Norma finally forged ahead to get to forgiveness, she found herself in a rocky, but forward-moving boat!

Boat Rockers:
Confront painful situations
Allow themselves to get angry
Speak the truth
Let people get frustrated with them

People Pleasers:
Avoid conflict
Soften their opinions, adjust to others
Don't allow themselves to get angry
Keep their feelings inside

Are you a boat rocker or a people pleaser? _______________

OK, here's a boat-rocking challenge. Take a step forward. Initiate a conversation, write a letter, do something to get your thoughts and feelings out on the table so they are not bottled up inside.

3. Our crazy logic

Most of us are fairly willing to offer conditional forgiveness. We'll forgive others if they will (a) feel really sorry, (b) beg for forgiveness, (c) do something nice for us, (d) start showing us they're changing, or (e) _____________________________ (*you fill in the blank*). Part of learning to be better forgivers is to notice our crazy logic. Jesus's forgiveness is unconditional while often our forgiveness is conditional. Think for a moment about people or situations that are bothering you right now. Write down the first thing that comes to mind.

I'd be more willing to forgive _________________ **if they** _______________________________.

I'd be more willing to forgive _________________ **if they** _______________________________.

I'd be more willing to forgive _________________ **if they** _______________________________.

What did you learn about yourself from this exercise? How can you remove any conditions that might be interfering with your ability to forgive?

MIX IT UP

1. Bring a gift to the group that everyone might like to get (a Starbucks gift card, nice lotion, or so on).

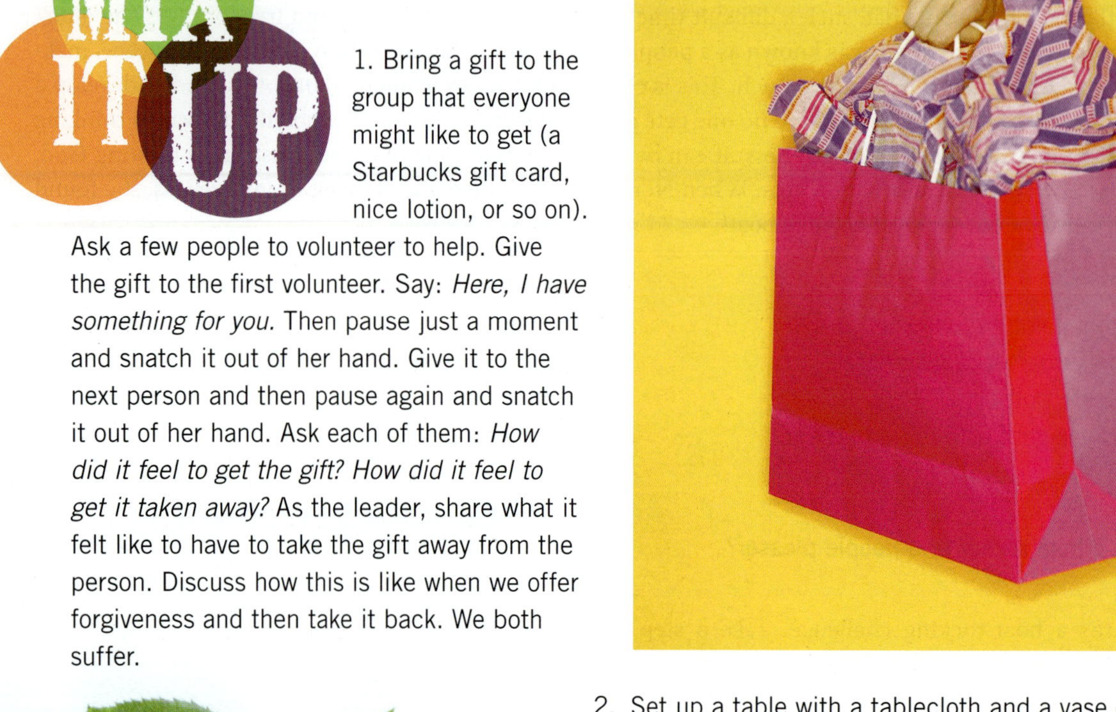

Ask a few people to volunteer to help. Give the gift to the first volunteer. Say: *Here, I have something for you.* Then pause just a moment and snatch it out of her hand. Give it to the next person and then pause again and snatch it out of her hand. Ask each of them: *How did it feel to get the gift? How did it feel to get it taken away?* As the leader, share what it felt like to have to take the gift away from the person. Discuss how this is like when we offer forgiveness and then take it back. We both suffer.

2. Set up a table with a tablecloth and a vase of roses. Scatter rose petals on the table. Place a large bowl and small paper squares on the table. Consider playing soft music in the background. Ask the group members to go to the table, write down who or what they need to forgive, and place their papers in the bowl, surrendering their issues to God. As they leave the table, tell them to take a rose petal. This is a reminder of God's beauty and also the fragrance of forgiveness; how God can take things that are ugly and painful and turn them into something beautiful. When everyone is done, consider lifting up the bowl, offering these prayers to God as a fragrant offering.

3. Consider taking Communion together and thank God individually for His forgiveness of our sins.

Verbatim What about forgiveness?

"Good character and bitterness will not live in the same heart, and the resolution to bitterness always involves forgiveness."

—Gary Fenton, *Good for Goodness' Sake*

1. Who or what are you harboring bitterness and resentment against right now?

Is God stirring in you a desire to forgive someone or some thing? What is it? How can the group encourage you to keep moving through this process?

2. Is it easier for you to forgive yourself or others? Why?

3. If you feel comfortable enough, share with the group some of the things on your forgiveness list as a praise to God for the good things He has done for you.

4. Closing round: Go around the circle and finish this sentence: *The thing that surprised me about working through this chapter was . . .*

Check These Out . . .

Good for Goodness' Sake
by Gary Fenton

The Power of Forgiveness: The Story of Karla Faye Tucker DVD

The Christmas Child
by Max Lucado

Bold Love
by Dan B. Allender and Tremper Longman III

Learning to Show Up

Instead of shut up

Janette's concentration on the tennis

ball completely unraveled when the baby let out a loud cry. "Just a minute, Michael," she called over her shoulder and darted off the court before her husband could say anything. Her four daughters were scrunched inside a playpen underneath a sprawling oak tree to the side of the tennis court. She had filled the pen with an assortment of toys and snacks; but after an hour of confinement, the girls were restless.

"Mommy, I tried to give her the bottle but she wouldn't take it," six-year-old Kelsey cried, knitting her brows together.

"It's OK, honey. Let's give her a cookie." Janette dug out a box of animal crackers from a nylon tote bag and handed a hippo-shaped cookie to one-year-old Lizzy.

"Come on!" Michael barked.

"Coming," she answered dutifully as all eight eyes looked up at her. With anxiety rising in her chest, she forced a reassuring smile for her girls. "Just a few more minutes. Here, sweetie," she handed the bag of cookies to Kelsey, "keep handing Lizzy these. That'll keep her happy."

Scurrying back onto the court, she looked up to see Michael lob a ball into the air. "I hate lobs," she muttered. Raising her racquet over her head, she swung down and the ball went careening into the net.

"You're hitting it too late. I've told you this a hundred times." Irritation oozed through Michael's words.

Janette nodded and walked to the net, retrieving the ball. She stole a glance at the girls and silently winced at the pitiful sight of them.

"Let's not do any more lobs," Janette said as she hit the ball to Michael. He didn't answer but returned her ball with another lob. Janette kept her eyes glued to the ball and swung when it was still well above her head. Sailing over the net, it landed just inside the white line. "Whew," she blew out her cheeks.

When Michael said he was done playing, Janette made a beeline for the girls. "All done!" she grinned, scooping Lizzy up into her arms.

"I'll be back in a minute," Michael announced and walked toward a group of people standing outside the clubhouse. Janette disassembled the playpen and loaded everyone and everything into the car. When the baby began fussing, Janette popped a pacifier into her mouth and watched out the car's rear window, hoping Michael would hurry.

On the short drive home, Michael sped through traffic, weaving in and out of cars. "Please slow down," Janette said softly, clenching her jaw.

He made a sharp turn and the tires screeched. "I'm the driver here."

Janette looked over her shoulder at Lizzy. "The baby is sleeping. Please, Michael."

Ignoring her, he sped down a narrow two-lane street toward their neighborhood. "You remember Liz and her family are coming over for dinner tonight?"

"Yes. I have a pork roast. But, Michael . . .," Janette hesitated, "I was going to ask you . . . it seems like having so much company over is hard on our family. I'm wondering if . . ."

"Janette," he underlined her name with reproach. "You know Liz is going through a hard time. It's not easy on her and she doesn't have a lot of people to turn to."

"I know. It's just I . . ."

"This is part of our Christian calling, to open our home to others."

"I was only saying . . ."

"We have a God-given responsibility to take care of others in need."

Janette's mind flashed to all the people "in need" in Michael's life. He invested most of his spare time into people outside their family. A wave of sadness flooded her heart.

"Janette, it's the least we can do." Shaking his head, Michael swerved the car into their driveway. "Your attitude surprises me."

His reprimand stung. "You're right. I'm sorry. I shouldn't have brought it up."

"No. You shouldn't have."

Janette lifted the baby out of the backseat and carried her into the house for a nap while Michael lay down on the family room couch for his nap. After the baby was settled, Janette set the girls up at the kitchen table with crayons and coloring books so she could concentrate on cleaning the house and cooking dinner before their company arrived. She

seasoned the roast, chopped lettuce and tomatoes for a salad, and began setting the table in the dining room when a fierce fight broke out in the kitchen.

"I had it first!" four-year-old Trish screamed.

"Mine!" squealed three-year-old Lauren.

"Owww!"

A shrill cry rang through the house.

"I'm trying to sleep in here!" Michael roared from the family room.

Flinching inwardly, Janette hurried into the kitchen. "Shhh!" She raised her finger to her mouth and her eyes grew narrow as she glared at the girls. "If you can't be quiet, you're all going to your rooms!" she urgently whispered.

Trish stuck her tongue out at Lauren and threw a blue crayon down. "Fine." She picked up a yellow crayon and continued coloring, but Lauren laid her head down on the table and kept crying.

"Shhh!" The panic in Janette's voice made her daughters look back up at her. "Daddy is sleeping. You have to be quiet!" She lifted Lauren out of her chair. "Shhh," she said more softly. "You're tired, sweetie." How 'bout you lie down for a few minutes?"

Janette stroked her daughter's braids as she carried her down the hall to her bedroom. After tickling her for a couple of minutes, Lauren fell sound asleep. Padding softly out of the room, Janette checked her watch and mentally reviewed everything she still needed to do before company arrived. Balls of tension had gathered at the base of her neck and she fought the fatigue that beckoned her to lie down for a few minutes. After she finished setting the table, she pulled potatoes from the cupboard. Slicing the potatoes into cubes, her thoughts slowly sank.

I wish we weren't doing anything tonight. A loud sigh seeped out her mouth. Staring at the pile of potatoes, she stopped slicing as her thoughts drifted to Liz and the rocky time she was going through. A stab of guilt jarred her. *I have such a bad attitude. Michael's right.* Frowning, she rolled a potato toward herself and cut it in half. "Forgive me, Lord. I want to obey You and be a good servant tonight. Help me make a nice meal for these people."

Later that evening, the company sat around her dining room table, complimenting Janette for the good meal. "Thanks," she smiled, piling plates into a stack. The tension in her neck had moved upward and her head throbbed. "Who would like coffee?" she asked, injecting a false cheerful note into her voice. After she cleared the dishes, she served decaffeinated coffee with cherry crumb cake while Michael

charmed their guests with entertaining stories. When she set Michael's coffee and dessert in front of him, he patted her backside. "I'm going to get Janette a three-way mirror in the bathroom," he looked up at her and grinned, "so she can see what her butt really looks like." He threw his head back and laughed.

Humiliation crawled up Janette's skin, reddening her face. She shrugged, "He's right. Ever since my fourth baby I haven't been able to bounce back."

I need to lose weight, she told herself as she walked into the kitchen to get cream for the coffee. *He's right.*

As the years rolled by, Janette's marriage didn't improve. Michael continued to treat her poorly and Janette allowed it through silent compliance—which she wholeheartedly believed was her job as a Christian wife. However, when she was 37, an unexpected friendship marked the beginning of change inside her.

The friendship was with Jessie, a teenage boyfriend of her oldest daughter. Jessie came from a dysfunctional family and had few stable adults in his life. Janette had been involved in her church's youth ministry for years and had a heart for sharing God's love with confused youth; so when Jessie began opening up to her about his family problems, it was natural for her to befriend him.

As their friendship grew, Janette and Jessie began running together. Janette used their running time to listen to him talk through the confusing, tangled mess of his family and voice his questions about God. They talked about all sorts of issues and a bond was formed through their rich conversations. Janette found herself looking forward to their runs for more than just an opportunity to support a hurting teenager. The kind companionship and mutual respect they had for each other felt like a cold cup of water on a blistering hot summer day. And like an archaeological dig, she began to make discoveries about herself that had been buried for a long time.

One day after they ran together, Janette went home to take a shower. A smile spread over her face as she thought about some of the things she and Jessie had discussed. He was always asking her opinion and, unlike Michael, valued what she had to say. As she went over their conversation, her heart pricked. *This is what it's like to connect with another person.* The thought made a direct hit on Janette's heart. *This is what Michael and I should have.*

She turned and faced the shower faucet, closing her eyes. Another thought poked her like a hot iron and she winced. *Jessie likes being around me more than my husband does.* Pain shot down her throat and lodged in her chest as tears began to trickle down her cheeks.

Later that night, when Michael told Janette he was going to a horse show over the weekend, the pain in her heart mounted again. "But the girls have their tennis tournament," she retorted. "I was hoping you could come with me."

"Nope. I've already committed to going to the show."

"But . . . I thought . . ." Emotions thickened Janette's voice.

"I said I can't, Janette." His words were clipped.

Before she could stop herself, Janette burst into tears.

Unaccustomed to his wife crying, Michael frowned over at her. "What is *wrong* with you?"

Cupping her face inside her hands, she sobbed harder.

"You better get a grip on yourself." He shook his head and left the room.

Janette shuffled down the hallway to their bedroom and fell onto the bed. She buried her head into a pillow, trying to drown out the sound of her sobs. *Why do I hurt so much?* After an hour, the crying finally waned and Janette dragged herself into the bathroom and rinsed her face with cold water.

Making dinner that night, she moved slowly around the kitchen in a fog. *What is wrong with me?* she wondered as a torrent of emotions lurked close to the surface. Biting her lip, she pulled vegetables from the refrigerator. *I feel so empty.* As she chopped an onion and a few stalks of celery, confusion swirled inside her head and weariness wrapped around her like a wet wool blanket.

Later that week, another unexpected burst of tears came flooding out of Janette when Michael was in a bad mood and spoke harshly to her on the telephone. This time she couldn't stop crying for two hours. Over the next several weeks, her emotional outbursts increased and Janette found herself crying for days at a time.

One morning, after Michael left for work and the girls went to school, tears spilled down Janette's cheeks as she roamed around the house trying to get things done. *What's wrong with me, God? Am I going crazy?* She ambled into the bathroom and tried to rein in her emotions. Staring at her reflection she cried harder. *What is happening to me?* Gray circles outlined her eyes and her skin was pasty. *I've always been so in control. Now I'm an emotional basket case.*

Swallowing hard, she rinsed a washcloth with cool water and rubbed it up and down her face. She brushed her eyelashes with mascara and swept her cheeks with powder blush. *I've got to get this under control.* She stared at herself again in the mirror. She looked a little better on the outside, but underneath the makeup she knew all her pain was still there. *Lord,*

I'm dying inside. Help me figure this out. I don't know how long I can function like this. She bolted from the bathroom before fresh tears could leak out.

A few weeks later, Janette's confusion completely erupted when she found out Michael had gone on a business trip with a female co-worker. She knew Michael was not romantically involved with the woman, but, nonetheless, the trip made her uncomfortable and she had bravely spoken up and told Michael about her reservations, asking him not to go. Michael had agreed to her request.

Later that month, Janette called Michael at his office to ask him about a bill they had received. "By the way, did Colleen ever go on that trip with you?"

"Yes, she did."

A thud pounded in the depths of Janette's chest. "I've gotta go," she said, dropping the receiver as if it was on fire. Sinking onto the floor, choking sobs erupted from her angry soul. With a trembling hand, she picked the receiver back up and called her brother, Alex. "This marriage is a joke," she croaked hysterically over the phone line. "I'm not doing it anymore."

"Stay put," Alex commanded, "I'm coming over."

Alex and his wife, Susan, came right over and Alex called Michael, with whom he had been friends for many years. That afternoon, Janette spent hours crying and talking with Susan while Alex and Michael talked. When the four of them finally gathered together in the kitchen to talk, Janette was pale and listless and Michael stoned-faced.

Alex tried to get Michael to talk, asking probing questions. "Michael, what's going on? Look at your wife. She is dying and broken. Why you are sitting there with no response?"

Silence. Michael sat unmoved.

Alex pushed further. "Why do you treat her this way? Do you want to be married to Janette?"

Michael's face twitched and he looked down. After a long moment he drew a shaky breath. "I love Janette. I don't know why I treat her like this." He covered his face and his shoulders began to shake.

Alex and Susan looked at Janette, hope lighting up their eyes.

Janette shook her head. Like a dried-up well, she was utterly empty. "I don't care anymore."

"I want to be married to her." Michael wept louder.

Janette's swollen eyes stared blankly at Michael. Nothing inside her wanted to reach out to her husband. "I just want out."

Alex's eyes filled with compassion. "Janette, I know a woman, Cindy. She's a Christian counselor and I think you would really like her. She could help you walk through your feelings and talk about where to go from here."

Numb, Janette nodded.

Janette began meeting regularly with Cindy, trying to figure out what to do with her marriage. Through long conversations with Cindy, she began to see how her upbringing influenced her married behavior. "For so long, I believed being a good Christian wife meant I needed to 'shut up and put up.' For me, a good wife meant a happy husband. So, to make him happy, I went along with whatever he said or did."

After forcing herself to begin to think differently,

she began to open her eyes to her destructive patterns. "I began to understand that I was as big of a problem in my marriage as Michael because I *allowed him* to treat me that way. I put up with it and never said anything, which created a monster that I intentionally kept feeding!"

It took a very long time for Janette to learn she had a choice in how she allowed herself to be treated. "I never considered it was something I could stop. I just existed, hollow of thoughts and opinions. And, I hated conflict because I was taught by my church and my family to believe that conflict meant I was a bad wife."

After many weeks of talking with Cindy and a few other close friends, Janette was convinced she wanted to do life differently. "I told Michael I wanted to grow and change. I also told him I believed loving God looked different than how I had been living." Janette knew the unspoken rules of their marriage would have to change and she explained to Michael that if she felt she was being controlled or manipulated during a conversation, she would walk out of the room instead of silently endure it.

She used the support and input of a few close, godly friends to help her process through episodes and conversations with Michael. "I had been in denial for so long that I needed a few insiders to tell me the truth about myself so I wouldn't slip back to my old ways. They could see the unhealthiness much more clearly than I could."

Change inside Janette was slow and she had to fight for it. "In a lot of ways it was much easier to not think about stuff or have to deal with it. But I knew I couldn't do that anymore. Really what I needed to learn was how to show up in my marriage, how to have a voice. Part of that process was learning to pay attention to what was going on inside me."

The changes she made in her marriage spilled into her other relationships, too, especially with her children and close family members. For the first time, Janette began expressing her own needs and opinions. It was uncomfortable for some of them at first because they weren't used to Janette saying no. But, over time, people close to her began respecting the changes she was making.

Janette also learned a lot about her relationship with God. "I still love God with my whole heart but I have learned that I can love God better and serve others better as a whole person. Before, I wasn't whole; I was only bringing part of me into my relationship with God and other people, the part that I thought I was *supposed* to be."

Janette is still in the midst of her journey. Her marriage is far from perfect but she has seen changes in Michael. He is more respectful, less controlling, and willing to hear Janette's thoughts and feelings without dismissing them. But more importantly, Janette has seen significant changes inside her own heart.

"I am a very different person. I set up boundaries. I make choices. I speak truth from my heart. I 'show up' instead of avoid. It feels like I am living as a grown-up instead of as a little girl. And living this way, I feel full and whole with God instead of lonely and empty inside a hard marriage." ❀

Truth and the Transforming Consequences

"No one can make you feel inferior without your consent."
—Eleanor Roosevelt

A muted voice.

A toned-down response.

An opinion held back.

Anything to keep the peace. Not all of us are peace-makers, but if we were to take a poll, the percentages of women who are good at keeping the peace in relationships would be fairly high. There's a tendency ingrained into many of us, especially those who have been raised in the church, to avoid conflict, serve (quietly), try not to complain, and to make sure that others' needs are met before our own. Isn't that what good Christian women do?

This can be an extremely confusing question. Clearly, in the Bible, a servant's heart is an honored virtue. Jesus modeled humble servanthood as He washed His disciples' feet, and He challenges us to live the same way.

Read John 13:12–15.

When he had finished washing their feet, he put on his clothes and returned to his place. "Do you understand what I have done for you?" he asked them. "You call me 'Teacher' and 'Lord,' and rightly so, for that is what I am. Now that I, your Lord and Teacher, have washed your feet, you also should wash one another's feet. I have set you an example that you should do as I have done for you. **(NIV)**

But often, to some women, humble servanthood equates with keeping a false peace. Interestingly, Jesus does not see it this way In fact, He makes it very clear that, to follow Him, we sometimes have to make a few waves. Look at what Jesus says about Himself in Matthew 10:34.

"Do not suppose that I have come to bring peace to the earth. I did not come to bring peace, but a sword." **(NIV)**

Jesus is telling us that there is something more valuable than maintaining peace for the sake of peacefulness. John the Baptist, whom Jesus called the greatest man who ever lived, was not what people would call a peacemaker. He stirred people, challenged the status quo, and spoke truth that many people didn't like to hear. Yet, he was a humble servant of Christ.

The truth is that peacekeeping is often the easy way out. It was for Janette. For years, it was easier for her to be quiet and allow her husband to treat her poorly than to speak the truth.

What happened in Janette's life happens to many women. In an effort to be a good wife, friend, sister, employee, or daughter, women confuse servanthood with peacekeeping and become lost in the mix. They stuff away their thoughts, feelings, opinions, reactions, and feedback. But all too often the day comes, as it did in Janette's life, when a woman who lives this way finally reaches her limit and wakes up one morning and says, "I'm done . . . I can't do this anymore." Broken relationships usually follow.

Another common outcome of a life lived this way is bitterness. I (Laura) know a woman, Joyce, whose husband worked in youth ministry and was a workaholic. Joyce believed in the ministry as much as her husband and worked alongside him until they began raising their own children. Night after night, Joyce found herself home alone with the children as her husband was out doing ministry. He'd come home bursting with excitement because of the changed lives he was witnessing.

Joyce never said anything because she wanted others' lives to change as much as he did. She was afraid that if she spoke the truth, he wouldn't think she was supportive. But slowly, resentment crept into her heart and festered until she became infected with bitterness. She is now bitter toward the ministry she once loved, toward her husband, and even toward God.

So how can we avoid this? How can we learn to live as humble servants, putting others first, yet not compromise the truth inside us? How can we become like John the Baptist and like Jesus? How can we be humble and gracious truth speakers who don't sell out to keeping the peace for the wrong reasons?

Here are a few verses to chew on that can help us to get us started.

Read Psalm 139:23–24.

Search me, O God, and know my heart; test me and know my anxious thoughts. See if there is any offensive way in me, and lead me in the way everlasting. **(NIV)**

Spend time right now and pray this specific psalm, asking God to reveal ways in which you might compromise by being silent when, in fact, He wants you to speak truth in a graceful and loving way.

What areas of your life or relationships come to mind?

Have you ever put peacekeeping over truth speaking as the easy way out? How so? How did you feel?

Jesus wasn't an avoider. He modeled a better way for us, a life of humble truth and trust. We are called to speak the truth in love, to lovingly address issues instead of pretending they don't exist, and to trust God with conflict instead of avoiding it.

Read Ephesians 4:15.

Instead, we will hold on to the truth in love, becoming more and more in every way like Christ, who is the head of his body, the church. **(NLT)**

What does "speaking the truth" mean to you?

Is there something you've stuffed that has the potential of festering? Be honest. Take a deep look.

Speaking the truth doesn't mean pointing the finger, telling others all the things they are doing wrong, judging, or criticizing. Rather, it's learning how to be more honest, present, and humble about what's really going on inside of us and being willing to share that with the significant people in our lives, whether they agree with us or not.

Now read Matthew 7:3–4.

"And why worry about a speck in your friend's eye when you have a log in your own? How can you think of saying, 'Let me help you get rid of that speck in your eye,' when you can't see past the log in your own eye?" **(NLT)**

It would have been easy for Janette to point the finger at Michael. After all, she felt he continually disrespected her. But Jesus makes it clear this is not the way He wants us to go. Instead, He wants us to focus on the work we have to do in our own life.

Think of a relationship you are or have been in where you focused on the other person's problems. What was it like for you? Did they ever change?

Smashing Down False Idols

The Israelites always struggled with worshipping false idols, hoping that maybe the idols would take better care of them than God. Gold, wood, silver, clay—it didn't really matter. They just wanted something to put their hope and trust in that seemed a little more tangible. Of course, false idols are just that, false. They are counterfeits for the true and living God.

Often, we worship false idols too. We worship what people think of us more than what God thinks. We worship our image and reputation as "good Christians" more than honesty and truth. We worship behaviors passed on to us by our parents and churches instead of living free in Christ.

Take a look at this list of idols. Which ones do you sometimes "worship"?

- The "But Good Christian Women Don't Rock the Boat" Idol
- The "Conflict Is Bad" Idol
- The "Nobody Cares What I Have to Say" Idol
- The "I Am Supposed to Always Be Nice" Idol
- The "Everyone Else's Needs Are More Important than Mine" Idol
- The "It's Selfish to Ask for What I Really Want" Idol
- The "Others Expect Me To" Idol

Which of these would you like to begin to smash down?

Focusing on others rather than ourselves is easier. However, when we focus on others and try to change them it usually backfires. They don't change, and we get angry and bitter. So God tells us to do the harder thing for our own good—to focus on the work we have to do in ourselves. He can do a work in us if we get our attention off the other person and onto our own stuff. This doesn't mean we should neglect the reality of how we feel and never speak truth. It simply means we must stay focused on what we can change—ourselves.

Reread what Jesus says in Matthew 7:3–4.

Like Janette, we have to look at the log in our own eye and take responsibility for what we *can* change.

Take a look at the log pile below. Think of relationships you are in right now. What are some of your logs, the things that you might tend to do in close relationships? Look at the list and write the number of the ones with which you identify on the logs below.

1. Be defensive.
2. Silently punish.
3. Feel ashamed.
4. Be emotionally distant.
5. Disrespect and put down.
6. Be overly submissive.
7. Avoid conflict.
8. Be self-righteous.
9. Harbor hurt.
10. Lash out in anger.
11. Resent.
12. People please.
13. Judge.
14. Show bitterness.
15. Feel insecure, inadequate.

I can tend to . . .

Sometimes it's hard to admit these things, but honesty and humility are the paths to change. None of these attitudes and behaviors will go away quickly, but with God's help these logs can be whittled down.

As we seek God's strength and help to change ourselves, life can become different. We can become humble truth tellers, willing to say hard things and lovingly take responsibility for our own thoughts, feelings, and actions.

But we need to remember that real change can be very slow. True transformation into Christ's image is a lifelong process, but it always starts with an open heart that is willing to listen to God and do what He is asking us to do or change, even when it's hard, scary, or shakes up the status quo.

Digging Deeper

1. Strength training: building the truth muscle

As women, many of us (sometimes unknowingly) live from a place of very low self-esteem. In order to reposition ourselves and live from a strong and confident place, we need to begin a disciplined training rooted in Christ's truth about us.

Just like good weight lifters don't start with the biggest barbells when they train, we won't get strong right away. Good lifters start with a lower weight and keep increasing. An essential exercise to build spiritual and emotional strength is memorizing and relying on the promises in the Scriptures, allowing God to embed their powerful truths into our core so that we can draw from them as we engage in life.

"All Scripture is inspired by God and is useful to teach us what is true and to make us realize what is wrong in our lives. It straightens us out and teaches us to do what is right" (2 Timothy 3:16 NLT). As women trying to make changes in our lives and relationships, there are many Scriptures that can strengthen us. Challenge yourself to memorize at least one of the following Scriptures, allowing the words to take root in your heart.

I can do everything with the help of Christ who gives me the strength I need. **Philippians 4:13 (NLT)**

Out of all the peoples on the face of the earth, the LORD has chosen you to be his treasured possession. **Deuteronomy 14:2 (NIV)**

For you did not receive a spirit that makes you a slave again to fear, but you received the Spirit of sonship. And by him we cry, "Abba, Father." **Romans 8:15 (NIV)**

How great is the love the Father has lavished on us, that we should be called children of God! **1 John 3:1 (NIV)**

Which of these bring you some strength? Why?

2. We reap what we sow

In the Book of Galatians, there is a very small passage packed with great punch. It says, *"You will always reap what you sow!"* (Galatians 6:7 NLT). If we sow (plant) seeds of silence and insecurity, it is unlikely we will reap (bring in) peace and strength.

Sowing matters. We need to be very intentional about what we sow because it affects what we "bring in," not only to our own lives but into the lives of those we love.

• **Think about something you are reaping in your life that you don't like (anxiousness, impatience, anger, or another attitude or behavior).**

• **What are some things you can intentionally sow to reap a different harvest? Taking a walk and memorizing a Scripture; reading a faith-building book; writing down your prayers and how God answers them; attending a group get-together or Bible study; asking for prayer and encouragement from good friends; thanking God more than asking Him for things; and other positive actions.**

• **Take a moment and ask God to help you sow these good things into your life.**

Celebrate the growth!

3. Growing up is hard to do

Sometimes the reason we don't speak up is that we are still stuck in childish ways of relating to each other. Some of us are still little girls in grown women's bodies! Part of spiritual maturity is growing up and learning to love others well. The Apostle Paul puts it this way when talking about maturing: *"When I was a child, I talked like a child, I thought like a child, I reasoned like a child. When I became a man, I put childish ways behind me"* (1 Corinthians 13:11 NIV). Getting our voice as women means we need to put childish ways behind us.

Look at the list below. Check which of these "childish" things you might tend to do.

❑ Go with the flow even when you don't agree.

❑ Rarely express your own desires or needs.

❑ When there's trouble in a relationship, assume it must be your fault.

❑ Throw fits.

❑ Pout and sulk when things aren't going your way.

❑ Hope that people can read your mind because you are too afraid to say what you're thinking.

❑ Stop expecting anything from other people and do it all yourself.

❑ Bottle up thoughts and feelings until they explode in anger.

If we are going to grow up to be strong, God-centered women, these childish ways have got to go! It is childish and immature to be unwilling to speak up and share our thoughts, feelings, and opinions out of fear. Part of living as an adult is speaking the truth in love to each other and trusting God will take care of us. When we silence our voice and fail to "show up" in our relationships, we are not loving well. God wants us to put these childish ways behind us.

How are you "growing up"? What are some victories you've recently had in responding to a situation like a grown-up instead of like a child? Be specific.

Shout It Out!

1. Safe yelling

"In your anger do not sin." **Ephesians 4:26 (NIV)**

Yelling is usually never a good idea. It gets us into trouble. The Bible makes it clear that in our anger we shouldn't sin. Yet many of us have a lot of pent-up anger inside from years of not learning appropriate ways to express it.

The Bible doesn't say "don't get angry." It is a God-given emotion. Jesus got angry throughout His ministry; He just didn't "sin" in His anger.

A safe way to express anger is to pour it out on paper, a paper that no one will necessarily ever read. It is cathartic and a great release for pent-up feelings that stem from stuffing and silencing. You can do this on the computer, in your journal, or on a piece of notebook paper. It can be a letter to God or to a person with whom you are struggling. The purpose is to ramble as much as possible and spill your heart out, unedited.

Use these journaling launches to get started.

Dear God,

I am so angry about . . .

I feel so hurt that . . .

Dear ___________,

I wish I could tell you face-to-face that . . .

I am afraid that if I do tell you the truth, you will . . .

2. A few tricks of the trade

Need to have a difficult conversation but are afraid to try? Here are a few suggestions for speaking up in a conversation without finger pointing:

1. Concentrate on feelings, not thoughts, in the conversation.

   I feel . . . versus *I think you are . . .*

2. Stick with your own experience.

   "Here's what it's like for me . . ."

3. Avoid the statement "You make me feel . . ."

   We are responsible for our own thoughts and feelings. Blaming will only get us into trouble and create defensiveness.

4. Own your own part of the feelings; acknowledge your "log."

   Admit when you are being oversensitive or defensive. Admitting the log in your own eye goes a long way toward breaking down the walls in a difficult conversation.

5. Be specific! Be specific! Be specific!

   Often we make generalized statements like "You always" or "You never" instead of just stating the specifics of an immediate experience.

If you know there are some things you need to say to a person, take a few moments and write it out, using the preceding guidelines.

Pray about when, if, and how you need to have this conversation. If you decide you need to talk face-to-face, make sure you ask a friend to pray for strength, courage, and wisdom for you during the conversation.

3. Playing all your cards

Early on in Janette's journey, her spiritual mentor handed her a deck of playing cards. She said to Janette, "In your relationship with your husband, you are not playing with all of your cards. You use certain ones all the time, but much of the deck is missing.

"Part of being in a real relationship is using all of our cards—our weak ones and strong ones, our good character qualities and our not-so-good character qualities, our desires and dreams, our frustrations and disappointments. Janette, it's time to play all your cards."

Often, like Janette, we don't play certain cards out of fear. We worry that if we play them all, our opponent might get angry and walk away from the game. Part of growing up and showing up is playing our full deck of cards and not just the ones we think others want us to play.

Think of some of the cards in your deck. Fill in what comes to mind in each of these areas:

Which of these cards are you afraid to play?

Why?

Which one(s) do you need to put back in your deck and start using?

1. Pass out a piece of Warheads candy to every woman in the group. Have the women put the candy in their mouth and suck on it until the sweetness (finally) starts to seep through. Talk about how sometimes speaking up and finding our voice is like a piece of Warheads candy. We want to avoid the sour and get straight to the sweet; but the truth is, in order to get to the sweet, you have to suck on the sour long enough to get to the sweetness inside.

2. Give everyone a piece of paper and have them write something they wish they could say out loud to a person right now but are afraid to try. This could be a spouse, family member, friend, co-worker, or other. Give some examples: *"It hurts me when you ignore me." "I feel unloved when you always watch the football game." "I feel unimportant to you." "It seems like you never listen to me"* Tell them not to write their name or the person's name. Have everyone put the sentences into a basket and have two readers read each of them out loud. When all have been read, pray for the women, for courage and wisdom to know what needs to be said and what needs to go unsaid.

Your Opinion Matters!

In college, I (Laura) was a peer counselor. It was a great paid job in which I helped other students with everyday campus life issues. I'll never forget when my boss, Darcy, gave me my performance evaluation. She said, "You're doing a great job, but we'd like to hear from you more in staff meetings. Your opinion matters." More than 20 years later, that conversation still sticks with me because it helped me trust that what I had to say was valuable. What about you? Do you think your opinion matters? Take this quick survey and see for yourself. Circle the ones that best describe you.

1. If you are in a meeting with co-workers, you contribute to the discussion:

A lot   Somewhat   A little

2. If you disagree with your boss, you speak up and say something.

Usually   Sometimes   Hardly ever

3. If a close friend does something you don't think is a good idea, you tell her your true opinion.

Usually   Sometimes   Hardly ever

4. If your husband or partner does something that you don't like, do you tell him?

Usually   Sometimes   Hardly ever

5. If someone close to you says something to you that hurts your feelings, do you let that person know?

Usually   Sometimes   Hardly ever

6. When you have a creative idea on how to improve or change something for the better, do you share it with the people who matter?

Usually   Sometimes   Hardly ever

SCORING

Each answer gets 1, 3, or 5 points:

A lot/Usually = 1
Somewhat/Sometimes = 3
A little/Hardly ever = 5

Total your score and see how you are doing on learning to share your opinion.

A score of 20 + = Need some practice.

Give yourself one small goal a day, such as giving your opinion in a meeting or in class.

A score of 11–19 = Getting there.

You have found your voice and you need to continue challenging yourself on productive ways of speaking up and stepping out.

A score of 6–10 = You know that your opinion matters.

You believe what you have to say is of value. And you're right! Encourage women around you to believe the same about themselves.

in living color

A Mom's Legacy

We learn our unhealthy patterns from our families. Intentionally or unintentionally, the ways our parents related to each other, us, and the world get passed down. Does this mean we are stuck forever with the unhealthy patterns of our parents and grandparents? No, through Christ all things are made new. This means God can break the bonds of family patterns and create a new legacy for our children. Even though Janette changed, her children were out of the house by the time significant transformation occurred.

Danielle, Janette's daughter, was unintentionally taught by her mom to keep her opinions to herself and not rock the boat. She had a low self-esteem and so entered into a marriage like that of her parents. But, seeing what God was doing in her mother's life inspired her to begin her own spiritual journey at the age of 25 instead of 45. The result has been a fresh, alive walk with God and a persistent battle in her marriage to live differently. It has required a lot of looking at the log in her own eye. Here's what Danielle has to share:

"From as early as I can remember, my aspiration as a little girl was to be a godly woman and wife. I saw my mom as the ideal Christian woman and I strove to be one too. However, I had no idea how difficult it would be! I found myself in a marriage where I struggled to fulfill my husband's desires. No matter what I tried—whether it was losing weight, working harder around the house, agreeing with everything he said—it was never quite good enough for him. I found myself empty, tired, and not measuring up to either my husband's or my own unbelievably hard standards.

"I was married less than a year when I realized this couldn't be God's heart for my marriage. One of the main reasons my eyes were opened was I watched my mom developing more of herself as an independent person. She had stopped trying to be exactly what my father wanted her to be and she was beginning to say what she wanted and needed. I saw her begin to have opinions about things and stand up for herself.

"My mom struggled through 25 years of marriage before making these changes and she was determined not to let that much time go by for me. She began encouraging me to look at my own patterns, notice how low my self-esteem really was, and become aware of how willing I was to do absolutely anything to make my husband happy. Seeing my mom change gave me hope and I began to pray that God would show me how to live differently.

"So here I am, finishing my third year of marriage. These years have been much harder than I thought they would be, but I am beginning to offer more of me and who God made me to be in my marriage and in other relationships. God sees me as unique, loving, caring, and captivating, and I am learning to live from that truth.

"God has definitely been working on me and I have learned so much from my mom. Even though it has been a painful process, I have never felt more at peace and assured of God's love and His future for me. I hope the work God is doing in me will help prevent my children from someday getting stuck in the same trap."

1. What part of this chapter resonated with you?

2. Is it hard for you to speak the truth to the people you are in significant relationship with? Why or why not?

3. Share with the group some of the "logs" you have in your own eye. Which ones seem like they are giving you the most trouble in your relationships?

4. How can the group help encourage you to keep looking at this log? What can they do to keep you moving toward God and change?

4. Closing round: Go around the circle and finish this sentence: *Please pray for me to learn to speak up more in my relationship with* _______________.

Check These Out . . .

Changes That Heal
by Henry Cloud

Leave the Mud and Learn to Soar
by Elaine Martens Hamilton

Love Is a Choice
by Robert Hemfelt, Frank Minirth, and Paul Meier

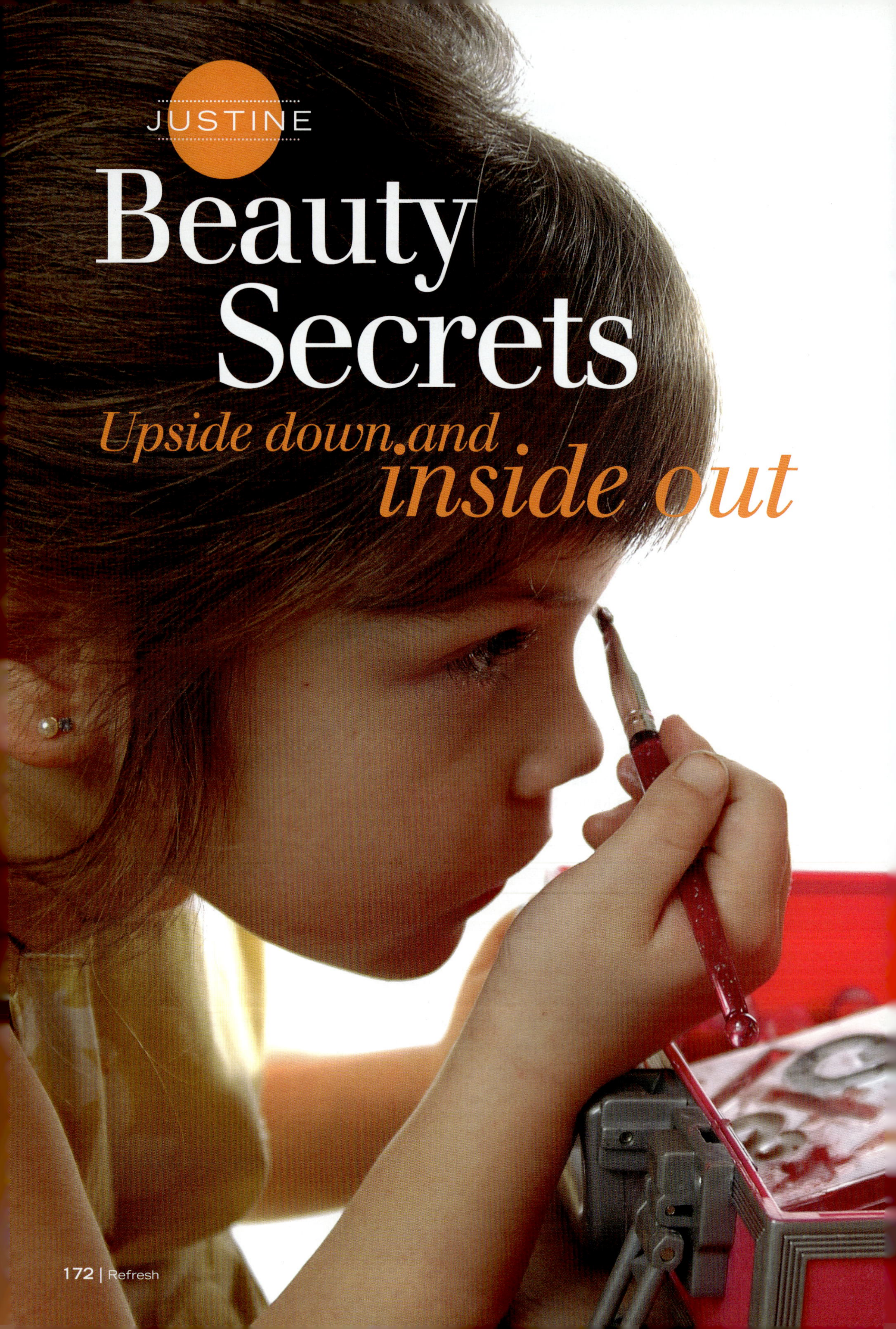

JUSTINE
Beauty Secrets
Upside down, and inside out

about your hair," Justine's mom frowned and tugged a strand of her hair. "It's just so mousy."

Justine shrank inside.

"And I hate those pants on you. Makes you look so thin."

Looking down at her tan corduroy pants, Justine shrugged.

"I'm going to go shopping this weekend and try to do something about the way you look."

Justine's heart sank and she turned and walked out of the kitchen. She slipped into her room, shut the door, and sat down at her piano. Her fingers glided over the keys and a low, sorrowful sound resounded through the room, echoing Justine's heart.

Later that week, they went shopping and Justine's mother bought Justine padded bras, frilly shirts, and pants that somehow were supposed to make her look more shapely. The shopping expedition wasn't too bad until they got to the shoe department, where things took a turn for the worse.

"You've got such ridiculously big feet," her mother laughed, browsing through the shoe department. "How are we ever going to find nice shoes for feet that big?"

Certain everyone in the store was staring at her feet, Justine looked down, following her mother at a distance.

"No one I know wears a size 10," her mother said too loudly.

Shame smothered Justine and she wanted to melt into the floor like the Wicked Witch of the West.

Later that week, Justine's mom called her into the family room.

"Yes, Mom." Justine obediently came into the room where her mom and dad sat side by side on the couch.

"Just stand there," her mom said, elbowing Justine's dad. "See what I mean? She's so skinny. Her hip bones just stick out." She shook her head with disgust. "And her overbite is awful."

Justine's dad chuckled. "Where are her breasts? Isn't she supposed to be developed by now?"

Flaming heat rose up Justine's face as her parents snickered. Tears burned on the inside of her eyes. *Don't cry. Don't cry.*

"I know," her mom nodded with a laugh. "She looks pitiful." Her mom brought the tips of her fingers together. "She's got a Bob Hope nose, doesn't she? It just slopes right off her face."

The heat in Justine's face turned her cheeks crimson. She swallowed and dug her nails into her hand. *Don't cry.* She bit her lip and focused on the pain from her sharp fingernails.

"And her hair is so stringy. I have to do something about it."

That night, when Justine lay in bed, the humiliation she felt standing in front of her parents still seared her heart, and the tears she had refused to let her parents see seeped onto her pillow. Their words took root in her 12-year-old heart and a harvest of insecurities began to blossom inside her.

By the time Justine entered high school she had one goal—to get noticed by members of the opposite sex. She had discovered that the shame and humiliation inside her was alleviated when boys found her attractive. She took sewing lessons and learned the art of making outfits that turned heads. Justine found herself never really wanting to date or get intimate with the boys that pursued her. She just wanted their attention and approval.

One weekend, a carnival came to town. Justine worked hard on a revealing outfit she could wear to the big event. Friday afternoon, she put the finishing touches on her pink hip-huggers and slipped them on. A smile spread across her face when she checked herself out in the mirror. This should work. She had made the hip-huggers nearly two inches lower than the sewing pattern had called for and, with the fitted gray and pink polka-dot tube top, she had plenty of skin showing.

That evening, she and her friend, Dawn, hung outside of the beer tent because they were too young to go in. Sailors, who had come to the carnival on their night off, kept buying the girls beers and hanging outside the tent with them. Justine had men nearly twice her age standing in line to get her a beer. She lapped up the attention like a kitten drinking milk. When she and Dawn went home at their curfew time, she couldn't suppress a wide grin. "That was so much fun." She twirled around on the sidewalk.

"I feel dizzy," Dawn said, bobbing along after Justine.

"I feel great!" The beer mixed with the attention sent a ripple of exhilaration down her arms.

When she opened her eyes the next morning, her forehead throbbed and she felt nauseated. She closed her eyes and pulled a pillow over her head as memories from the night before began to trickle in. In spite of feeling lousy, a smile pushed up her lips as she thought about all the guys who had flocked around her the night before.

Fast-forward 30 years. Justine's quest to feel acceptable through attracting men remained, but life's demands as a single mom of three children sapped her energy. Her husband, whom she met in high school, had left when their children were young. But Justine had become a Christian and depended on her intimate relationship with God to help her through the fallout of bad relationships and the difficulties of single parenting. Life wasn't easy. Financial stress. Parenting rebellious teenagers. Yet, through all the trauma and drama, Justine pursued a love relationship with God.

Justine had to turn to the Lord, and not a man, for strength. She would need it. One afternoon, she was at work when she received a phone call.

"Hi, Justine. This is Dr. Walker, a surgeon down at St. Joseph Hospital. The results of your mammogram last week indicate we need to do some further checking and I am wondering how soon you can come down for a biopsy."

Justine's heart skipped inside her chest. "You mean come right now?" A nervous laugh sputtered out of her mouth.

"Yes. Can you?'

"Uh, OK."

"Let me put you through to the front desk to see when we can get you in."

"OK." *If the surgeon is calling me, this can't be good.* An icy quiver ascended to the nape of her neck.

Justine wasn't able to get scheduled that day, but the next day a doctor conducted a core biopsy. Justine, in pain, kept trying to read the doctor's face for any clues to her condition.

"I know you're not supposed to share the test results but is there anything you can tell me without telling me?"

"Well, you're right. Until the biopsy is officially analyzed, we can't tell you anything."

Justine waited. Maybe there was more the doctor would say.

"What I will tell you is that it will be extremely important for you to have a positive attitude." The doctor looked into Justine's eyes and Justine heard the unspoken words. In that moment she knew.

I have cancer.

"OK. Thank you," Justine heard herself say.

Driving home after the procedure, Justice thought about how she would look bald. The image in her mind made her wince and she squeezed the steering wheel. *Oh Lord, I know You are going to use this.* She inhaled a deep breath and let it out slowly.

The next day when Justine got the call from her doctor, she knew what he would tell her. "There is a large tumor in the left breast and also a tumor in your lymph nodes which means it has spread."

Justine's tongue felt thick and her words seemed to come out in slow motion. "OK. So now what?"

"I need you to make an appointment so we can go

over the different treatment options you have."

Justine made an appointment and hung up the phone. Still staring at the receiver, the hazy reality of cancer buzzed inside her head. *Lord, I know You are with me in this. Give me Your peace and lead me to make the best decision about the treatment plan.*

After meeting with the doctors and carefully praying over all her options, Justine decided to have surgery to remove the tumors and undergo a series of different chemotherapy treatments. Out of all the turbulent emotions that saddled her, Justine found herself fixated most on the fact that she was going to lose her hair. She couldn't stand the idea of being bald and began obsessing over it.

One afternoon she went into the bathroom and wrapped her head in a towel. Staring in the mirror she tried to picture herself hairless. A deep sadness consumed her. "I don't want to lose my hair, Lord!" she whispered at the mirror. Tears sprang to her eyes and she walked into her bedroom collapsing on the bed. *What is wrong with me?* She cried into her pillow. *I have cancer and all I can think about is losing my hair! It's not like I'm losing a child or something.*

But no matter how much she scolded herself, she couldn't shake the grief she felt over losing her hair. Ten days after she began chemo, she sat alone with a cup of tea on her back porch. Her Bible sat in her lap but she felt too nauseated to even open it. Fighting the bile that threatened to rise up her throat, she ran her fingers over her hair. When she pulled her hand away from her head, there was a mass of brown hair in the palm of her hand. "Oh no," a trembling rose from inside her. "It's happening."

She ran her hand over her hair again. Another wad of hair came out and she felt like someone had kicked her in the stomach. "Oh Lord, help," she whispered. Unable to stop, she kept running her hand through her hair, dropping clump after clump onto the porch. When a soft wind blew over the backyard, sweeping her hair onto the lawn, she closed her eyes and tears flushed down her cheeks. With anguish gripping her heart, a sudden memory flooded over her and there she stood in front of her parents as a little girl:

"Look at her mousy brown hair . . ."

"What about her flat chest . . ."

"She has huge feet . . ."

"What a ski-slope nose . . ."

Justine opened her eyes and shuddered as the words replayed in her mind. She felt like that preteen girl all over again—shamed, ugly, and insecure. A sob rose up her throat. *Oh God, I haven't remembered that since I was a little girl. Could that be why this is all so painful?*

She sat there for a long time and cried. And as her tears poured out, something took place inside her heart. Slowly, she was warmed by a comfort, a balm caressing that broken piece inside her—the little girl who was never accepted for how she looked. Later that evening, when her daughter came over to shave the little hair that was left on her head, Justine shared the memory with her. As Justine talked about it, her heart felt lighter. Something had shifted and the agony of her hair loss no longer seemed to have its stronghold.

Looking back on that evening today, Justine describes how God actually has used cancer in her life to restore her and give her a self-acceptance she had never known before. "I had never thought about that childhood memory until I was sitting there with my hair literally falling out of my head. Through the process of losing my hair, God reminded me of that shamed and dark corner of my heart. It had never really been healed and He used that moment, when handfuls of hair were clutched in my hand, to bring me healing."

As Justine cried and prayed over the hurt of her childhood memories, she began to see that most of her life she had carried with her the belief that she was "OK" based on her outward appearance. She realized that by the time she was a teenager she had learned to package herself through clothes, makeup, and accenting her positive features. She became excellent at using those avenues as a means to secure her self-worth.

Although more subtle, even as a grown woman, she unconsciously continued to rely on others' approval to give her some sense of self-acceptance. When she faced losing important components of her outward appearance—her breast and hair—the grief, shame, and agony of her "ugly" childhood came rushing back.

"God is so good. He heals us in our most broken places that even we have forgotten are there. The process of losing my hair was like a doorway into a room full of peace and satisfaction about who I am in God. And the thing is, once I went into that room, I felt truly pretty! There I was without any eyebrows, eyelashes, or hair, and for the first time in my life I discovered an acceptance of myself as God had made me and as God saw me. I think when you see yourself through God's eyes, you truly know what it means to feel beautiful—and I felt beautiful."

Justine is still in the midst of battling for her life through cancer treatments. She is physically weak and weary from the battle, but her spiritual life soars. She continues to marvel at how God actually used her cancer to heal something so deep and embedded in her; she had not been aware of its damaging effects.

"In a million years, I never would have thought God would use cancer and baldness to give me an idea of how beautiful and worthy I am to Him. I just hope He knows how thankful I am." ❁

Beauty: Turned Upside Down and Inside Out

"The challenge with beauty is that we attempt to see it with our eyes; but that is only possible after we have first seen it with God's heart."

—Sharon Saul

Do you think I'm beautiful?

We usually don't ask the question out loud, but we've thought it many times. Somewhere deep inside all women want to feel alluring, be treasured, valued, accepted, and thought of as beautiful in someone's eyes. Here's a quick internal test. *How do you define beauty? Close your eyes and think of a "beautiful woman." What is the first image that pops into your mind?*

Often, when we think of the word *beautiful,* we think of external beauty, the kind the world values and affirms. There's this ideal out there that is extremely deceiving; in fact, it's literally impossible to achieve. Ask any top model and we bet she'll tell you that she never feels beautiful enough.

I (Laura) have a friend, Amber, who used to be a model. One day at church she was in a brown wrap dress with an aqua scarf. I told her how much I loved her outfit and how beautiful she looked. She stared at me stunned and speechless. Later that day Amber called her mom and gushed, "Mom, someone thinks I'm beautiful." When Amber told me she had done this, it was my turn to be stunned and speechless. How could she not know she *was* beautiful? Her face was perfectly symmetrical and porcelain. Her body was lean, yet curvy. Her hair was shiny, thick, and long. I wondered what in the world she saw when she looked in the mirror. What ideal of beauty is she trying to measure up to?

The more important question for all of us is why can't we see our own beauty? Our media-focused culture has damaged all women across colors, shapes, and sizes by commercializing an unrealistic view of what is deemed "beautiful."

The real problem is that when we as a culture talk about beauty, we talk about the exterior. And let's face it. God never has—never will—care about the outside like He does the inside. He has always been

concerned with our heart. True beauty has nothing to do with our hair color or cut, our blue jeans size, or the shade of our skin. True beauty is believing we are a beautiful, unique, and wonderfully made creation fashioned by the God of the universe.

So how do we get there? How do we get to a place of radical self-acceptance? How do we let go of the messages that haunt us from the past and learn to silence the voices in our head that tell us we're not pretty enough, smart enough, or thin enough? How do we get to a place where we're firmly planted in the soil of God's amazing acceptance of ourselves just as we are?

Looking Back . . .

Sometimes we have to look back in order to move forward.

Think back to your childhood and teenage years. Think of some statements that people have said to you that hurt or caused you to view yourself in a negative way. I (Kathy) have a painful memory that happened in middle school. I can speak freely about it now, but these ugly words affected how I viewed myself for many years. A boy in my class called me "Jell-O butt"

Launching Forward . . .

When we launch forward into adulthood, often we are completely unaware of deep childhood wounds that influence our self-acceptance. Justine had no idea as a grown woman that she had buried the painful words and actions of her parents. As her hair started to fall out, she was confronted with the profound question that we all need to ask ourselves:

Who am I, really?

Who are you?

I am . . .

....

....

....

when I was in the seventh grade. Imagine the pain of those words! I always struggled with never being as thin as the other girls. Looking back, I see how these words seared a scar on my young heart and left me feeling bad about myself, especially my body.

Think back to your childhood. What were some of the messages passed on to you about your outward appearance? Think of remarks that parents, friends, siblings, and others said to you either directly or indirectly.

....

....

....

....

We don't know what you wrote down, but our guess is that most of us answered with one of the world's definitions. If we answer with the world's words, we will be stuck with answers like:

I am a mom. I am a nurse. I am a struggling college student. I am a runner. I am a girlfriend. I am a wife. I am a volunteer at my kids' school. I am a woman who keeps getting used by men. I am a failure as a parent. I am fat. I am a person who keeps making the same mistakes. I am a divorcée.

But how does God want us to answer the question, Who are you?

In Hosea 1:10 (NLT), God says, "You are children of the living God."

This is who you are:
a child of God—a beautiful, loved, treasured child of God.

Wouldn't the fabric of our hearts look different if we could freeze-frame ourselves before the "Jell-O butt" comments entered our lives? I (Laura) see what this looks like in my young daughter who, deep in her soul, believes she is beautiful on the inside and out! She lives in a place of utter self-acceptance. Why? Because the world hasn't perverted her self-image yet. No one has called her too fat or too skinny, stupid or a brainiac, flat or top heavy. And she isn't old enough to start comparing her outward appearance to that of supermodels. So there she lives, in a place where she celebrates how God created her instead of picking herself apart.

Traditional African American song

Read Deuteronomy 7:6.

For you are a people holy to the Lord your God. The Lord your God has chosen you out of all the peoples on the face of the earth to be his people, his treasured possession. **(NIV)**

He was talking to the Israelites in this passage but His words are also for us today.

Now reread this paraphrased passage and insert your name.

For you, _______________, are a person holy to the Lord your God. The Lord your God has chosen you, __________, out of all the peoples on the face of the earth to be one of his daughters, his treasured possession.

What if the question, Who are you? always led to one simple answer?

I am a unique, wonderfully made, treasured, and beautiful child of God.

We would live differently. We would know freedom. We'd be less afraid. We'd need less from people and more from God.

> "You are a child of God. Your playing small does not serve the world. There is nothing enlightened about shrinking so that other people won't feel insecure about you. We were born to manifest the glory of God that is within us."
>
> —Nelson Rockefeller

Read 1 John 3:1–2, 19–20.

How great is the love the Father has lavished on us, that we should be called children of God! And that is what we are! The reason the world does not know us is that it did not know him. Dear friends, now we are children of God, and what we will be has not yet been made known. . . . This then is how we know that we belong to the truth, and how we set our hearts at rest in his presence whenever our hearts condemn us. For God is greater than our hearts, and he knows everything. **(NIV)**

May our daughters know the truth!

If you have a daughter, a sister, a niece, then you know how desperately you don't want anyone younger than you to live with a broken, damaged self-image. We want the next generation to grow up believing the truth about who they really are in Christ. Here's what some women said they want their daughters to know.

We want our "daughters" to know that they are:

- Precious, irreplaceable treasures
- Beautiful
- Accepted and loved in His eyes
- Perfect jewels
- His sweet, precious daughters
- Totally worthy
- Able to do anything they dream of doing
- Made in God's image, they bear His character
- Not what the world says they are
- Worthy of respect and honor
- World changers

If you have a daughter, what do you want her to know?

Take yourself out of the picture for a moment and think about this: *How do you think a "child of God" feels?* Write your answers below.

A child of God would probably feel . . .

Do you feel some of these things? When?

Which ones do you long to feel more?

In order for us to feel and live like children of God, we have to align ourselves with His truth—His truth, not the world's lies, our own self-criticism and condemnation, or other people's "Jell-O butt" commentary.

And here's the truth:

You are a unique, wonderfully made, treasured, and beautiful child of God! Do you feel it?

Beauty . . . What's It Worth?

- Since 1997, there has been a 446 percent increase in the total number of cosmetic procedures.

- People aged 35–50 had the most procedures—5.3 million and 47 percent of the total.

- Racial and ethnic minorities, as of 2005, had approximately 22 percent of all cosmetic procedures.

American Society for Aesthetic Plastic Surgery 2006 Statistics on Cosmetic Surgery

1. One of a kind!

Imagine this: Among the billions of people that God has created through history, *every single one of us* is unique. There has never been anyone made just like you. Your fingerprint is proof. God gave us each a certain body and hair type matched with a specific eye and skin color, making the perfect combination that makes you, *you*. So whether we like what He made or not, Scripture makes it clear that God definitely *knew what He was doing* when He made each of us.

Take a look at Psalm 139, a beautiful picture of God's intimate connection with us, His creation. The focus of this psalm is how God knows and understands *what's inside*. But it also is a reminder that He created each of us exactly how we are supposed to be.

Read verses 13–16.

For you created my inmost being; you knit me together in my mother's womb. I praise you because I am fearfully and wonderfully made; your works are wonderful, I know that full well. My frame was not hidden from you when I was made in the secret place. When I was woven together in the depths of the earth, your eyes saw my unformed body. All the days ordained for me were written in your book before one of them came to be. **(NIV)**

What's unique about you? Think about some of your characteristics that make you, *you*.

Now follow David's lead when he authored this psalm and praise God for how He created you.
God, I thank You that you made me to be . . .

2. God knows . . .

Because Jesus came to earth and was fully human, fully God, He knows what it is like to struggle with feeling loved, valued, and treasured in the world's eyes. In fact, of all the people in the world, He was the loveliest, the most beautiful, the King of all kings (Isaiah 9:6; Psalm 97:9; Philippians 2:9–11) and yet He was looked upon as unlovely, unworthy, and unacceptable by the people of His time.

So when we are feeling unaccepted, ugly, and unloved in the world's eyes, we can cling to the truth of God's Word and find comfort in the fact that we have a Savior who *knows the feeling.*

Read Isaiah 53:2–5, a description of Jesus in the Old Testament:

There was nothing beautiful or majestic about his appearance, nothing to attract us to him. He was despised and rejected—a man of sorrows, acquainted with bitterest grief. We turned our backs on him and looked the other way when he went by. He was despised, and we did not care. Yet it was our weaknesses he carried; it was our sorrows that weighed him down. And we thought his troubles were a punishment from God for his own sins! But he was wounded and crushed for our sins. He was beaten that we might have peace. He was whipped, and we were healed! **(NLT)**

What does this passage cause you to remember about Jesus?

Now read Hebrews 4:14–16.

That is why we have a great High Priest who has gone to heaven, Jesus the Son of God. Let us cling to him and never stop trusting him. This High Priest of ours understands our weaknesses, for he faced all of the same temptations we do, yet he did not sin. So let us come boldly to the throne of our gracious God. There we will receive his mercy, and we will find grace to help us when we need it. **(NLT)**

How does remembering that Jesus knows what you are feeling, experiencing, and struggling with help you?

Woman in the Mirror

1. Mirror, mirror, help me see beyond you!

Often when we look in the mirror, we don't like what we see. We see too many wrinkles, gray hairs, a nose that isn't quite what we had hoped for, and skin that's far from smooth. We see lumps, bumps, and bruises. We see the mistakes from our past and our current struggles. It is hard for most of us to look in the mirror for too long and feel good about it. Yet, God says that he loves us *just like we are.* He knows the lumps, the bumps, and the bruises; but He sees far past them. He looks into the heart.

This will be a difficult exercise, but we think it's worth trying.

Set aside five minutes (that sounds short, but trust us, it'll feel long!). Sit or stand in front of your bathroom mirror and just look at yourself.

Look deep into your eyes. Breathe deeply. Allow yourself to see all of the bumps and lumps and things that you don't like; but keep looking, go further. Look past them and see if you can find some things you like. As women we have a difficult time talking about positive things about ourselves, but they exist. Now find them!

What are some things you like about your physical beauty? (You have to write down at least one thing—your eyes, noses, skin, teeth, hair . . .)

If you look beyond the physical, look deeper past just the color of your eyes or the texture of your skin, what do you see? Finish this sentence.

I am a woman who is . . .

(a survivor, wise, smart, industrious, committed, faithful, steady, strong, brave, honest, authentic, loving, caring, and . . .)

I may be older, but certainly not wiser. No, I take that back. I am wiser. But have I listened to my own wisdom? Not often. I still struggle with beauty and age. I struggle to remember that it's my heart that's important, not my face, my body, my former youth. I remember my mother telling me when I was young to look around me and notice that every elderly person looks somewhat the same. All have aging bodies. Just by looking at them, I can't tell who was the homecoming queen, the 20-something beauty, nor which one had the best body in a bikini.

She told me that it's harder for beautiful women to age because that's all they have. For those of us not stunningly beautiful, we must learn to develop depth and inner beauty. It sounds so cliché, but the truth is, inner beauty is the most important value we can present to the world. But how do we get there? Loving others, even those who seem unlovable. Being kind to everyone. Standing and living for truth—even when that means I have to be truthful about my failures. I take responsibility for my choices, and make better ones next time. I share my heart, be myself, and most of all, pour out my time in a love relationship with God.

I want to say that outward beauty isn't important. Honestly, I think I'm in transition right now. I'm finally beginning to believe it in the depths of my spirit—not just spouting the Christian party line. I can see it in the women around me. I'm slowly beginning to see that being loved, and loving, do not ever depend on how one looks, but on how one acts. I hope that if you ask me the same question in five years, when the gray has taken over, and the extra pouch won't go away, that I'll be able to tell you I've arrived and I know true beauty.

Lissa, 51

2. Conditional beauty … it's gotta go!

I feel beautiful when . . .

I have a new haircut and an outfit on that truly is the right size for me.—Ann

I'm well put together.—Susan

I am outdoors doing the things I love.—Leslie

People compliment me on the way I look or how I am dressed.—April

I easily fit into my favorite pair of jeans.—Donna

When do you feel beautiful? Now you fill in this blank.

I feel beautiful when . . .

....

....

....

So what happens when the right "conditions" aren't available to us? What happens when we start to lose our hair, our kids rebel, we gain 20 pounds, or we lose our job? How beautiful do we feel then? The secret to real beauty is to have it mirror the true essence of Christ's love—which is *unconditional*. Beauty comes through Christ's Spirit working in our heart, reminding us of the real truth. Remember? *You are a unique, wonderfully made, treasured, and beautiful child of God!*

3. Chosen

Remember when we were young and on the playground picking teams for a game, that feeling of "Choose me! Choose me!" roaring inside our hearts? Some of us were chosen first. Others of us knew the feeling of being chosen last. Here's the reality: God chooses all of us first. We aren't at the bottom of the lineup. In His eyes, we are all at the top. It is so easy to buy into lies about ourselves and deny the truth—that we are chosen by God, beloved and precious in His eyes. It's time to embrace our "chosenness" in God's eyes and live from that place instead of staying stuck on the playground begging inside to be chosen.

Write down on a notecard lies about yourself with which you struggle.

....

....

....

....

....

Now, take a lighter or match and burn the notecard. On a new notecard write:

"I am the chosen child of God, precious in God's eyes, called the beloved from all eternity, and held safe in an everlasting embrace."

Put the notecard on your mirror.

1. Ask the women to open their purses and take out one item of makeup. Ask each of them to describe how she uses it, and what it does for her. Have each women tell how it feels when that piece of makeup is "on" as opposed to when it is "off." Now brainstorm what we can "put on" in the morning with God. (His truth about who we are in Hosea 1:10; His armor from Ephesians 6; and so on). What difference would it make in how you went about your day if you had these things "on" instead of the makeup?

2. Bring a stack of magazines to the group and have the women flip through them to find advertisements that use beautiful women to sell products. Show each other what you find. Discuss why beautiful women are used to sell cars, power tools, food, alcohol, and everything else under the sun. Ask: *How do these images make you feel? How are these images affecting how you view yourself? How can we guard our hearts against the powerful messages these advertisements are sending?* As soon as you are done with the discussion, have all of the women rip their pages up in unison.

3. Read through the "Infusion." Process together as a group the question: *Who have you been letting define you?* Then lead the group in a guided prayer to confess how we allow the world and other people to define us instead of Jesus.

in living color

Flawed in the World's Eyes, Beautiful in God's

David Roche was born with a severe facial disfigurement. On the left side of his face is an extensive cavernous hemangioma, a benign tumor consisting of blood vessels. When he was young, surgeons tried to remove the tumor, but in the process removed his lower lip; and then gave him such extensive radiation that the lower part of his face stopped growing and he became covered with radiations burns on his temple and eyelid. In his mid-50s now, David is an inspirational speaker. Listen to what he tells other people as he shares his journey. *"My face is unique. But my experiences are universal. I have learned that every person has feelings of being disfigured, of feeling different and in some way unacceptable. We all, no matter what our appearance or life circumstances, have to learn to value ourselves and the gifts we bring to the world. I have had to learn to find my own inner beauty and power. What seemed to be my 'flaws' have been revealed as a wonderful source of strength."* (www.davidroche.com) Used by permission.

A Father's Love Letter to His Daughters

My Child,

You may not know me, but I know everything about you. Psalm 139:1 *I know when you sit down and when you rise up.* Psalm 139:2 *I am familiar with all your ways.* Psalm 139:3 *Even the very hairs on your head are numbered.* Matthew 10:29–31 *For you were made in my image.* Genesis 1:27 *In me you live and move and have your being.* Acts 17:28 *For you are my offspring.* Acts 17:28 *I knew you even before you were conceived.* Jeremiah 1:4–5 *I chose you when I planned creation.* Ephesians 1:11–12 *You were not a mistake, for all your days are written in my book.* Psalm 139:15–17 *I determined the exact time of your birth and where you would live.* Acts 17:26 *You are fearfully and wonderfully made.* Psalm 139:14 *I knit you together in your mother's womb.* Psalm 139:13 *And brought you forth on the day you were born.* Psalm 71:6 *I have been misrepresented by those who don't know me.* John 8:41–44 *I am not distant and angry, but am the complete expression of love.* 1 John 4:16 *And it is my desire to lavish my love on you.* 1 John 3:1 *Simply because you are my child and I am your Father.* 1 John 3:1 *I offer you more than your earthly father ever could.* Matthew 7:11 *For I am the perfect father.* Matthew 5:48 *Every good gift that you receive comes from my hand.* James 1:17 *For I am your provider and I meet all your needs.* Matthew 6:31–33 *My plan for your future has always been filled with hope.* Jeremiah 29:11 *Because I love you with an everlasting love.* Jeremiah 31:3 *My thoughts toward you are countless as the sand on the seashore.* Psalm 139:17–18 *And I rejoice over you with singing.* Zephaniah 3:17 *I will never stop doing good to you.* Jeremiah 32:40 *For you are my treasured possession.* Exodus 19:5 *I desire to establish you with all my heart and all my soul.* Jeremiah 32:41 *And I want to show you great and marvelous things.* Jeremiah 33:3 *If you seek me with all your heart, you will find me.* Deuteronomy 4:29 *Delight in me and I will give you the desires of your heart.* Psalm 37:4 *For it is I who gave you those desires.* Philippians 2:13 *I am able to do more for you than you could possibly imagine.* Ephesians 3:20 *For I am your greatest encourager.* 2 Thessalonians 2:16–17 *I am also the Father who comforts you in all your troubles.* 2 Corinthians 1:3-4 *When you are brokenhearted, I am close to you.* Psalm 34:18 *As a shepherd carries a lamb, I have carried you close to my heart.* Isaiah 40:11 *One day I will wipe away every tear from your eyes.* Revelation 21:3–4 *And I'll take away all the pain you have suffered on this earth.* Revelation 21:3–4 *I am your Father, and I love you even as I love my son, Jesus.* John 17:23 *For in Jesus, my love for you is revealed.* John 17:26 *He is the exact representation of my being.* Hebrews 1:3 *He came to demonstrate that I am for you, not against you.* Romans 8:31 *And to tell you that I am not counting your sins.* 2 Corinthians 5:18–19 *Jesus died so that you and I could be reconciled.* 2 Corinthians 5:18–19 *His death was the ultimate expression of my love for you.* 1 John 4:10 *I gave up everything I loved that I might gain your love.* Romans 8:31–32 *If you receive the gift of my son Jesus, you receive me.* 1 John 2:23 *And nothing will ever separate you from my love again.* Romans 8:38–39 *Come home and I'll throw the biggest party heaven has ever seen.* Luke 15:7 *I have always been Father, and will always be Father.* Ephesians 3:14–15 *My question is . . . Will you be my child?* John 1:12–13 *I am waiting for you.* Luke 15:11–32

Love, Your Dad

1. What were some of the messages passed on to you about your outward appearance? Think of things that parents, friends, siblings, and others said to you either directly or indirectly.

2. How have these things affected how you view yourself?

3. When do you feel most beautiful?

4. If you felt fully accepted just as you are, without changing a thing, what do you think might be different in your life? What would you feel more of? Less of?

5. Closing round: Finish this sentence with two to three words: *Through this chapter, God reminded me that I am ___________ in His eyes.*

Check These Out . . .

Do You Think I'm Beautiful?
by Angela Thomas

Captivating
by John and Stasi Eldredge

The Allure of Hope
by Jan Meyers

Body. Beauty. Boys.
by Sarah Bragg

Conclusion

We hope that *Refresh* has met you in the place where you live—the real everyday muck and mire of your life as well as the places of victory, laughter, and beauty. We also hope after reading *Refresh* you know you are not alone. Whatever your story is, there are other women who share some of your same emotions and struggles and are also finding God's hope and peace in the midst of their journeys.

It is also our desire that through the pages of this book, women recognize how much they can learn from each other and in that process become better askers and listeners. We pray, too, the truth of God's Word lifted off the pages and was written on your heart. We encourage you to forge ahead—dig deeper into the Bible, trying to apply God's Word in your life, and seek out a community of safe women to accompany you as you pursue change and growth.

We want to thank the women in these stories who courageously shared pieces of their journeys with us. They believed in our vision of using real-life, redemptive stories as a wide boulevard leading to God's truth for the lives of women everywhere today. It wasn't easy for them to trudge through some of the mess and pain in their own lives but they did it for you! And we thank them.

We also want to thank you! Thanks for going on a new ride with us in the realm of women's Bible study. We hope this was an adventure that took you to new places you have never been before.

We are praying for you!

Love,

Laura and Kathy

More Refreshment

Born to Be Wild
Rediscover the Freedom of Fun
Jill Baughan
ISBN-10: 1-59669-048-8
ISBN-13: 978-1-59669-048-6

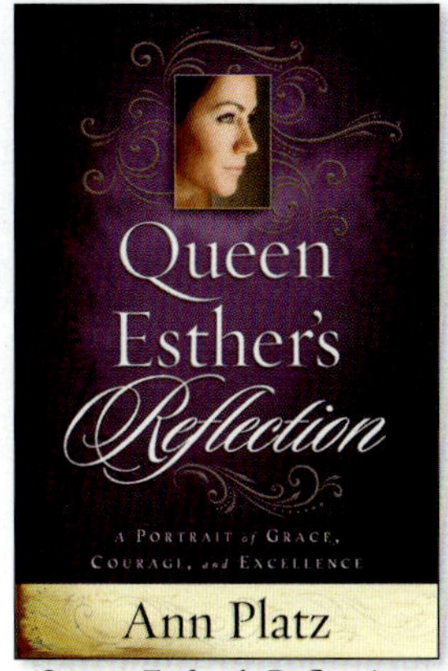

Queen Esther's Reflection
*A Portrait of Grace, Courage,
and Excellence*
Ann Platz
ISBN-10: 1-59669-012-7
ISBN-13: 978-1-59669-012-7

Made for Paradise
*God's Original Plan for Healthy Eating,
Physical Activity, and Rest*
Dr. Patricia Hart Terry
ISBN-10: 1-59669-085-2
ISBN-13: 978-1-59669-085-1

Trolls & Truth
*14 Realities About Today's Church
That We Don't Want to See*
Jimmy Dorrell
ISBN-10: 1-59669-010-0
ISBN-13: 978-1-59669-010-3

The Mentoring Mom
*11 Ways to Model Christ
for Your Child*
Jackie Kendall
ISBN-10: 1-59669-005-4
ISBN-13: 978-1-59669-005-9

Intentional Living
Choosing to Live for God's Purposes
Andrea Jones Mullins
ISBN-10: 1-56309-927-6
ISBN-13: 978-1-56309-927-4

Raising Moms
*Daughters Caring for Mothers
in Their Later Years*
Rhonda H. Kelley
ISBN-10: 1-56309-992-6
ISBN-13: 978-1-56309-992-2

Splash the Living Water
Sharing Jesus in Everyday Moments
Esther Burroughs
ISBN-10: 1-59669-002-X
ISBN-13: 978-1-59669-002-8

Stronger Still
*A Woman's Guide to Turning Your Hurt
into Healing for Others*
Edna Ellison
ISBN-10: 1-59669-090-9
ISBN-13: 978-1-59669-090-5

Be Restored!
God's Power for African American Women
Debra Berry
ISBN-10: 1-59669-007-0
ISBN-13: 978-1-59669-007-3

More information about New Hope books may be
found at www.newhopepublishers.com. New Hope
books may be purchased at your local bookstore.

The Art of Hope

Sewing, jewelry making, weaving, papermaking, soap making, beekeeping, farming, metalworking, wood carving, beading, and painting are among the skills artisans use to create a wide variety of native handcrafts. Many skills are passed down through generations while others are newly learned.

REFRESH OTHERS

WorldCrafts[SM] imports and sells handmade crafts from around the world. Since 1996 WorldCrafts, a nonprofit ministry of WMU®, has worked with select artisan groups to benefit individuals, families, and communities.

WorldCrafts
- works with local contacts,
- discovers one-of-a-kind artistry,
- learns about living conditions,
- partners with artisan leaders who abide by the Fair Trade Federation guidelines.

What You Can Do

WorldCrafts grows when you spread the word; purchase products; or give to the Jackson/Reese Endowment. Telling others about WorldCrafts and purchasing products boost artisans' income and build their hope. Making a tax-deductible gift helps expand the work to new artisans.

- Host a WorldCrafts party at home or church.
- Include products and stories in programs.
- Purchase meaningful gifts for friends and family.
- Place catalogs on display tables or in magazine racks.
- Register online to receive notification of specials.
- Contribute to the Jackson/Reese Endowment.
- Lift up the artisans, contacts, countries, and their projects.

Behind every WorldCrafts[SM] product is a unique story of hope. Many items are made in villages where earnings help provide better living conditions for artisans and the whole village. Other items are made in cities and towns where it is very difficult for people to find work. Artisans' earnings can be used to purchase essentials such as food, education, homes, and medicine.

Visit www.WorldCraftsVillage.com to learn more.

WorldCrafts[SM]

P. O. Box 830010
Birmingham, AL 35283-0010
1-800-968-7301 (Call this number for a free catalog.)
(205) 991-8100

Making a World of Difference®
WorldCrafts is a ministry of WMU®.

Your purchases of handmade WorldCrafts items give artisans and their families around the globe hope for a better life.

More Refreshment *Coming Soon*

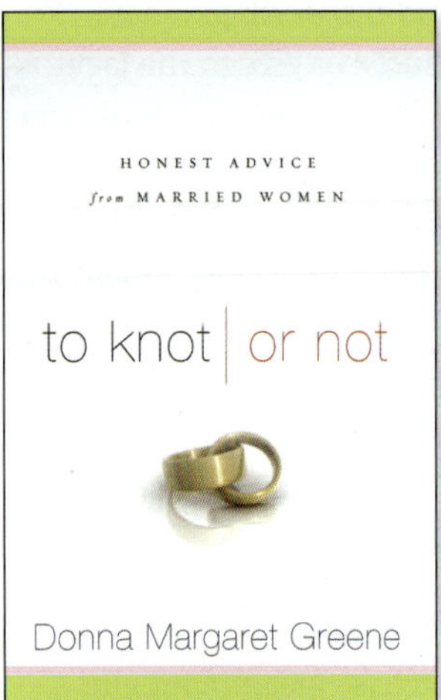

To Knot or Not
Honest Advice from Married Women
Donna Margaret Greene
ISBN-10: 1-59669-093-3
ISBN-13: 978-1-59669-093-6

Behind the Scenes of Breast Cancer
*A News Anchor Tells Her Story
of Body and Soul Recovery*
Brenda Ladun
ISBN-10: 1-59669-091-7
ISBN-13: 978-1-59669-091-2

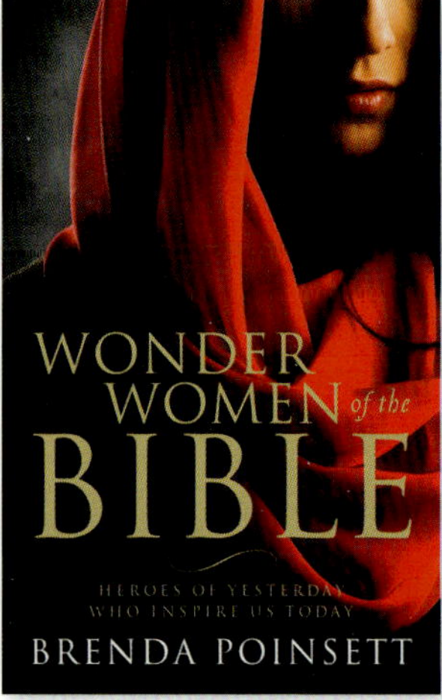

Wonder Women of the Bible
*Heroes of Yesterday
Who Inspire Us Today*
Brenda Poinsett
ISBN-10: 1-59669-094-1
ISBN-13: 978-1-59669-094-3

Wounded by Words
Healing the Invisible Scars of Emotional Abuse
Susan Titus Osborn, MA; Jeenie Gordon,
MS, MA, MFT; and Karen L. Kosman
ISBN-10: 1-59669-049-6
ISBN-13: 978-1-59669-049-3

Winds of Hope
Healing Devotions for Life's Storms
Rebecca J. Hughes
ISBN-10: 1-59669-074-7
ISBN-13: 978-1-59669-074-5

Wonderlust
*A Spiritual Travelogue for the
Adventurous Soul*
Vicki Kuyper
ISBN-10: 1-59669-076-3
ISBN-13: 978-1-59669-076-9

A Month of Miracles
30 Stories of the Unmistakable Presence of God
Author: Women by Design
ISBN-10: 1-59669-209-X
ISBN-13: 978-1-59669-209-1

New Hope Publishers is a division of WMU®,
an international organization that challenges
Christian believers to understand and be radically involved in God's mission. For more
information about WMU, go to www.wmu.com. More information about New Hope books may be
found at www.newhopepublishers.com. New Hope books may be purchased at your local bookstore.